CAPE TO CAIRO

MARK STRAGE

Cape to Cairo
RAPE OF A CONTINENT

A HELEN AND KURT WOLFF BOOK
HARCOURT BRACE JOVANOVICH, INC., NEW YORK

FOR MY FATHER

960.2
St1c
86259
Jan 1974

Library of Congress Cataloging in Publication Data

Strage, Mark.
Cape to Cairo.

"A Helen and Kurt Wolff book."
Bibliography: p.
1. Africa—History—19th century.
2. Railroads—Africa. I. Title.
DT28.S8   960'.2   73-13958
ISBN 0-15-115450-3

First American edition

B C D E

CONTENTS

ILLUSTRATIONS
Between pages 128 and 129

32 The Victoria Falls Bridge under construction, 1905 (*National Archives of Rhodesia*)

33 The first train crossing the Zambezi on the Victoria Falls Bridge, 1905 (*National Archives of Rhodesia*)

34 Stanley's first house in the Congo, showing railway-building equipment (*Royal Geographical Society, London*)

35 Track-laying in the Upper Congo (*Royal Commonwealth Society, London*)

36 The first train into Elizabethville (*Royal Commonwealth Society*)

37 Railway construction in the Sudan desert (*Sudan Archives, Durham University*)

38 Sudan railway scene, 1898 (*Royal Commonwealth Society*)

39 The defences of Alexandria after the bombardment, 1882 (*National Army Museum*)

40 Scottish solders in Egypt, *c.* 1890 (*National Army Museum*)

Picture research by Robyn Wallis

MAPS

Prologue

WELL into the second half of the nineteenth century, long after the rest of the world, including the great landlocked mass of Asia, the hidden corners of the Americas, and even the scattered islands of the Pacific had been explored, evaluated and picked over, there still remained one entire continent virtually untouched by white men. On the map, it hung like an enormous ripe pear, sketched in tantalizing outline.

It was largely to geography that Africa owed its immunity. In the north, easily accessible across the Mediterranean, an endless desert greets and discourages visitors. Along the ocean coasts, the mountains drop sharply to the sea, leaving only a coastal shelf which seldom exceeds thirty miles in width. Other continents had been betrayed by rivers which offered easy access to their interior. The great rivers of Africa present wide, inviting mouths to the intruder, but then quickly defeat him with churning rapids and impassable cataracts.

Passage overland was difficult. The mountains themselves, the dense vegetation, the stifling climate, all conspired to shield a vast elevated plateau where the weather was fair and the soil rich with hidden wealth. Across this plateau, great human migrations inched tracklessly; civilizations rose and fell, some documented and others conjectured. Much of what took place we will never learn for certain. But this we do know: in 1870, Africa still belonged to the Africans; more than nine-tenths of the continent's territory was ruled in one fashion or another by its natives.

Within thirty years, this proportion was reversed. Except for a few undesirable enclaves, the entire continent had been opened up, haggled over, parcelled out among the powers of Europe. That this could all happen so quickly is testament to the white man's enterprise, his skill at organizing resources, his determination in the face of awesome adversity, and his unquenchable greed.

How it happened – how rape on such colossal scale was planned and perpetrated – is the subject of this book.

All stories have a beginning. This one, for reasons which will be apparent, can be said to start on the first day of September 1870.

On that day, had a traveller been transported over the full length of Africa, from southern tip to northern coast, he would have seen something like this:

First, directly beneath him, was the Cape itself, shadowed by the headless shoulders of Table Mountain. At its foot lay the only substantial white settlement south of the Sahara – the capital of the Cape Colony, a Cinderella without prospects in an imperial household which included India, Canada and Australia.

To the right rose the Drakensberg range, 10,000 feet tall to catch the rain which made the coastal valley lush and fertile. Vasco da Gama, who first sighted it on Christmas Day 1497, named it Natal. Dutch settlers had fought the native Zulus for possession of the land, and had in turn been followed by the British, who brought trade and established the nucleus of a struggling colony.

To the left, there was nothing. Here, rainfall amounted to less than 15 inches a year; a rocky, riverless coast stretched for 800 miles, needlessly protecting the emptiness of the Kalahari Desert. North and east, straddling the Orange and Vaal rivers, were the ample farms of the Boers, descendants of the emigrants who had come to the Cape during its 150-year ownership by the Dutch East India Company. The Boers liked room – a man felt crowded if, from the stoop of his house, he could see the smoke rising from his neighbour's chimney. Long ago they had loaded their wagons and moved north in search of more land. Now their sleek cattle grazed on the banks of the Limpopo, the white man's border.

Beyond it crouched the dragon of the Matabeles, professional thugs with a national economy based on plunder and a social order regulated by brutality. Their newly crowned king, Lobengula, was hugely fat, slow of movement, intensely black, and dressed in a loin-cloth of monkey skins which scarcely served its function. Yet one of the few Europeans who had visited his private court, a dung-strewn goat enclosure, described him as the most imposing monarch he had ever seen, with the exception of the Tsar Alexander.

Another European, the gentle David Livingstone, had walked to the far end of the Matabele kingdom, the Zambesi river. There he had come upon one of nature's wonders. The river, a mile-wide sheet of placidly moving water, spilled over a rocky 340-foot drop, emitting a constant low-throated rumble and sending up dense columns of vapour. The natives called it *musi-oa-tunya* – the smoke that thunders. Livingstone renamed it in honour of his monarch.

To the west was the Congo. Its mouth had been discovered by Diego Cam in 1482. He could hardly miss it, since it was seven miles wide and spewed a rush of silt that stained the ocean for thirty miles. Cam was sufficiently impressed with his find to mark it with four massive stone pillars, but it was not until 1816 that a concerted effort was mounted against it. Twenty-eight Englishmen under Captain J. K. Tuckey of the Royal Navy battled the current, carried their boats overland around cataracts, and managed to reach a point less than 200 miles from the coast. There, exhausted, they stopped. On the way back, seventeen of them died, of disease, hunger, and probably heat prostration. They had attacked the jungle in full battle-dress – leggings, field packs and regimental jackets. For another 61 years, the place they had reached was to be known as Tuckey's Farthest, and no one in the world had the remotest idea that beyond it lay 2,800 miles of the world's second largest river.

Survivors of Tuckey's expedition gave an account of what little of the country they had seen: a dense forest populated by pygmies who kept a respectful distance. They also spoke of a strange aquatic animal which none of them had seen before, but which from their description a schoolchild now could identify as a hippopotamus. Later, others such as Chaillu, Schweinfurth, Speke and Grant, and in time the extraordinary Italian-turned-Frenchman Savorgnan de Brazza, hacked their way through the forest, bringing back useful information, unbelievable tales, and occasional conversation-pieces such as a tree sap which, when solidified, would bounce if dropped.

For all these exertions, however, the white men had little in the way of permanent results to show. Along the western coast, there were a few settlements: Luanda and Benguella, where Portuguese traders bartered for the trickle of goods issuing from the interior; Boma, at the mouth of the Congo, where an odd half-dozen British, Belgian and French merchants, late-comers to the market, sat and rotted. To the east, on the Red Sea coast, there were two specks of European enterprise, recently established in anticipation of the maritime traffic which it was hoped would result from the opening of the Suez Canal. One was a French colony, Obock. The other did not even have official status; it was merely a commercial coaling station owned and operated by the Rubattino Shipping Company, whose home offices were in Genoa.

Beyond the forest began the desert, not gracefully sculpted dunes of fine sand but enormous reaches of stone and metal-hard baked clay, and bare rocks that piled into tier after tier of mountain ranges. On the far side of the tallest range, at last, lay the sea. Here, at its edge, the traveller could finally see a European flag.

It flew over the city of Algiers, and to hoist and keep it there had cost the French more than 160,000 lives and the expenditure of $600 million. They had been there for forty years in 1870, engaged in what the historian Louis Thiers, soon to become the first president of the new Republic, described as 'not colonization, nor even occupation on a large scale, but war, badly made'.

East of the desert ran the Nile. Once its course had been charted and the great geographic exercise of tracing its source completed, the European powers had no further interest in it, or in the Sudan, the territory through which it ran for 2,300 miles, more than half of its total length. Soon enough, the struggle for control over this territory would bring all Europe to the brink of war, but for the present Egypt claimed it as its dependency by right of conquest.

North of the last cataract at Aswan, the Nile uncoiled itself and prepared for the last leisurely miles to the sea. Just above the point where the river fanned out into its delta, stretching for more than three miles along the eastern bank, lay Cairo. Its 320,000 inhabitants, of every colour, religion and degree of probity, made it the largest city in Africa. Most of them lived in the narrow alleys of the old city, but there were new quarters as well – impressive buildings which had been put up for the opening of the Suez Canal less than a year earlier. The Canal had not yet enriched Egypt – it was never to do that – but it had made the city into a glittering attraction. One visitor, Winwood Reade, wrote: 'Cairo, like Rome and Florence, lives upon tourists, who, if they are not beloved, are welcome; the city is lighted by gas; it has public gardens in which a native military band performs every afternoon; new houses in the Parisian style are springing up by the streets.'

In the midst of all this splendour, already mortgaged to the hilt, sat its proprietor, the 39-year-old Khedive Ismail. On the throne only seven years, he could bask in the spiritual reward of knowing that he was the greatest builder in Egypt since the Pharaohs or, should that be his inclination, in the more palpable gratification available in his harem, by repute the best-stocked in the world.

It is to be hoped that he enjoyed both fully, because harder days lay ahead – for Ismail and for all Africa.

Elsewhere in the world, other men and one woman who would play vital roles in those days were going about their business.

For several of them, that business was war. On September 1st, 1870, Kaiser Wilhelm of Prussia was at the head of his troops in France. In the evening, he retired to his tent and composed a telegram to his wife, Queen Augusta, in Berlin: 'Since 7.30 this morning, a battle, victoriously progressing, is taking place around Sedan. The enemy has been almost entirely driven back.'

Two hundred miles away, in Dinan, General Chanzy's Second French Army was preparing to move up. Within a few days it would be joined by a 20-year-old cadet named Herbert Kitchener, freshly passed out of the Royal Military Academy at Woolwich and eager for a first taste of battle.

Another soldier, Colonel Charles George Gordon, was languishing on garrison duty as commanding officer of the coastal defences at the mouth of the Thames. This was dull work after his heroics in the Crimean campaign and as commander of the Ever-Victorious Army in China.

Leopold II, 35-year-old King of the Belgians, was at his summer residence in Ostend, but his mind lay elsewhere as he stared out at the grey expanse of the Channel. Nine years earlier, as heir to the throne, he had travelled the world and written: 'The sea bathes our coasts, the world lies before us. Steam and electricity have annihilated distance. All the non-appropriated lands on the globe can become the field of our operations and our successes.' It did not matter to this complicated man that his country was an insignificant speck wedged between the giants of Europe. And it did not take much of a geographer to see that of all the non-appropriated lands on the globe, the most conspicuous was Africa.

Across the Channel, Leopold's first cousin, bereaved these last nine years, was in residence at Balmoral. For her, in whose name blood would be spilled in every corner of the world, this was an ordinary Thursday. 'The Queen went out in the morning,' the Court Circular read, 'attended by Lady Churchill, and Her Majesty drove in the afternoon with Princess Louise.'

Nathan Meyer Rothschild, head of the London branch of the family, was at his desk at New Court, in St Swithin's Lane. In the village of Thoissey, in the Department of Ain, a seven-year-old boy named Jean-Baptiste Marchand was probably at play – history had not yet begun recording his movements.

The last major actor in the story was just completing a long ocean voyage. On September 1st, 1870, the wooden barque *Eudora*, 72 days out of Gravesend, dropped anchor beyond the sandbar blocking the entrance to Durban, the principal seaport of Natal. Among the twenty-odd passengers, mostly German emigrants, was a tall, pale-faced English boy who had celebrated his seventeenth birthday at sea. The fifth of nine children of a Hertfordshire clergyman, he was being sent to southern Africa because he suffered from a touch of consumption. His name was Cecil John Rhodes.

Rhodes quickly regained his health in Africa, established the basis for a modest income, and returned to Britain to complete his education.

In Oxford, Oriel College still rang with the echoes of John Ruskin's great Inaugural Lecture.

> There is a destiny now possible to us, the highest ever set before a nation ... will you, youths of England, make your country again a royal throne of kings; a sceptred isle, for all the world a source of light, ... ? This is what [England] must either do, or perish. She must found colonies as fast and as far as she is able, ... seizing every piece of fruitful waste ground she can set her foot on and there teaching her colonists that their chief virtue is to be fidelity to their country, and that their first aim is to be to advance the power of England. ...

As a student, Rhodes was older than most of his classmates, more experienced by far, yet far less worldly. While they, to the extent that they paid attention at all, accepted Ruskin's words as the proper backdrop against which their own preordained careers would comfortably unfold, he conscientiously measured himself against Ruskin's challenge:

> It often strikes a man to enquire what is the chief good of life. To one the thought comes that it is a happy marriage; to another great wealth; to a third travel. ... To myself, thinking over the same question, the wish came to render myself useful to my country.

Rhodes was to live only another twenty-five years, but every moment of that quarter-century he single-mindedly dedicated to the goal he had chosen. Many years later, when he was Prime Minister of the Cape Colony, and taking one of his customary evening walks, a friend drew his attention to the brilliance of the stars. Rhodes looked up absently and said, 'I would annex them if I could.'

At the beginning, however, his ambition was slightly more modest. He completed his studies and returned to Africa with the intention of securing as much of that continent as he could for the Queen. Edwin Arnold, an editor on the London *Daily Telegraph*, had coined the phrase 'Cape-to-Cairo'. It had a nice ring to it, and some degree of geographic logic. Britain already held the Cape, and had a firm hand in the affairs of Egypt; in between lay an enormous empty space. All that was needed was some master hand to fill that space, to paint it with the imperial red which map-makers traditionally reserved for Britain and her dependencies.

Rhodes had no doubt that he could do it. That the idea was someone else's, that others had tried before him and failed did not bother him in the least. 'What was attempted by Alexander, Cambyses and Napoleon,' he once told a meeting of shareholders, 'we practical men are going to finish.'

His practical mind fastened on a practical device – a railway. A railway which would run from the Cape to Cairo, climbing up and down mountain ranges, slicing through jungle and over swamp, across desert and plains and Heaven knew what else lay in its path. Such a railway would be 6,000 miles in length, more than a third of the world's girth from pole to pole. With branches sent out to reach the oceans on both sides, it would be the sturdy armature on which an empire could be assembled, shaped and cast.

This was the project Rhodes undertook in order to render himself useful to his country. But others, impelled by equally lofty motives or by the desire for private gain, had looked at Africa, too, and fashioned schemes and devices of their own.

Unprepared for their attention, the continent shuddered and endured, secure in its massiveness. But so extraordinary were these men, so audacious their dreams, that Africa has not to this day recovered. Long after the last of them has gone, it is still shaking from their deeds – vivid, bloody, heroic, shameful.

PART ONE

Cape Town to Kimberley

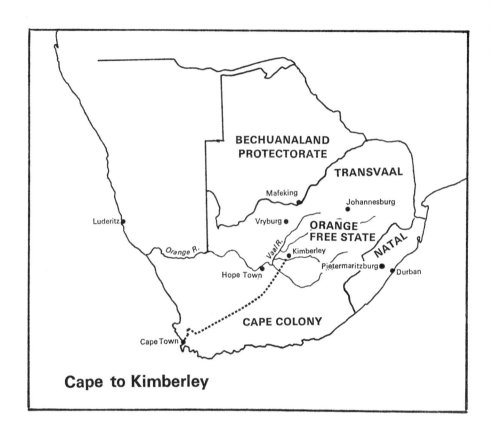

Cape to Kimberley

THE southern Africa to which Rhodes came in 1870 was the least likely place anyone seeking his fortune could have chosen.

It had been discovered at almost the same time as the New World, and for the same reason. Bartolomeu Diaz, too, was looking for the Indies in 1488, but his orders had been to sail eastward. He had clung to the coast, past the farthest point described by earlier explorers, until a thirteen-day storm blew him far out to sea and brought him back ashore to a sheltered cove on whose banks cattle placidly grazed. Although both the animals and the natives herding them fled inland at his approach, Diaz wished to continue along this new coast, pleasantly green and washed by a propitiously warm current. Fearful for their dwindling rations, however, his crew forced him to turn back. On the way home, he sighted to his starboard the great headland to which he gave the name Cape of Storms. In Lisbon, King John II overruled him and changed it to Cape of Good Hope – a touch of royal optimism which remained for Vasco da Gama to justify. Profiting from Diaz's experience, he doubled the Cape in a wide seaward sweep and proceeded up the coast as far as the Arab port of Melinde. There, he took aboard a pilot named Malemo Cano who, running before the monsoon without navigation instruments, guided him to Calicut, on the south-western coast of India. The day, marked with 'great rejoicing and the sound of trumpets', was May 16th, 1498; the search for a sea passage to the Indies was over.

For a century, the Indian Ocean remained a Portuguese lake, only occasionally trespassed upon by foreigners such as Sir Francis Drake, who wrote in 1580: 'We ran hard aboard the Cape, finding the report of the Portuguese to be most false, who affirm that it is the most dangerous Cape of the world, never without intolerable storms. ... This Cape is a most stately thing, the fairest we saw in the whole circumference of the earth, and we passed it on the 18th June.'

But then Portuguese dominion withered, sapped by over-extension abroad and indolence at home. The annexation of Portugal by its more powerful neighbour, Spain, in 1580, and the loss of Philip II's fleet eight years later at the hands of the English created a vacuum which competitors eagerly rushed in to fill. Within four years, three companies – English, Dutch, and French – were organized to satisfy Europe's acquired taste for pepper, cloves and cinnamon. There was national pride involved, of course, but there was another spur as well: more than 600 per cent profit could be made on each cargo.

The Cape of Good Hope and the sheltered Table Bay which lay at the foot of its unfinished-looking bulk, two miles long and 3,500 feet high, became the halfway house on the long, difficult voyage from Europe to the Indies. Ships put in to take on water, barter with the natives for cattle, and leave messages for each other, depositing them wrapped in linen or canvas under flat rocks – the 'post office stones' which can be seen in almost every South African museum. Some visitors lingered to take a look round. John Jourdain, a merchant on the British East India Company's *Ascension*, arrived on July 14th, 1608, and stayed two months. He commented on the excellent fishing – one cast of his seine brought up '300 fishes, $1\frac{1}{2}$ foot or longer, and tasting like bream' – and the fertility of the soil: 'If it were manured, I am of the opinion that it would bear anything that should be planted on it.' In all, he found the Cape 'healthful and commodious for all that trade the East Indies'. The only drawback was the native population – 'The world doth not yield a more heathenish people and more beastly.'

Twelve years later, six ships under the command of Andrew Shillinge and Humphrey Fitzherbert put into Table Bay, joining nine Dutch vessels which were already there. After civilities had been exchanged and the Dutch had left, the two British captains climbed part way up the mountain, planted the flag of St George, and took possession of the land 'as far north as the next white settlement' in the name of James I. Improvidently, the sovereign declined to accept, and thus lost an entire continent.

The British persisted. In 1626, Sir Thomas Herbert dropped by and noted: 'To what peculiar Potentate it belongs, I dare not determine. ... Nor is the land not worth the challenging, for in all my life I never saw ground more pleasant for view or healthful for use. ... The people are of a swarthy dark colour, well limbed and proper, nor want they courage. ... Their heads are long, their hair curled, and seemingly rather wool than hair; it is black and knotty.'

And, saving the sincerest compliment for last: 'Though these savages be treacherous, yet doubtless they esteem more of an Englishman than of a Portugal or Fleming.'

Possibly so, but they were not given the opportunity to choose. The contest over the East India trade ended with a clear victory for the Dutch. Once satisfied with picking up western-bound cargoes in Lisbon, and retailing them around northern Europe, they took advantage of Portugal's weakness – and the loss of the Armada – to capture the Spice Islands: Malacca, Macassar, Ceylon, Banda, and the great prize of Java, where Batavia became the capital of their new empire. As for the Cape, a Dutch East India Company ship, the *Haarlem*, had been driven ashore and wrecked there early in 1647. While waiting for rescue – a matter of eleven months – its crew had of necessity been obliged to test the early reports of the land's ability to sustain life. Finding them fully accurate, two of the officers proposed on their return home that the Company establish a permanent fort and garden – the first merely to guard the second which, in turn, would protect travellers against the greatest hazard of long sea voyages, scurvy.

It was therefore not conquest but the cultivation of cabbages which brought the first permanent European intruders into southern Africa. Lest there be any mistake about that, the Company chose carefully the man to head the project. Neither a soldier nor a statesman, Jan Anthonissen van Riebeeck had demonstrated during nine years of service in the East Indies the kind of industry and attention to detail which had earned him promotion to the rank of Senior Merchant. He was quiet, sober, 33 years old, married and the father of a young son. Furthermore, for what it was worth, he had already spent time on the Cape – eighteen days while his homeward-bound ship picked up the *Haarlem*'s survivors.

On Christmas Eve of 1651, the 200-ton *Drommedaris* with two smaller ships trailing cleared the roadstead in the Texel and headed south. After a successful voyage – only two deaths, one birth – the little fleet sighted its objective during the afternoon watch of April 5th, 1652. The following day, having sent one of his ships ahead to peek past the point and make sure no unfriendly callers were in harbour, van Riebeeck sailed into Table Bay and came to anchor, shortly after sunset, in five fathoms of water.

The next day was the Sabbath, but on the 8th work started and, judging from van Riebeeck's *Journal*, did not stop for a decade. There was a fort to build, gardens to plant, a brick kiln to be constructed, trees to be felled – some, witness to visitors' incurable habits, bore carved dates such as 1604, 1620, 1622. Later, with relative affluence, there were cattle to tend, fences to build, grapes to press, butter to churn. Mindful of the Company's instructions, exploration was discouraged, but van Riebeeck himself investigated a small island which lay within sight off the Atlantic coast. He found it covered with shells, which yielded useful lime, and crowded with seals, and penguins.

From the first, van Riebeeck's men – he had about 90, of whom a few including himself had been allowed to bring their wives and children – showed little inclination for pioneering. They were, after all, Company employees and not, like their compatriots who had chosen to make the long voyage westwards, settlers working on their own behalf. To underline the distinction, the Company had expressly forbidden such unproductive diversions as private bartering with the natives for ivory, hides, or whatever else might be sold to crews of passing ships. The men grumbled but obeyed: punishment, ranging from fines to public lashings and an infrequent keel-hauling, was severe.

As for the natives, they were less than useless. About two dozen of them had watched the boats unloading, after which their leader, whose name was Herry and who had somewhere picked up a smattering of English, offered himself as an interpreter. Neither he nor his colleagues, whom the Dutch named *strandloopers* – beachcombers – had anything of value; they lived off whatever edible roots the tide washed up. But there were other natives – Hottentots* – who lived on the far side of the mountain and who, like their ancestors who had shied at Diaz's coming, kept cattle. Herry managed to convince them to barter a cow and a calf for three small plates of copper. After that fine start, trade suffered because the Hottentots discovered that they could steal whatever they coveted. Van Riebeeck complains that they even coaxed children away from the fort, causing them no harm but wishing only to tear the copper buttons off their coats. His own preferred solution would have been to seize the Hottentots' cattle and ship off its owners as slaves to the East Indies, but this was beyond the scope of his orders, which required that he develop 'a good understanding with the natives in order to make them accustomed to intercourse with you'. Faced with an unforeseen problem, van Riebeeck at first proposed to dig a canal which would have cut off his settlement from the rest of the peninsula. When that was shown to be impractical, he settled instead for a thick thorn hedge.

It proved no more effective in regulating relations between the races than anything which has been tried since. Pilfering continued, and van Riebeeck complained in his *Journal* that the natives were 'black, stinking dogs'. Actually, they were dark yellowish to brown, and their worst offence was not dishonesty but a stubborn unwillingness to trade away their cattle, or to do work assigned by the whites.

On April 2nd, 1654, still thinking of the tidy manner in which things had been done in the Indies, van Riebeeck mused: 'If it could be agreed upon, it would be very much cheaper to have the agricultural work and all the other necessary work done by slaves in return for a plain fare of rice and fish or seal and penguin meat alone, and without pay. They could be obtained and brought very cheaply from Madagascar, together with rice, in one voyage.'

The Company agreed to try the idea. The first shipment of slaves, three males and eight females, arrived in June 1657. Other, larger batches followed, first from Madagascar, then from the East Indies. During the same year of 1657, the Company tried another experiment: in order to improve productivity, it acceded to the demand of nine of its employees that they be allowed to settle down on their own farms as free burghers. Thus, black and white immigrants received an even, if unequal, start in south Africa.

Free enterprise proved as successful as slavery. By May 1658, there were 57 free burghers, their land stretching as far out as they could push the Hottentots. (The full population of the settlement as of that date was recorded as: 'Garrison, 80; Sick, 15; Dutch women and children, 20; Healthy and sick Company's slaves, 98; Freemen, 57; Slaves of private parties, 89; Prisoners, 7.') With prosperity came amenities: a lumber mill,

---

* This too was a Dutch term, meaning 'stutterer' or 'stammerer'. The natives' own name for themselves was Khoi-khoi – 'man-man' – possibly to distinguish themselves from the Bushmen, a Stone-Age race of stunted hunters who were pushed by black and white alike into the arid wastes of the Kalahari where they still survive in protected areas, like other disappearing species.

a bakery, an enormous communal granary known as Groote Schuur, a brewery and four taverns to handle the passing trade. Van Riebeeck himself, the stern work of founding a colony behind him, turned gentleman farmer and planted 1,200 vines of grapes. The vintage of 1659, his first, was pronounced 'of fine flavour and taste, glory be to God'.

None of this sat well with the Company, which viewed it as irrelevant to the running of a refreshment station for its ships. Van Riebeeck was informed: 'From your letters we have remarked that you are gradually tending towards the building of a town there, and the enlarging of the colony; but as we look at it here, this idea should be abandoned.'

It was easier said than enforced. Rather than retrench, the free burghers added to their land holdings, and formed a Council which met regularly to discuss such matters of common interest as the best way to guard against Hottentot cattle raids, and the most effective punishment for recaptured fugitive slaves.

In July 1661, van Riebeeck asked to be relieved, and his request, turned down five years earlier, was granted. As he boarded ship, on March 8th, 1662,* he could look back on a useful, productive decade. He had built the beginning of a town – De Kaap possessed three streets. He had acquired cattle – they fattened contentedly in the Company's kraal. He had planted 500 acres of wheat and corn, 42 acres of gardens – its plump Dutch tomatoes, carrots, beets, onions, radishes and lettuce were the admiration of visitors. And he had sown another crop, which was still some years from harvesting.

For the next century and more, nothing happened. In Europe, and even in the New World, nations and ideas clashed. Voltaire wrote, as did Adam Smith, Rousseau, Kant, and Tom Paine. Reason and revolution flourished in turn. The Iron Age gave way to steel. At the Cape, the single most significant event was the arrival, in 1688, of 185 French Huguenots – one of the mildest ripples to result from the revocation, by Louis XIV, of the Edict of Nantes. As a group, they were vastly better educated, better informed, more skilled in every art than the 600-odd Dutch, employees and burghers, who were already there. Yet such was the stifling social climate of De Kaap that the newcomers rapidly lost their verve, their identity, and even their most precious possession. In 1701, the use of French was forbidden in all public matters; twenty-three years later, services of the Church were last allowed to be performed in that language. All that remained – and remains – were the names: de Villiers, du Toit, Malan.

Little by little, the Company lost its grip on the settlement. In 1691 it made the concession of permitting the ranking Senior Merchant to call

---

* Despite his latter-day differences with them, the Company promoted van Riebeeck to membership on the Court of Justice to Java. He died in the East Indies on January 18th, 1677, never having returned to Holland.

himself governor; in turn, he tried to check the outward press of the burghers, who had now started calling themselves *trekboeren* – frontier farmers – and pleading soil exhaustion as a pretext to appropriate new land. In handing the governorship over to his successor in 1699, Simon van der Stel warned prophetically: 'Should you be weak enough to gi e way to such sinister tricks, the whole of Africa would not be sufficient to accommodate and satisfy that class.'

This warning was ignored, with the result that the community grew in area much faster than in population. Land was free, or virtually free, for the taking. A farm of approximately 6,000 acres cost a nominal £25 a year in rent, but officials seldom came around to collect it, and the trekboer, who might journey down to *Kaapstad* once or twice in his lifetime, was unlikely to volunteer it. There was, however, one price which had to be paid: if the Company did not prevent a man from adding to his holdings, or providing a full-scale start for each of his sons, the natives sometimes did. The results were countless minor skirmishes, cattle raids and, in 1779, a major fight – the first of a century-long series of native wars.

Labour was no problem. Trekboers only put three or four of their acres to the plough, enough to grow fruit and vegetables for themselves and a little corn for barter. The rest was for cattle-raising, a task which could be entrusted to slaves. At the Cape, where there was little productive work for them to do, their existence attested mainly to their owners' wealth and social position. But on the frontier, they fulfilled the role conceived for them by van Riebeeck: they did all the work for no pay other than their meagre keep, and permitted their owner to enjoy the fruits of contentment.

In time – 1781 – the great events of the world did reach far enough south to touch the settlement on Table Bay. At the tail end of a global struggle between France and Britain which caused great parts of North America and Asia to change hands, a small contingent of French troops arrived to occupy the Cape. The immediate local effect of their presence was that prices rose by 50 to 100 per cent, a theatre suddenly opened, and the ladies of *Kaapstad* began to wear their best dresses on weekdays as well as Sundays. For three years, the town blossomed as troops spent their pay in the waterfront taverns, while their officers sought more refined pleasure in the substantial stone houses and country residences of the town's leading citizens. Then a truce was negotiated in Europe and the troops departed as suddenly as they had come. When the hangover had worn off, a loyal Dutch patriot named Jacob Abraham de Mist complained that the 'giddy and godless' French 'had entirely corrupted the standard of living at the Cape, and extravagance and indulgence in an unbroken round of amusements and diversions have come to be regarded as necessities.'

Or possibly, since the French were not really French at all but mainly Luxemburger and Swiss mercenaries, the time had simply come for a little corruption.

The town's merchants, saddened to see the soldiers go, did not have to wait long. They were back in 1795, and it mattered little that this time they wore British uniforms.

War was raging in earnest now across Europe, with revolutionary, republican France on one side, and virtually everybody else on the other. In quick order, the French invaded Holland and destroyed its fleet, ice-bound at anchor; King William of Orange fled to London where he established a government-in-exile; Holland emotionally proclaimed itself a republic and declared allegiance to France; Britain looked at the Cape and decided that 'what was a feather in the hands of Holland will become a sword in the hands of France.'

The British stayed for eight years, then dutifully departed when peace again descended in 1802. They came back in 1806.

Much had happened in the intervening four years, including the battle of Trafalgar. More than any other event, Nelson's decisive victory opened Britain's eyes to the fact that, for the taking of a few strategic points, she was now, by elimination, mistress of the seas. One of these points was the Cape. No longer needed as a cabbage patch – lime juice had taken care of that – it now had a far more important role to play: it had to guard the road to India, the focal point of Britain's new empire. In 1795, the British had sent a light squadron of nine ships. In 1806 they came in a fleet of 63, with every intention of staying permanently.

The British inherited a mixed bag. Of the Cape's population, 25,757 were white. With the demise of the Company, which had quietly sunk into bankruptcy in 1795, all of them had automatically become freemen. There were 29,545 slaves, and another 20,000-odd human beings whose status was uncertain – freed or runaway slaves, the remains of a Hottentot population which had been decimated by smallpox in 1713, the half-breed product of energetic intermarriage. There was one single city, now called Cape Town, and a few fair-sized, comfortable villages laid out in neat, tree-shaded squares. Beyond them, the farms stretched and thinned out to the distant Vaal and Orange rivers. Along the east coast, the Great Fish River, some 500 miles from the Cape, had been designated as the boundary between whites and natives – not meek Hottentots this time, but Xhosas who could defend themselves, and attack as well. The river was supposed to keep them apart; it served instead to provoke continuous raids, reprisals, and counter-reprisals.

Culturally, the colony was nearly as barren as the Great Karroo desert which lay beyond the mountain passes to the immediate north. The only art which flourished was architecture, still represented by fine houses with graceful porticos and gables. Of literature or music there was none; nor even a newspaper until John Fairbairn started the *South African Commercial*

Advertiser in 1824. Schools barely taught students their letters, and the sole library was so poorly stocked that its assistant librarian, John Pringle, wrote to a friend in England asking for 'a copy of Euclid, a few of the more elementary books on Arithmetic, French, Latin, Greek, *Mother's Cate-chism*, a pair of small globes and a good atlas'. Like other mail from the Cape, Pringle's letter waited for the monthly packet and reached its destination in just under 100 days.

Still, the Cape was not a bad place to live, either for its inhabitants, who enjoyed the false boom of providing garrison amenities to four or five thousand British troops, or for the troops themselves, who could have drawn far harsher duty at some other outpost. The succession of British governors were uncomplicated men who had no desire to make sweeping changes or antagonize the Dutch. Certainly, not even the sternest of them could imagine that he was behaving in such a fashion that some day a distinguished South African – perhaps the most distinguished of all, Jan Christiaan Smuts – would label their collective stewardship as 'The Century of Wrong'.

Circumstance – the ripening of the seeds planted by van Riebeeck, the thrust of ideas conceived on another continent – this, rather than premeditated British devilry, conspired against the Dutch; and particularly against those who had chosen to live on the land rather than close by the docks and markets of Cape Town. No Boer would accept that explanation then, and none of their descendants is probably willing to do it today. The pattern was too neat.

The British had arrived in 1806; during the following year, they prohibited trading in slaves. The Bill had passed only after long debate, and because of parliamentary manœuvring unrelated to the moral issue involved, but the Boers saw it as a direct attack against their way of life. On the heels of the soldiers had come missionaries. Not satisfied to stay in town, they had appeared on the frontier, asking questions and interfering with the time-honoured relations between white and black. And when the Boers attempted to undo the trouble they had caused, the British sent out magistrates – the infamous Black Circuit – to punish not the meddlers or the fractious servants who had deserved their punishment, but the masters.

In 1815, a Boer named Frederick Bezuidenhout, charged by a magistrate with cheating and abusing a servant, refused to appear in court, and was killed in a gunfight with the soldiers – Hottentot soldiers no less – sent to arrest him. Swearing revenge, his brother precipitated a small rebellion which was quickly and forcefully put down with the public hanging of five white men. The site of their execution – Slagter's Nek – is one of the shrines of contemporary South African history.

In 1820, the first large group of English-speaking colonists arrived. There were 5,000 of them, their passage had been paid by a special £50,000 Parliamentary grant, and they were settled on good land cleared of natives.

Quite possibly, the British intended to start stocking the colony with their own kind, though unemployment at home was probably a more likely reason. In any case, they chose the wrong breed; most of the immigrants were town folk who knew nothing of farming and quickly abandoned their homesteads for the new communities of Port Elizabeth and Grahamstown, where they reverted to more congenial occupations as shopkeepers and artisans. Nevertheless the preferential treatment they had been accorded was duly catalogued in the 'Century of Wrong'.

Far more damaging to Boer interest was another British act eight years later which had no self-serving, imperial motive whatever. It was in fact so much the work of a single man – a missionary named John Philip – that his name is still invoked by the present proprietors of South Africa as the embodiment of the ill-will which the outside world has always borne them. Philip's act – Ordinance 50, to give it its proper name – abolished the pass system under which Hottentots and other non-whites who were not slaves were nonetheless effectively bound to their masters' land for life, and moved towards securing for them a measure of fundamental civil rights.

The British governors, their troops and their magistrates, merely enforced these new rules of relationship. Their inspiration came from London, where a new tide had begun to run. Castlereagh had died in 1822, and there would never again be another monarch such as George III. Ten years of turmoil and soul-searching had produced the Great Reform Act, and let loose the evangelical, humanitarian zeal of which Wilberforce, Wesley and Buxton were only among the most visible symbols.

According to many historians, the final blow which tore South Africa was the abolition of slavery throughout the British Empire, voted in 1833 and made effective the following year. True, it deprived Boers of the labour supply on which they and their forefathers had relied. But perhaps even more impelling was the sentiment expressed by a Boer woman, Anna Steenkamp, sister of Piet Retief. She wrote: ' … it is not so much the freeing of our slaves which drove us to such length, as their being placed on an equal footing with Christians, contrary to the laws of God, and the natural distinctions of race and colour, so that it was intolerable for any decent Christian to bow down beneath such a yoke; wherefore we rather withdrew in order to preserve our doctrines in purity.'

These doctrines, their purity preserved, are presently the order of the day in Pretoria, Johannesburg, and Cape Town as well. As for the withdrawal, it is recorded as the Great Trek.

Whatever connotations it may have acquired in English usage – great distance, slow progress, arduous passage – the word *trek* had a specific meaning in Afrikaans. It was not merely a journey, but a one-way journey; its direction might veer, and its destination be uncertain, but the traveller was not expected to return. This finality, coupled with the patriarchal mantle draped over the Boers by their descendants, has caused the story of the Great Trek to take on, in the re-telling, the aspect of an Exodus – the spontaneous rising of half a nation, turning its back on the enemies of God and marching northward in stately procession toward deliverance.

That is not how history records it. In May 1835, Louis Trigardt, 53 years old and with a price on his head for intriguing against the Colony, decided to move north, taking with him a party of six families, numbering some fifty people. They travelled in nine ox-drawn wagons, accompanied by saddle horses, about 500 head of cattle and some 3,000 sheep and goats. Moving at the rate of six miles a day – less when the ewes were lambing or there was good grazing – they met by prearrangement another group of about the same size led by Janse van Rensburg and, together, forded the Orange River just before the New Year of 1836. But even that defiant gesture – crossing the Orange was forbidden – was not the true start of the Trek. As early as 1833 and 1834, small scouting parties had ventured ahead – quietly, for Slagter's Nek was still fresh in the mind – to report that good land was to be had in abundance. (The information did little good. The leaders quarrelled and went their separate ways. Van Rensburg's group vanished without a trace, presumably wiped out by hostile tribes. Trigardt's party, their gunpowder exhausted, tried to reach the coast by crossing the Drakensberg range. Only one of the men – Trigardt's eldest son – and a few of the women and children made it; the rest died.)

The great, remembered names began leaving in late 1836 and 1837: Andries Potgieter and Sarel Cilliers, leading a party of 65 families which, as every South African history notes, included a ten-year-old boy named Paul Kruger; Gerrit Maritz, a well-to-do wagon-maker from Graaff-Reinet; Piet Retief, the finest natural leader among the trekkers and, by virtue of his fate, their tragic hero. He, too, crossed the Drakensberg, to find the lovely, rain-blessed valleys which sloped to the sea. Possibly they reminded him of the Promised Land, whose description he could recite by heart. But the Bible had made no mention of Zulus, nor of their king, Dingaan, who signed a treaty of peace with Retief and then, during a celebration of friendship, treacherously slaughtered him and his 68 unarmed companions. Their death was avenged by another of the great names: Andries Pretorius. This time the Boers were armed, and well-entrenched at Blood River. The Zulus attacked, as they always did, in waves. But after three hours they stopped and went away, leaving 3,000 dead piled in front of the laagered wagons, 'like pumpkins on rich soil'. That happened on the morning of December 16th, 1839. And because, before the battle, the Boers had sworn that if God gave them a victory they would build Him a church, the date is still celebrated as The Day of the Covenant.

Blood River temporarily broke the back of Zulu resistance. In the first two years, perhaps 4,000 people had gone north; afterwards, another eight or ten thousand followed. But they too went in small groups – families, friends, neighbours. Rather than a great outpouring, the Trek was a collection of individual movements, more characteristic of Boer custom and, ironically, far more courageous if not as epic as the legend. Nor was it quite an Exodus. By 1845, when the last of those who wished to go had left, four-fifths of the Afrikaans-speaking population of Cape Colony remained behind.

Nevertheless, the Great Trek was the most important event south of the Sahara since the coming of the Europeans. The letting loose of a thin layer of determined, land-hungry men to spread over vast territories dissolved the fabric of a native civilization woven around the free use of land. With the decimation of its herds, penned into ranges too poor to sustain them, tribal life withered. But the native himself prevailed. Too strong to be killed off by disease, alcohol or hunger, too numerous to be pushed out, he was left to fend for himself and, in the absence of authority or guidance, find a place among the whites. The relatively small number of whites in present-day South Africa, compared to other former colonies such as Canada and the United States, is conventionally explained by the lack of immigration. That, too, is not exactly true. South Africa did have her immigrants but, as Professor de Kiewiet has pointed out, they were black.

Politically, the Trek resulted in the Balkanization of south Africa into four white states, two of them British – Cape Colony and Natal – and two Dutch – the Orange Free State and the Transvaal. Having allowed the Boers to leave, the British were powerless to prevent them from establishing their own republics. Nor did anyone in Cape Town or London strenuously care. The Boers had been, on the whole, undesirable subjects – unprofitable to tax, and, because of their constant border quarrels, expensive to govern. As for their new domains, there was little beyond the Orange River for a sensible white man to covet.

In any case, the Cape had ample problems of its own. Started as a seaside boarding-house, it had never progressed far beyond that role. In 1821, its economy had been so fragile and dependent on the outside world that the removal of the British garrison from nearby St Helena Island, made redundant by the death of its most famous occupant, had caused a serious slump. Blessed with one of the finest natural anchorages in the world, it was not until 1860 that Cape Town could afford to build the breakwater and docking facilities needed to make it an efficient harbour; for two hundred years after van Riebeeck's arrival, freight was still handled by a single wooden jetty, and passengers ferried ashore in rowboats. Wool, which replaced wine as the colony's chief export, provided subsistence if not prosperity for a few years. But then, in 1865, the end of the American Civil War caused a world-wide collapse of wool prices. With no natural resources and nothing left to attract new capital, the imminent prospect was that the Cape would fulfil the prediction of one of its governors, Sir George Grey, and drift, 'by not very slow degrees, into disorder and barbarism'. Clearly, what was needed was some kind of miracle.

*

The miracle, when it arrived, looked unprepossessingly like a pebble and weighed just a shade under 21½ carats.

Picked up by a child named Erasmus Jacobs on his father's farm near Hopetown, on the Orange River, it caught the eye of a neighbour named Schalk van Niekerk. He had in the past earned a few shillings by selling an odd garnet or topaz which turned up in the gravel at the river's edge. Erasmus's pebble, decidedly neither a garnet nor a topaz, passed through several hands before ending up on the laboratory bench of a Grahamstown physician named Dr W. Guybon Atherstone. Having dulled his keenest jeweller's file on it, Dr Atherstone, who was also an amateur mineralogist, pronounced it to be a diamond – a daring diagnosis in view of the fact that no diamond had ever been found closer to south Africa than India or Brazil. It was, however, good enough for Sir Philip Wodehouse, the Governor of Cape Colony. He paid £500 for it and shipped it off to the Paris Exposition of 1867 in the hope, unrewarded, that it might spark interest in investment or immigration. Locally, the windfall – van Niekerk received £350 for the stone, and shared it with Mrs Jacobs – caused farmers to look more closely at their children's playthings, and even occasionally stoop down to pick up something that glittered. But any organized attempt at prospecting was frustrated by Erasmus's inability to remember, even vaguely, where he had found his pebble.

A second stone turned up in March 1869. By then, the price of pebbles had gone up; van Niekerk was obliged to pay the native who had found it the bulk of his wordly goods – 500 sheep, 10 oxen and a horse, worth in all about £400. He then sold the stone, which turned out to be a flawless white diamond weighing 85·8 carats, to a jeweller named Gustav Lilienfeld for £11,200.*

In a more prosperous country, the discovery of two diamonds within a span of two or three years, and in a remote, inaccessible corner – Hopetown was some 700 miles or two months by ox-cart from the Cape, and half that distance from Natal – might have attracted a few treasure hunters. In poverty-ridden south Africa, thousands made the trip – no count was kept, but estimates vary from 5,000 to 10,000 for the first two years. A few were lucky, including a party of army officers sent from Natal to preserve order; once on the scene they dropped their swords, picked up shovels, and returned home in seven months with a small pouch worth between £12,000 and £15,000. Most, however, found little. The value of diamonds discovered in 1869 was officially set at £28,413. Even allowing for illicit trading, which began immediately, this did not average out to very much – certainly not enough for the discomfort of standing hip-deep in a river all

* Named the *Star of South Africa*, it eventually reached London, where it now rests among the Crown Jewels. There is a story that before it left its homeland, Sir Richard Southey, the Colonial Secretary, laid it on the table of the Cape Assembly and declared, 'Gentlemen, this is the rock on which the future of South Africa will be built.'

day long and scraping away at its bottom. (In 1871, the yield was £300,000 – better, but still something under £60 per man for a year's work.)

One problem was that no one had the remotest idea where to look for the diamonds. Experts at the Cape had not been helpful; one expressed the opinion that diamonds were not native to the region, but had been brought by ostriches who had carried them in their gizzards. Many of the prospectors simply imagined that the diamonds would be lying on the ground, waiting to be picked up. There was, indeed, a lot to be picked up – pebbles, stones, boulders, as far as the eye could see in every direction – but scarcely a soul among the searchers had the vaguest idea what a diamond looked like in its rough state. The ground itself was flat, dry, uninvitingly hard and covered with patches of short, thorny bush. The only landmarks were two rivers – the Orange itself and, thirty miles upstream from Hopetown, the Vaal. Remembering that gold had been found in streams, the diggers attacked the banks, using a long frame fitted with three sieves of varying meshes fixed on swinging rockers to separate out sand, gravel and, it was hoped, diamonds. (The contraption, invented on the spot by an American veteran of the '49 California gold rush named J. L. Babe, was called a cradle, and gave rise to the inevitable *mot* that he was the only Babe who had ever rocked his own cradle.)

A few diamonds were found in this fashion, just enough to encourage further search and cause both banks of the rivers to become covered, from hilltop to water's edge, with tents, lean-tos, sorting tables, outdoor kitchens, and accumulating mounds of discarded dirt. Meanwhile, other diggers, the more adventuresome and those who had arrived too late to stake out desirable claims near the water, began boring holes in dry land. There was no system or logic to their choice – any rumour of a find would send parties scurrying in that direction – but by sheer statistical probability one of those diggings, in the middle of a dry pan on a farm owned by a man named du Toit, yielded a yellowish, crumbling clay which contained diamonds. Here, at last, was a clue, and woe betide the poor Boer on whose acres it was subsequently found. Within days or even hours, his land would be swarming with excited men armed with shovels and picks, digging holes, hammering in wooden stakes, trampling crops and frightening the cattle. Nothing was sacred: one of du Toit's neighbours had had the misfortune to build his house out of yellowish clay, and it was picked apart with pocket knives. Two other neighbours, a pair of brothers named Dietrick and Johannes de Beer, owned a dusty farm which they had optimistically named *Vooruitzicht* – foresight. When the human locusts descended, they sold out for the staggering sum of £6,000, piled into their wagons and, probably shaking their heads at both their own good fortune and the insanity of the rest of the world, trekked off to find peace farther out on the veld.

If the distinction of discovering the south African diamond fields can be attributed to one man – van Niekerk does not qualify, for he never found a

diamond himself – it would have to go to a young Englishman named
Fleetwood Rawstorne. The son of the town magistrate of Colesberg, in the
Cape Colony, he had been 24 years old in 1869 when he joined the first rush
to the fields. From a rare photograph, one imagines him as somewhat dashing, with long sideburns and a trim, sloping moustache, but with a wistful
side as well – high forehead, far-focused deep-set eyes. His luck, for the
first two years, had not been spectacular, but neither so grim that he and
his companions did not gather in his tent for an occasional evening of card-
playing. It was during one of these games – on a Saturday night in July
1871 – that his Cape boy servant, Damon, burst into the tent. In silent
apology for having interrupted the game, he held out an upturned palm on
which rested two or three small diamonds. One of the players, a minister's
son named Henry R. Giddy, recalled: 'Needless to say, the effect on us all
was electrical, and there was an immediate rush and scramble out of the
tent. Having quickly secured stakes and hatchets, the whole party, led by
Damon, made haste to the spot where the diamonds had been found.'

It turned out to be a *kopje*, a flat-topped hillock about 20 feet high and
measuring some 180 feet by 220. In the clear moonlight, 'with just a twinge
of frost in the air', the men made the agonizing decision of where to stake
their claims; each could have two, 31 feet square; as the discoverer,
Rawstorne was entitled to four. He was also entitled to name the *kopje*,
which he called Colesberg, after his home town. To the thousands who
began arriving with daybreak, however, it became known as New Rush.
They quickly pegged out every square inch for miles around, and bid the
price of claims from the legal 10 shillings to £20 and, within three months,
to three and four thousand pounds each. Even that turned out for some to
be a bargain, because Colesberg Kopje, or New Rush, or *Vooruitzicht* – for
it was located on the old de Beer farm – was to yield up more than £100
million in diamonds during the next twenty years, and became better known
under its present-day name of Kimberley.* As for Fleetwood Rawstorne,
fate dealt him a poor hand on that moonlit night. A late-coming digger
named Arie Smuts, who paid £50 for half a claim less than 100 feet from
his own, found diamonds worth £20,000 in ten months, then sold out to
another man who proceeded to dig up 657 stones, including two weighing
more than 100 carats each. Rawstorne found almost nothing. Well-liked and
cheerful, he drifted around and died, penniless, in 1886.

Among the earliest arrivals at the fields was another Englishmen, a 25-year-
old cotton planter from Natal named Herbert Rhodes. Hearty, fond of
adventure and good at games – at Winchester, he had taken six wickets

---

* The reason for the change was that the new Colonial Secretary found the Afrikaans
names unpronounceable, and New Rush insufficiently elegant. His own name was Lord
Kimberley.

against Eton – he was the kind of young man who was universally expected, with a bit of luck, to make his mark somewhere. In September 1870, he was too preoccupied pursuing that luck to take time out in order to meet, as promised, a younger brother being shipped out into his care. He did, however, remember to arrange for the boy – his name was Cecil and he was just 17 – to be put up by friends, Dr P. C. Sutherland, the Surveyor-General of Natal, and his wife, a motherly woman with no children of her own. The choice had been dictated by Cecil's health, which was the reason for his coming.

If he was disappointed by his welcome, Cecil did not complain. Rather, his first letter home describes the wonders of the trip – whales, flying fish, albatrosses with a 20-foot wing-span – and of his new surroundings – sugar cane, cliffs rising from the sea, natives who carried their snuff-boxes in holes bored through their ears. The rainy season was about to start, and farmers were burning the coarse, dried grass; Cecil was impressed by the spectacle, at night, of flames rolling along the crests of the hills. But the biggest wonder was still unseen, 350 miles away. 'People out here', he wrote, 'do nothing but talk of the diamonds,' and repeated some of the current stories: one digger had tried unsuccessfully to sell his claim for 15 shillings, and on the very next day had found a stone worth £11,000; another had traded a native a roll of tobacco for a diamond which sold for £800; one buyer alone was disbursing £6,000 in cash a week. Herbert, he heard, had done extremely well and was expected back within the month.

Herbert did arrive, cheerful as ever, but with only one or two diamonds worth, Cecil reported, 'from five to ten pounds'. The cotton plantation, too, probably fell short of whatever he may have imagined such an exotic enterprise to look like. As an emigrant, Herbert had qualified for a grant of 200 virgin acres in a deep fold of the Unkomaas valley, some 30 miles from the capital, Pietermaritzburg. The soil was, if anything, too fertile. Before leaving, Herbert had cleared less than one quarter of his land and, inexperienced, had planted the rows of cotton too close together. The crop, weed-choked and worm-ridden, did not cover expenses. Nevertheless, the brothers set about clearing another 50 acres, devising better methods of cultivation, ordering new seeds from America. Living in two small huts, one for sleeping, the other for eating, they started to build a brick house, 60 feet by 20 and circled by a wide verandah.

It was not a bad life, nor, by pioneering standards, very strenuous, since all the work, even the cooking and cleaning, was done by Kaffirs – the term applied indiscriminately and disdainfully by whites in south Africa to describe all non-whites. There was ample time for social calls, rides into the country, even weekly dances and an occasional cricket match. Cecil met a young neighbour his own age with whom he dutifully read the few books he had brought along – Plutarch, Marcus Aurelius, Gibbon. His great ambition was to continue his studies, if possible at Oxford and, of necessity in a family of nine children, on his own resources. At a shilling a pound, the price Herbert expected to get for the crop, now planted properly and thriving, the prospect did not seem impossible. 'Cotton', Cecil wrote home, 'is decidedly the best thing in Natal.'

But Herbert was a man with an unslaked thirst. In March 1871, he packed off for another try at the diamond fields, taking five Kaffirs with him and leaving Cecil in charge of the rest to harvest the crop. It was much better this time, winning honourable mention at an agricultural show. But the price had fallen. Instead of a shilling a pound, Cecil received fivepence, making the season's exertion profitless and ending his brief agricultural career. Possibly, as his many biographers claim, it had long-lasting significance as the character-builder – 'Ah,' he is quoted as saying in later life when told something was impossible, 'they told me I couldn't grow cotton.' But the immediate effect of the plantation's failure was to leave him with no choice except to follow his brother to the fields.

The notion had already occurred to him. Diamonds were a risky business – Herbert was proof enough of that. But there was a sensible way to approach it: 'You want to have money to last you for a good six months or a year's digging. ... If you would only look at diamond digging like cotton growing, and wait a year for your crop ... you are bound to succeed.'

In October 1871, he packed his gear – a few staples, a pail and shovel, his slim library – and set off to test his theory. By the time he arrived at Colesberg Kopje, there were 10,000 people at work. Of the many descriptions of their activity, one of the best is his own, in a letter to his mother:

> Fancy an immense plain, with right in its centre a mass of white tents and iron stores, and on one side of it, all mixed up with the camp, mounds of lime like anthills; the country round is all flat with just thorn trees here and there. ... I should like you to have a peep at the *kopje* from my tent door at the present moment. It is like an immense number of antheaps covered with black ants, as thick as can be, the latter represented by human beings. ... Take your garden, for instance, and peg the whole off into squares or claims 31 feet by 31, and then the question is how to take all the earth out and sort and sieve it. All through the *kopje* roads have been left to carry the stuff off in carts. ... There are constantly mules, carts and all going head over heels into the mines below.

He then described the procedure of meshing and sorting, and provided a homely analogy for the diamond-bearing soil: 'It works just like Stilton cheese, and is as like the composition of Stilton cheese as anything I can compare it to. ... They have been able to find no bottom yet. ... '

The letter then discussed his own progress – he had found a $17\frac{5}{8}$-carat stone which, unfortunately, was slightly off in colour – and concluded on a more business-like than filial note: 'I average about £100 a week. Yrs. C. Rhodes.'

What he did not describe for his mother, probably because he had no interest in them himself, were the many diversions which, even at that early date, were available to the miners. They included some twenty hotels, and saloons beyond number – one chronicler reckoned there was one per 16 inhabitants, with names such as 'Harp of Erin', 'Auld Lang Syne', and 'London Town'. There were gambling parlours, half a dozen billiard rooms, and girls of every colour, description and price. Nightly auctions were held at which it is recorded that a new arrival who billed herself as 'The Blonde Venus' went to a Dutch buyer for £25 and six cases of champagne. There was cheating, stealing, brawling, and all the other attributes of a mining camp at the crest of a strike. Garbage and even the skeletons of dead horses and mules lay uncollected; a bath, in brackish water which cost more than beer did at the Cape, was a luxury. All of it had happened before, and would again. What did not fit in was Cecil John Rhodes.

There are many descriptions of him, too, during those early days: ' ... a tall, fair boy, blue-eyed, and with somewhat aquiline features, wearing flannels of the school playing-field, somewhat shrunken with strenuous rather than effectual washing. ... '

Or, ' ... a fair young man frequently sunk in deep thought, his hands buried in his trouser pockets, his legs crossed and twisted together, quite oblivious of the talk around him ... without a word, he would get up and go with some set purpose in his mind, which he was at no pains to communicate.'

Or one of the most famous of all, contributed by Gardner Williams, who went on to become Rhodes's principal mining expert: ' ... a tall, gaunt youth, roughly dressed, coated with dust, sitting moodily on a bucket, deaf to the chatter and rattle about him, his blue eyes fixed intently on his work or on some fabric of his brain.'

The aggregate picture is vivid, but too pat. One suspects that, like the yellowish clay itself, it has been sifted – if not intentionally then out of unconscious regard for a man who not only amassed a tremendous amount of money, but had the rare distinction of having a country named after him during his lifetime. Williams, for instance, did not even meet Rhodes until 1885, long after his bucket-sitting days were over. In 1871, Rhodes was 18 years old; all but the last of those years had been spent at a country parsonage. He had not even gone away to school; Herbert had been sent to Winchester and Frank, the next eldest, to Eton, but when Cecil's turn came family finances could stretch only as far as the local grammar school, and as a day student at that. The year in Natal, if it did not mould his character, no doubt did almost as much for his self-confidence as for his health, but it is fair to ascribe the uncommunicativeness, the deep thought and the aloofness as much to shyness as to the contemplation of any grand design.

But a design there was, or at least the goal of a design. Throughout his life, Rhodes had few confidants, nor was he given to writing the long, introspective letters which are the bread and butter of historians – and often read as if composed with that audience in mind. He did, however, leave an unmistakable trail of clues to his innermost thinking: a set of seven last wills and testaments. The final one, written in 1899 and running to 22 pages, provided detailed instructions to create the Scholarships for which he is today best remembered.* The first was written in 1872, on a single crumpled sheet of paper. In it, a 19-year-old whose total possessions could easily fit into a suitcase bequeathed ' ... all of which I might die possessed to the Secretary of State for the Colonies, in trust and to be used for the extension of the British Empire.'

By 1873, only a little later than the year he had allotted himself, Rhodes had earned enough to apply to Oxford. (University College, his first choice, turned him down as ill-prepared, but Oriel accepted him – 'considerably to its later advantage', as one writer noted.) In all the standard accounts of Rhodes's life, the years at Oxford are represented as the making of the man – the gentle channelling, in cloistered halls and cosy, fire-lit rooms, of ele-mental force into purposefulness. There was not much of that. Because of his age, his occupation, his lack of public school education, Rhodes was as much of an outsider here as he had been on the fields. He chose to live in 'digs' and take his meals out. Health was a problem; in his first year, he caught pneumonia as a result of a day's rowing on the Isis and was obliged to return to Africa, having seen a doctor's report that gave him 'less than six months' to live. Afterwards, business matters obliged him to shuttle back and forth so that it was not until December 1881, when he was 28 years old and many times a millionaire, that he received his degree. Rhodes's education, in addition to tuition, room and board, cost him £2,000 in steamship tickets.

Oxford had become accustomed to characters – Oscar Wilde was in resi-dence during Rhodes's time – but it is hard to imagine that it was ready for an undergraduate who, at every chance, brought up the subject of south Africa and, to demonstrate its bright future, would reach into his pocket and produce a handful of diamonds. As a student, Rhodes was indifferent, despite his Plutarch and Marcus Aurelius. He read a great deal, but to no particular end, less like a scholar than a man who has a formed idea in mind and is seeking to support it with outside opinion. The idea he had already expressed in his first will; the support he found in Ruskin, in

* They required a graded combination of literary and scholastic achievement, profi-ciency in 'manly sports', qualities of 'truth, courage, sympathy for and protection of the weak, kindliness, unselfishness and fellowship', moral force and character – a set of quali-fications which Rhodes himself, as his critics have pointed out, would have fallen far short of satisfying.

Darwin, and particularly in Winwood Reade's *The Martyrdom of Man*, a now-forgotten but then much-discussed mixture of mysticism, religion, and the creed of the survival of the fittest. He read deeply into the history of the Roman emperors – in later life, there was always a bust or print of one or another of them in his bedroom or study. Out of this hodge-podge, he crystallized the view that the English were instruments of some super-natural purpose.* It therefore was morally right and intellectually sensible that they should rule the world. Furthermore, he had determined how this could be done. His second will, written in 1877, asked that the whole of his estate be used

> ... to and for the establishment, promotion and development of a Secret Society, the true aim and object whereof shall be the extension of British rule throughout the world ... and especially the occupation by British settlers of the entire Continent of Africa, the Holy Land, the valley of the Euphrates, ... the seaboard of China and Japan, the ultimate recovery of the United States of America as an integral part of the British Empire ... and finally the foundation of so great a power as to hereafter render wars impossible and promote the best interest of humanity.

Rhodes's conclusion was wrong, and nowhere more wrong than in Africa, the only place where he had time to put it to the test. The implementation of the plan was naive; Rhodes soon learned that plain money, in sufficient quantities, could accomplish almost anything within the reach of a Secret Society. But as to the plan itself, having once set it down, he never deviated from it.

In addition to the far more detailed nature of the second, there was another significant difference between the two wills. The first had been, for practical purposes, only an expression of intent; by 1877, Rhodes was well on the path to substance. In the intervening years, the nature of diamond mining had changed, first physically then economically. If enough people dig away at the same spot, the result will be a hole, which will grow deeper as they continue to dig. When Rhodes had described the working of the mine to his mother, diggers used tin buckets, canvas sacks, or even slings made of rawhide to transport the ore to the sifting tables. As the bottom of the mine receded, it became necessary to rig up pulleys, winches and cables, one for each claim. A visitor to Kimberley in 1874 described them as forming 'a monstrous cobweb, covering the whole face of the vast pit'. It was an expensive cobweb, too. Many miners whose equipment had

---

* It was a view which, shorn of mysticism, was not unshared by many of Rhodes's compatriots. In this case, however, it sometimes found odd expression. Many years after he had left Oxford, Rhodes was camping out on the veld with a friend, whom he shook awake in the middle of the night. 'What's the matter? Fire?' the man asked. 'No, no,' Rhodes replied, 'I just wanted to ask you, have you ever thought how lucky you are to have been born an Englishman, when there are so many millions who are not?'

consisted of a shovel and unlimited hope were obliged to sell their claims to those who had the money to work them. Rhodes had the money – not only from diamonds, but from other enterprises as well. He had, for instance, purchased and dragged up to Kimberley the largest pump available in Natal – in anticipation that the seasonal rains which flooded the mines would provide him with predictable, and profitable, employment. (Between rains, he used the pump to manufacture ice cream, an expensive delicacy at the fields.) When the regulation limiting the number of claims a man might own was amended in 1876, Rhodes was able to begin consolidating his holdings.

Kimberley, too, had changed – for the worse. Anthony Trollope passed through in 1877, gathering material for a travel book on south Africa. There had been, he reported,

> ... no rain for a year, not a tree within five miles, not a blade of grass within 20. ... When a gust of wind would bring the dust hiding everything, ... and when flies had rendered occupation altogether impossible, I would be told, when complaining, that I ought to be there in December, say, or February ... if I really wanted to see what flies and dust could do. I sometimes thought that the people of Kimberley were proud of their flies and their dust.

Though Kimberley was by now the second largest city in south Africa, most people still lived in tents, or in their wagons. What buildings existed were made of corrugated iron, 'probably the most hideous material that has yet come into man's hands'. The ensemble promoted Trollope to note that ' ... there are places to which men are attracted by the desire of gain which seem to me to be so repulsive that no gain can compensate for the miseries incidental to such an habitation.'

He was not very impressed with diamond mining as a profession either: 'I can conceive no occupation on earth more dreary, hardly any more demoralizing than this of perpetually turning over dirt in quest of a peculiar little stone which may turn up once a week or may not. I could not but think ... of the comparative nobility of the work of the shoemaker who by every pull of his thread is helping to keep some person's foot dry.'

Trollope's description did not exactly fit Rhodes's manner of operation. He did live in one of the corrugated iron houses – a two-room cottage which he occupied with total disregard for comfort or appearance long after he could have afforded to import and reassemble a marble mansion. But his diamond mining was done on 'halves' – which is to say that as the owner of a claim he took half its profits and left the rest to a digger who did all the work and paid the expenses. Shortly, he also undertook another career which Trollope would have found much more suitable: politics.

At the start of the diamond rush, it had bothered no one that the land where the stones were being found actually belonged to neither the British nor the Dutch. Poor and useless, it had been given to the Griquas, a tribe of mixed white, Bantu and Hottentot parentage who did odd jobs for neighbouring farmers, kept a few scrawny head of cattle of their own, and were generally referred to as 'the Bastards'. In 1870, when it looked as if there might be something to the diamond business, the Orange Free State reached out to claim the land by sending a commissioner to help the Griqua chief, Nicholas Waterboer, administer it. As soon as news reached Cape Town, the British objected. Protracted litigation, the outcome of which was never in doubt, ensued. The diamond fields, with a comfortable margin for new finds (17,800 square miles in all), became the Crown Colony of Griqualand West. For whatever costs it had incurred, the Orange Free State was given an indemnity of £90,000. (The award was made in 1876, when the year's diamond yield exceeded £2 million.) Four years later, Griqualand West was annexed by the Cape Colony and awarded six seats in its Parliament. It was for one of these seats that Rhodes, still an under-graduate but wealthier than most 27-year-olds in the world, and far more powerfully motivated, decided to run. For sentimental reasons, he wanted to stand as candidate for Kimberley, but had to settle instead for Barkly West, a neighbouring rural community which, despite its name, was pre-dominantly Dutch.

To candidate Rhodes, it made little difference. He identified with the voters by assuring them that his forebears, too, had been 'keepers of cattle'. Further, he told them, 'The Dutch are the coming race in south Africa, and they must have their share in running the country.' How prepared he was to help them secure that share, especially if it should be at the expense of British interests, is uncertain. But as the most practical of dreamers, he well knew that the population of Cape Colony was two-thirds Dutch, and that nothing could be done without their support – or at least their sufferance. The farmers of Barkly West liked what they heard. The descendant of cattle keepers was elected and, through two decades of controversy, success, dis-grace, regeneration and war, held his seat until his death.

As a public servant, Rhodes had no difficulty identifying the interests of his constituents, or his own. Sworn in on April 7th, 1881, he was on his feet on the floor of the House twelve days later, making his maiden speech. The subject under debate was disarmament of the Basutos – a native tribe whose skill at defending themselves had earned them the status of an island preserve within the Cape Colony. Rhodes was opposed to disarmament and marshalled a number of arguments in favour of his position, omitting only the most pressing: the diamond mines now depended entirely on black labour, and the greatest lure to employment was that, after their back-breaking stint, workers could use their wages to buy guns.

The next subject to which he addressed himself was railway-building.

In the second half of the nineteenth century, the laying of parallel metal tracks had become the symbol of progress in Europe. Nations vied for the honour of the greatest mileage of railway they could build, per square mile or per inhabitant. Belgium, for obvious reasons, was hands-down winner in both categories, but Britain was not far behind. So much confidence was placed in the locomotive as the bearer of civilization that an enthusiast suggested that coins of the realm should bear not a profile of a stately lady, but a full view of a smokestack, belching. The Cape Colony, caught up in the fever, had proposed building a railway in 1828, then again in 1845, and actual construction was begun on March 31st, 1859. The line had reached Worcester, 109 miles from the Cape, in 1876, but surveying crews reported the sad news that, while a way had been found through the mountains that lay ahead, it would be necessary to build a 200-foot tunnel. Such an undertaking was beyond local resources, but fortunately a British engineer named George Pauling had decided to practise his trade in south Africa. Pauling was only twenty when he arrived in 1875, but he knew his business. The mountain was pierced, and civilization reached Beaufort West, 339 miles from the Cape, in 1880. Here, it paused while lawmakers argued over which of their respective constituencies should next receive its benefits.

In Rhodes's mind, there was no doubt. 'Where else should any railway extension go than Kimberley?' he asked the House. 'The Opposition say they are in favour of a "moderate extension", and even a moderate extension must come to Kimberley.' There was civic pride involved, but also a little self-service. Kimberley's exports could be carried away in a man's pocket; its imports, including the new machinery needed to work the mines, were bulky and expensive. Wood, free for the cutting in some places, cost £20 a ton in Kimberley. The House voted the money to extend the railway, but did not commit itself to any destination.

Rhodes next turned to another delicate point: the use of Dutch in Parliamentary debate. He believed it should be enacted as a right, rather than a privilege. Relations between Boer and Briton, never good, had been deteriorating for a decade. The high-handed way in which Boer claims to the diamond fields had been dismissed had not helped, and neither had the size of the indemnity which, in the face of the inexhaustible wealth issuing from Kimberley, became increasingly condescending. In 1877, the British added injury to insult by annexing the Transvaal, an act which a speaker in Parliament – in London, not Cape Town – described as the result of 'force, fraud and folly'. Whatever the reasons for it may have been – and historians have not yet found a single creditable one – its result was to turn a nation of peaceful farmers, now led by a grown-up Paul Kruger as its President, into enemies. How effective they could be in this new role, the British were to learn during the long, bitter war which marked the turn of the century. They received a sharp sample in 1881, when a series of minor disobediences prompted Major General Sir George Colley to march over from Natal and show a little steel. With a trained eye for terrain, he selected the highest hill in sight and led his force – 1,200 men, including 240 kilted Gordon Highlanders – to the top where they dug in, presumably waiting to be dislodged. The Boers, as accurate with their Westley-Richards rifles as their fathers had been with flintlocks, did not bite. The fight on Majuba Hill, which took place on February 27th, 1881, a few weeks before Rhodes took his seat in Parliament, was not so much a battle as a turkey-shoot. The British lost 280 men to the Boers' six. They also lost the Transvaal, which was grudgingly given back its independence.

But it was geography above all else which preoccupied Rhodes. North of the Cape Colony lay Bechuanaland. *The Cambridge History of the British Empire*, which has a kind word to say for the remotest corner of its subject, describes it as 'enormous' and 'all very dry'. Most of its 275,000 square miles consist of the Kalahari Desert – hard limestone and sand so fine that it will hold virtually no surface water at all. The Sahara supports a rude, assimilated kind of life; even today, men die of thirst trying to cross the Kalahari.

To its extreme east, however, the desert yields a long, narrow strip of watered land. Deep wells, spaced out but replenished by the annual rain, provide the means for a marginal existence, and a chain of way-stations for the traveller. Rhodes told his colleagues in the House:

> I look upon this Bechuanaland territory as the Suez Canal of the trade of this country, the key of its road to the interior. ... The question before us is really this, whether this Colony is to be confined to its present borders, or whether in fact it is to spread its civilization over the interior.

Urgency to answer the question was precipitated by the Boers, who, landhungry as ever, had spilled out of the Transvaal and Orange Free State. They had shouldered the natives away from the wells, laid out farms for themselves, and given their intrusion the semblance of legitimacy by proclaiming the founding of two new republics, Stellaland and the hopefully-named Land of Goshen.

In vain, Rhodes warned, argued, prodded, and might well have suffered an early check to his career had it not been for the entirely irrelevant venturesomeness of a young German merchant named Fritz Luderitz. The son of a prosperous Bremen tobacco merchant, Fritz found life at home dull, and for 2,000 marks and a case of old muskets purchased a tract of land, some 240 square miles in all, at Angra Pequena, on the deserted Atlantic coast south of the Congo. His object was to open a private trading station, but, like any sensible businessman, he asked his government whether it was prepared to protect him should he run into trouble. Chancellor Bismarck's view of colonies was well known – he wanted no part of them. But in this instance he eventually relented, and on May 2nd, 1883, Luderitz hoisted a

German flag, the first to fly over territory anywhere outside of Europe.

The Cape viewed this development with concern. 'The general opinion here', the London *Standard* reported, 'is that there is not room for two flags in south Africa.' Concern turned to anxiety when it was learned that President Kruger, then touring Europe to borrow money, had visited Berlin where he was offered a superb banquet by the Kaiser. The plot was now clear: German and Boer, lumbering across Africa, were planning to shake meaty hands and throttle off the Cape. Unlikely? Did they not share a fondness for beer? And speak almost the same language?

Few people in the House were better qualified than Rhodes to lay this spectre to rest. He knew the Boers well enough to realize that their individualism, their fierce sense of personal liberty, would not permit a political marriage with Prussianism. He was not about to point this out, however. On the contrary, as he later said, 'I was never more satisfied ... than when I saw the recent development of the policy of Germany.'

But he had not allowed for the dust kicked up by diplomats at bay. In 1882, when Rhodes had tried to fight for his 'canal', Lord Derby, Her Majesty's Colonial Secretary, had assured the House of Commons that 'Bechuanaland has no value to us; it is of no consequence who owns it.' In Bismarck's change of mind, however, the British Ambassador in Berlin discerned an ominous portent: elections were coming up in Germany; the Chancellor had discovered an 'unexplored mine of popularity' – the German aspiration for colonies – and would exploit it. His successor disagreed, but found an even more worrisome motive: Bismarck did not care about Africa at all, but was being difficult in order to court the French, who hated the British. Secret cables moved back and forth. Lord Derby modified his view. On December 26th, 1884, in a communication marked 'Derby to Gladstone. Private', he advised the Prime Minister that Bismarck's actions were the 'deliberate expression, not perhaps of hostility, but of ill-will'.

It is not known what the appropriate response to hostility might have been; the reaction to ill-will was the dispatch of a military expedition. Its commander, a posturing fire-eater named Major General Sir Charles Warren, was already on the high seas. His orders, which he had written himself, were ' ... to remove the filibusters, to pacificate the territory, to reinstate the native on their lands ... and to hold the country until its further destination is known.'

The filibusters consisted of some 400 farmers in Stellaland, and perhaps 160 in Goshen. To remove them, Sir Charles had mounted a force of 5,000 men fully equipped with all the imaginings of an active military mind, including light artillery, supply battalions and three observation balloons. The moment he saw what was happening, Rhodes managed to wangle an appointment as Deputy Commissioner and go along on the expedition, but there was little he could do. Warren marched resolutely north as far as

Mafeking, 870 miles from Cape Town, bullying and antagonizing every Boer in his path. Having thus pacificated the territory, he proclaimed martial law and ordered that henceforth only settlers of pure British origin would be permitted to enter Bechuanaland, which would become still another British Protectorate. To his regret, none of the enemy had given him the pretext to fire a shot. On the contrary, many had cheerfully dropped their chores to help ferry him across the Orange River and, at £2 a day, help transport his baggage. It was more than any of them could earn in a month of farming.

Despite this inadvertent largesse, the Warren Expedition is, properly, inscribed in the Century of Wrong. It did, however, have one beneficial effect. As of November 3rd, 1884, the railway line had come as far as the south bank of the Orange and, again, stopped still. In flood, the river was nearly a quarter of a mile wide. Nobody in south Africa had ever built a bridge that long, which for many people was reason enough not to try. But Warren was not a man to be hobbled by precedent and neither, given the money, was George Pauling. That was no problem, a trifling £20,000 out of the million which the entire expedition had cost. The bridge, a sturdy structure 1,240 feet long and resting on nine low arches, was completed in time to save the conqueror the indignity of having to pay a final toll on his way home from war.

For Rhodes, who had resigned his appointment as Deputy Commissioner in protest, Bechuanaland proved to be a better school than Oxford. It taught him two lessons which Ruskin had neglected. First, that if you wanted something done properly you should not entrust it to Her Majesty's Government – 'Grandmama' as he was to call it. Second, that if you were building a railway, there was nothing like a small war to move it along.

Preoccupied as he was with other matters, Rhodes never neglected his business affairs. The making of money may not, as his admirers hold, have interested him, but it was far from incidental to his other activities. 'Pure philanthropy', he once noted, 'is all very well in its way, but philanthropy plus five per cent is a good deal better.'

In April, 1880, Rhodes combined his holdings into the De Beers Mining Company, with capital of £200,000. His partner was a quiet, cautious man named Charles Dunell Rudd who had also come to Africa for his health. (Herbert, as unsatisfied with success as with failure, left Kimberley to wander off in search of gold, and died in 1877, during a fire which destroyed his hut in the Shire highlands of what is now Malawi.) Nine years older than Rhodes and locally reputed to be a sound thinker – Harrow and Cambridge – and an astute businessman, Rudd readily accepted a back seat in the partnership, and would be totally unremembered but for one extraordinary chore which will be described in due course.

The purpose of creating the De Beers Company was to regulate the production and marketing of diamonds – a task which it still performs with near-total effectiveness today. Rhodes had had ample time, while sitting on his bucket, to muse on the irony that diamonds, the cause of so much exertion, had absolutely no intrinsic value. Only their rarity made them worth anything, so that success in finding them was in some degree automatically self-defeating. Later he determined that the possibility of selling diamonds depended on the ability of young men throughout the world to buy engagement rings. By means of calculations of his own, he estimated that this ability would remain at a stable £4 million a year. If the stones were cheaper, the young men would buy larger ones; if they were more expensive, the ladies would have to be satisfied with smaller ones. From this it followed that, however plentiful diamonds became, there would be no additional profit in trying to sell more of them – less, in fact, because as the mines became deeper it was more expensive to operate them.

De Beers was far from the largest of the mining companies, but it was the most aggressive in swallowing up smaller competitors. By 1885, its capital had more than quadrupled, and it faced only one serious rival: Barney Barnato's Kimberley Central Diamond Mining Company.

Barney Barnato was the same age as Rhodes, and he, too, had come to Africa to join an older brother. But here, all resemblance ended. Barney had been born Barnett Isaacs, the son of a shopkeeper in London's Whitechapel. After the sketchiest of schooling, he and his brother Harry had become boxers, acrobats, jugglers – the name change was inspired by the belief that all successful jugglers were Italian – a two-man show which commanded a shilling and a hot meal for an evening's performance. In 1871, Harry broke up the act by leaving to try his luck at diamonds. Barney carried on alone for two years, then decided to follow. Harry had not become a millionaire, but then he had not starved to death either. Travelling steerage in order to conserve his capital – £50 in cash and forty boxes of cigars so foul that his aunt could not sell them at any price in London – he arrived in Cape Town only a few days after Cecil Rhodes left to begin his studies at Oxford.

When he finally reached Kimberley after a 60-day trip by ox-cart Harry was not especially pleased to see him. Harry was a *kopje*-walloper, a speculator who made the rounds of the poorer, outlying diggings and bought rough diamonds for resale to the dealers in town. Business was terrible, largely because he never knew which diggers to approach; some of them despised wallopers, and Harry could waste many dusty days trudging the countryside only to collect curses heavily larded with anti-semitism. Barney, however, brought not only fresh capital but fresh ideas as well. For £27 10s, he bought a shaggy, spavined pony from a walloper who had made good and was leaving. The notion, or so the story goes, was that the animal, from long habit, would know where his former master had been accustomed to stop. True or not, the brothers' fortunes improved quickly after Barney's arrival, to the point that within a year they could give up the indignity of walloping and open up an office of their own. At Barney's suggestion, it was located in the corner of a saloon – Mahoney's – which stood at the extreme edge of Kimberley. The reasoning was that thirsty miners, heading for town, could be induced to make a fast deal. Within another year the firm had prospered enough to move to larger quarters of its own and hang up the hopeful sign: BARNATO BROTHERS, DEALERS IN DIAMONDS AND BROKERS IN MINING PROPERTY.

In 1876, a pall descended over the fields; the yellow clay which had been the source of diamonds began coming to an end. Underneath it was solid, ominously dark rock which dulled shovels, blunted picks, and exhausted even the most energetic Kaffirs. Diggers whose claims reached this level would quietly sprinkle a thin layer of clay over it, then go and look for gullible buyers. Barney, however, had worked out a theory of his own about how the diamonds had got there in the first place. Obviously they had not grown downwards from the surface, nor had they been deposited by rivers or, for that matter, by ostriches. By elimination, therefore, they must some-how have come *up* out of the ground. If some had found their way into the yellow clay, it stood to reason that there were many of them underneath, either imbedded in the dense blue stone, or beneath it. Barney did not know igneous rock from soapstone, but he had found the right answer. Over Harry's horrified objections, he paid most of their accumulated working capital of £3,000 for just four claims of worthless blue stone, located almost exactly in the middle of the Kimberley mine. Within a few months, the purchase price had been recouped, and the claims were yielding up stones at the rate of £1,000 and more a week. Much of it was immedi-ately re-invested, and re-invested again. Like Rhodes, Barney had luck; but unlike him, he had no Oxford or Bechuanaland to distract him. By 1885, when the battle for control began, Kimberley Central was bigger than De Beers, and he himself was earning perhaps four times as much as Rhodes.

Kimberley, appreciative of a good fight, sat back to watch. Barney Barnato had become one of the leading characters in the diamond com-munity, if not quite one of its leading citizens. Round-faced, with blond hair parted in the middle, protruding ears and a dapper, reddish wax-tipped moustache, no one detected in him the makings of an empire-builder. While Rhodes was busy safeguarding the Suez of the South, Barney's most signi-ficant act of statesmanship had been the creation of the Dutoitspan Amateur Dramatic Society. And if audiences did not fully appreciate the shadings of his interpretation of Othello, they knew enough to keep the judgment to themselves – tickets were free, and drinks on the house.

As expected, Rhodes made the first move, by trying to buy up a con-trolling interest in Barnato's company. The price of Kimberley Central shares shot up from £14 to £49. Barnato retaliated by dumping large quantities of diamonds on the market, forcing their price to below the production cost of 15s a carat; he knew he could outlast Rhodes and De Beers. Stung, Rhodes tried reason and persuasion, but Barney was not interested in being the number two man in the world's largest diamond company. Rhodes journeyed to London and enlisted the support of Nathan Rothschild, who had become interested in diamonds after talking to Gardner Williams, the great American mining expert. But even with such backing – Rothschild had offered an immediate £1 million, and more if necessary – the victory was bound to have Pyrrhic overtones.

Rhodes was fond of reminding listeners that he had never met a man he couldn't 'square'. Barney couldn't be 'squared' with money, with threats, or with the trappings of power. But he did have a weakness: underneath the clown's get-up, there was a yearning for respectability – a quality difficult to define elsewhere, but at the diamond fields automatically conferred by membership in the Kimberley Club. Rhodes, wearing stained veld clothes and dirty boots, could walk into the ugly brick building at any time; Barnato, in his customary striped morning trousers, frock coat with satin lapels and boutonnière, had to wait to be invited. Of all the gifts within Rhodes's power to bestow, this was one of the simplest, and far cheaper than others he had tried. To sweeten the pot, he even offered to sponsor Barney for a seat in the Cape Parliament, a position only proper for a Life Governor of De Beers Consolidated Mines – the title Barney would hold in the new company if he sold out.

His cup running over, Barney nevertheless still had one objection. Rhodes had spoken about making De Beers 'the richest, the greatest, the most powerful Company the world has ever seen'. That was fine, until Barney realized that he was being quite literal. In normal practice, the Deed of Trust of a company is a legalistic document which describes, in general terms, the nature of the business to be pursued. The De Beers Trust Deed, as drafted by Rhodes, empowered the company to 'acquire any asset it pleased, including tracts of country in Africa and elsewhere; to deal with Rulers or Governments of any nation'. It could 'build and operate tramways, railways, roads, tunnels and canals'; it could 'promote and establish any institutions'; it could 'raise and maintain a standing army, and undertake warlike operations'. Diamond-mining, mentioned in passing, was an insignificant part of the programme.

Barnato wanted none of it, but Rhodes, for whom everything else had only been a prelude, would not yield. The final bargaining session, according to all accounts, lasted an uninterrupted eighteen hours. To every objection, Rhodes simply replied, 'I want the power to go to the north' – a direction which in his mind included the whole of Africa. In the end, near four o'clock in the morning, Barnato capitulated. He had merely made a fortune in diamonds, but perhaps there was more to life than that.* To Rhodes he

* Perhaps there was. Barnato ran for Parliament and won, in a campaign 'awash with

said, 'Some people have a fancy for one thing, some for another. You have a fancy for making an empire. Well, I suppose I must give it you.'

He was one of the first, but far from the last man to come to that conclusion.

---

whiskey'. On June 14th, 1897, his affairs prospering, he was on his way with his wife and children to attend, as honoured guests, the Queen's Jubilee, when he rose quietly out of his deck chair and, without a word to anyone, jumped overboard.

PART TWO

Kimberley to Bulawayo

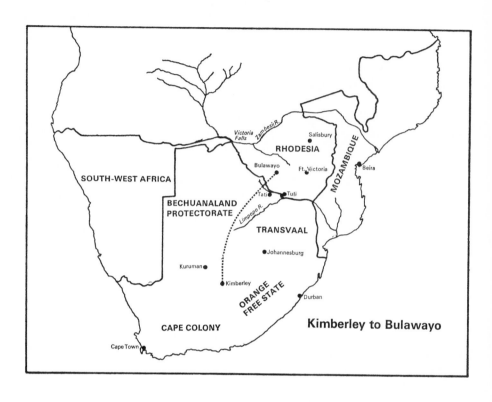

Victoria Falls · *Zambesi R.* · Salisbury · **RHODESIA** · MOZAMBIQUE · Beira

Bulawayo · Ft. Victoria

SOUTH-WEST AFRICA · Tati · Tuli

BECHUANALAND PROTECTORATE · *Limpopo R.*

TRANSVAAL

Kuruman · Johannesburg

Kimberley · **ORANGE FREE STATE** · Durban

CAPE COLONY

Cape Town

Kimberley to Bulawayo

WITH De Beers organized into a powerful instrument; with another fortune, amassed almost casually during the Witwatersrand gold strike of 1886, at his disposal; with his canal secured and his railway pushed through to Kimberley – the first train, its locomotive decked with bunting, had arrived on November 28th, 1885, and regular service from Cape Town 647 miles away quickly established; Rhodes was ready to go to work in earnest.

He was no longer the slim, gangling youth. Now, he looked more like the Cecil Rhodes of the photographs and the busts: heavy-faced, heavy-framed, with a blunt neck. The nose was heavier, and hooked between deep lines to a down-turned mouth and chin which could have belonged to one of his own beloved imperial Romans – not Marcus Aurelius, but Galba or Vespasian. He moved slowly, perhaps out of the unconscious economy of a man who knows his heart is bad. He abhorred women and frivolous men. Everything about him was of a piece, except for his voice. Listeners hearing it for the first time could scarcely hide their embarrassment. It was girlish, nasal, high-pitched, and, when he was excited or angry, would climb still higher and break apart altogether. Alfred Lawley, Pauling's partner, once interrupted a heated discussion by telling him: 'For God's sake, Rhodes, stop squealing like a damned rabbit.'

Among the friends he sought out during this period was Charles Metcalfe, a former Oxford classmate who had come to South Africa as a consulting engineer. Metcalfe's company was engaged in making something out of Bechuanaland, but that part of the continent no longer interested Rhodes. Cartographers were already correcting it to the proper shade of red. His thought now reached farther north, to the high country which stretched to the Zambesi. There was ample water there, clear air, the altogether splendid climate of a 4,000-foot-high pleateau. It was empty now, but it could easily and comfortably support enormous plantations, ranches for scientifically bred cattle, clean new cities teeming with vigorous Anglo-Saxon colonists. The soil was fertile, and covered still greater wealth. Among the few Europeans who had travelled the country was a German prospector named Carl Mauch, who had reported stumbling across a gold field '80 miles long by 2 or 3 miles in breadth'. He remembered that he had stood 'as it were transfixed, riveted to the place, struck with amazement and wonder at the sight so that he was unable, for a few minutes, to use his hammer.

Mauch had also found – and others had borne him out – the long-abandoned traces of ancient mines. For centuries, stories had been told about the mysterious land of Ophir, the domain of the Queen of Sheba. This is where it must have been, for did not another traveller, Adam Renders, find the massive, ruined circular walls, towers and terraces of a great city – Zimbabwe? It must indeed have been of imperial size and solidity to have withstood the relentless attack of jungle and the elements. Rider Haggard had believed the story, or at least found it compelling enough to use as the basis for his *King Solomon's Mines*, which had become the literary sensation of 1886.

But the gold was just a bonus; it was the land which counted. Immediately beyond the Zambesi, in the region of the great lakes, the first comers had included men with good, sound names such as Livingstone, Bruce, Baker, Grant, Speke. That was grounds for a claim. From the top of the continent down, Egypt was as good as another British protectorate. A few gaps remained, but not for long.

At Rhodes's urging, Metcalfe prepared a long article for the *Fortnightly Review*. Its title was *The British Sphere of Influence in South Africa*, and it began by resurrecting Rhodes's old bogey – 'The plans of the Transvaal Boers and the Germans to join hands and cut us off have been frustrated by the action of the British Government ... ' But then it took a mighty geographic leap to describe 'the passage of the iron track that must ultimately join the Cape with Cairo, and carry civilization through the heart of the dark continent.'

This was probably the first time that the idea of a railway running the length of Africa had been proposed in print, but already it bore the stamp of Rhodes's formula for philanthropy: 'The iron way is the great civilizer ... What has been done hitherto towards developing the mineral resources of South Africa may be set down as nothing compared with what must be done in the near future, for almost the whole of that vast zone to the Zambezi ... may be said to be auriferous.'

And Metcalfe even had, with Rhodes's prompting, a proposal for how the whole thing could be done: 'But what as to the government? ... Perhaps the best way of effecting what we are bound to do would be by granting a charter to some powerful company or corporation ... '

There it all was: plan, programme, reward. Only one minor detail stood in the way.

When Rhodes had described the country south of the Zambesi as being empty, he had naturally been thinking of white men. There were several thousand people living there, speaking different languages, observing different customs. Not one, however, was a reader of the *Fortnightly Review*.

The ruler of the land was Mzilikazi, one of the commanders of the great Chaka who, in the early years of the nineteenth century, had moulded his small tribe – the Zulus – into a single-minded war machine. Young men were trained only to fight, and could not marry until they had killed in battle. Chaka devised new weapons for them: the assegai, a broad, flat spear which was wielded by hand rather than thrown, and a large ox-hide shield for close combat. He taught a new way to fight: a crescent wave which reached out to surround the enemy and turn him inwards. Thus armed and motivated, the Zulus set out to devastate their neighbours, first in Natal and then beyond the mountain ranges. According to legend, it was during one such raiding expedition that Mzilikazi captured so much cattle that he decided not to share the booty with his chief, but to continue westward until he was far enough away to settle down in safety.

In their new home, his troops became known as the Matabeles – the men of the long shields – but did not change their way of life. Soon, Mzilikazi was himself king of a full-fledged nation. His impis – armed regiments – strode unchallenged from horizon to horizon. His black neighbours paid him the required tribute, and even the few white men who ventured this far north respectfully asked him 'for the road' – permission to enter his territory. Most of them were hunters or traders, but one of them, who first came to see him in 1831, was not interested in ivory or animal skins.

Robert Moffat had been a gardener's helper in Cheshire when, at the age of 19, he decided to offer himself to the London Missionary Society. After two years of study, he was sent to southern Africa, where he was to remain for 54 years. Tall, erect and full-bearded, he built his mission in Kuruman, so remote and barren a site that timbers for the church could only be found 300 miles away. He travelled even deeper into the interior, translated the whole of the Bible and *Pilgrim's Progress* into Tswana dialect, and fathered ten children, of whom eight survived infancy. The eldest of his daughters, Mary, married a young man who so admired him that he, too, elected to become a missionary: David Livingstone.

Moffat had no illusions about Mzilikazi. After a stay with him, he wrote:

> Here there is neither judge nor jury. Often, while the individual has not the shadow of an idea that he or she has done wrong ... he is transfixed with a spear or the head broken with a club and then dragged out to the hyenas. ... They think they are made or 'grow' only to eat, drink (I wish I could add dress) and live for Mzilikazi. ... Although one becomes accustomed to look upon them in comparative nudity, the Christian mind can never become accustomed to their savage songs, their boasts of bloody feats. ... I felt glad when the day came that I could return home.

Yet a friendship developed between the two men – so strong that when Mzilikazi, pushed by the tenacious Boers, decided to move again, he permitted Moffat to found another mission in the Matabeles' new homeland.

Its border on the south was the Limpopo, Kipling's 'great, grey-green, greasy' river, 'all set about with fever trees'. The trees – more accurately thorn and bush – were infested with tsetse flies. They had claimed much of his own cattle, and Mzilikazi counted on them to keep the white men out. Meanwhile, lest his new neighbours – peaceful Mashona tribes who had centuries ago seceded from the southward migration – think that the rules had changed, he named his new capital Bulawayo – 'the killing place' – and set his impis loose to assert his authority.

Built in the Zulu style, the town was essentially an enormous circular stockade. The outside was formed by conical huts, made of mud-filled layers of reeds and branches, and squeezed together to enclose a cleared space perhaps 500 yards in diameter. Inside was a smaller circle of huts and sheds: the royal palace with its women's quarters, sacred chambers and other dependencies. Here, Mzilikazi lived out his days in tranquillity unusual for Zulu kings. He died in 1868 and, following his wishes, was immured in a cave nestled in the great barren hills just south of his city. Surrounded by the symbols of his rank, his body was left propped in sitting position and turned to face north, where he was ready to lead his people again should the need ever arise.

He was succeeded by Lobengula, a son by a concubine. A missionary, T. M. Thomas, described the ceremony of installation:

> ... The soldiers numbered about seven thousand and constituted a semi-circle about twenty deep, ... Lobengula had a long staff in his right hand, an ample cape of black ostrich feathers and a bandeau of yellow otter skins. ... To a looker-on from the adjoining hillock, where I stood at the time, the view was a fine one. The motley, moving mass of people presented themselves with black and white, red and white, and other coloured shields in their left hands, ... swelling their songs of praise to their illustrious ancestors and former kings, like the chanting of a great cathedral.

Three months after his coronation Lobengula's legitimacy was challenged by one of the *indunas*, the great tribal councillors. The young king's reply was to collect his two best royal regiments and march against the insurgents' kraal. On the road, they encountered women of the tribe who rushed towards them, turned their backs and lifted their skirts to bare their buttocks. As a gesture of scorn, it was ill-advised; Lobengula took the kraal, scattered the enemy and finished them off at leisure.

This was the only attempt to question his authority. For the next eighteen years, he lived at peace, performing the rites which annually brought forth rain and crops, and collecting cattle and wives, of whom he had some eighty, selected by royal nod from groups presented annually for his choice.

As king, his principal concern was to dampen the impetuosity of his warriors, especially the younger ones who had been brought up on legends of Chaka and chafed to stick the blades of their assegais into something more challenging than the bodies of their Mashona neighbours. By choice, they would have tested their invincibility against the whites. But the whites stayed on their own side of the river. Those few who came north moved circumspectly, and made sure to placate Lobengula with gifts before wandering off in search of the rocks and pebbles which seemed to fascinate them. If the whites had any impis of their own, as some of the older men claimed, they were obviously afraid.

Rhodes had no impis, and he was not afraid of the Matabeles. In time, they would be squared. What worried him was that other Europeans would beat him across the Limpopo. The Portuguese, who had indolently settled in Mozambique 380 years earlier, when Henry VII was on the throne of England, were slowly bestirring themselves, pushing their ancient claims to the interior and making tentative forays into the safe Mashona country. The Germans, latecomers to Africa but hardly indolent, had long since burst out of Herr Luderitz's tiny coastal domain. In addition to all of southwest Africa, which they had demanded and received, their explorers – Carl Peters and others – were roaming west from Zanzibar, planting flags.

Then there were Rhodes's own neighbours in the Transvaal. Gold was of no interest to them – they had let the British take over and develop the rich mines in the Rand. But Paul Kruger could feel the noose tightening. Britons hemmed him in on two sides, the Portuguese on a third. All his attempts to gain access to the nearby Indian Ocean had been thwarted. But to the north lay land, millions upon millions of acres of it. It was, for him too, empty, and it was just the kind of land that the Boers understood and loved: rolling, well-watered ranges where a man could ride off a farm and settle down comfortably with his family to live the simple, undisturbed life prescribed by the Bible. In earlier days, the men – and boys like Kruger himself – would simply have packed up their wagons and rolled off, trusting to marksmanship to enforce their title deeds. But all that had changed. Now, white men were expected to sign treaties with the Kaffirs before taking over their land.

Late in 1887, President Kruger quietly let it be known that he had concluded such a treaty, binding 'the people and the state of the South African Republic, and Lobengula, great Paramount Chief of Matabeland' to 'everlasting peace and friendship'. In recognition of this bond, Lobengula formally consented to extend protection to travellers from the Transvaal, to render military assistance whenever called upon, and to accept the presence of a permanent representative of the Transvaal at his kraal. This representative was to be Pieter Grobler, a former cattle thief who had actually negotiated the treaty and, with his brother as the sole white witness, signed it.

Rhodes's reaction was to cry 'Foul'. It had to be a fraud because Lobengula did not stand to gain anything by agreeing to it, and besides who had
ever heard of Matabeles offering to fight wars on behalf of white men? Still,
a piece of paper could cause endless mischief. He therefore confronted Sir
Hercules Robinson, Britain's High Commissioner in Cape Town, with a
demand that something be done at once to eliminate this naked challenge to
British interests.

A quiet, reasonable man nearing the end of a distinguished colonial
career, Sir Hercules was at the time busy making preparations for Christmas.
He was willing to concede that the treaty was spurious, but, if so, would it
not collapse as soon as the Boers tried to take advantage of it? Furthermore,
he did not quite see where the threat to Her Majesty's interests lay; Britain
had no designs of her own on Matabeleland.

It is at this point, according to most lives of Rhodes, that he took the
High Commissioner by the hand, led him to a map, and explained his inten-
tions regarding Africa. 'But where will you stop?' Robinson is said to have
asked. 'Where the country has not been claimed,' was the reply. Having
thought it over, Robinson said, 'Well, I think you should be satisfied with
the Zambesi as a boundary.'

That was permission enough for now. The first job was to repudiate
Kruger's treaty; the second, to replace it if possible with a similar agreement, substituting Great Britain as ally. Rhodes knew the perfect man for
the job, possibly the only white man in South Africa who could carry it off.

John Moffat, born and raised at the missionary station in Kuruman, had
decided to follow his father's calling. As a child, he had watched the
preparations for Mzilikazi's great migration northward, and had followed
the tribe to its new home, helping to establish the first Christian mission at
Inyati, near Bulawayo. He and Lobengula were almost of the same age, and
had come to know each other well. Furthermore, Moffat had given up his
missionary duties and joined the British diplomatic service. He was therefore, with Robinson's concurrence, at Rhodes's command.

'Joni', as Lobengula called him, did it. He went to Bulawayo and returned
in four weeks with two fresh documents, both bearing Lobengula's name
and scrawled 'X' mark. The first repudiated unequivocally the agreement
with Grobler – 'the words are not true,' Lobengula stated, 'they are not my
words.' The second, dated February 11th, 1888, was a formal treaty of
friendship with Great Britain in which Lobengula promised to 'refrain
from entering into any correspondence or treaty with any Foreign State or
Power to sell, alienate or cede, or permit or countenance any sale, alienation
or cession of the whole or any part of the said Matabele country under his
chieftainship ... without the previous knowledge and sanction of Her
Majesty's High Commission for South Africa.'

This was all that Rhodes had hoped for. In commercial terms, he had
secured a free negative option on Matabeleland. Now, it was Kruger's turn

to protest and echo Rhodes's cry of foul play and misrepresentation. Under this new treaty, Lobengula had no more to gain than he had under the old one. And furthermore, since when did Matabele kings voluntarily agree to seek permission for their actions from some unknown, remote white personage?

Both men had excellent cases. Whether Lobengula did indeed sign the Moffat treaty, or the Grobler treaty, will never be known, and is not really important. More to the point is that there is no way to determine whether, if he signed, he understood what he was signing – not whether he could comprehend the sense of the legal phrases, which he certainly could, but whether the translation and verbal explanation given to him corresponded to the words on the piece of paper. Moffat himself noted that 'Treaties in which the signature of one of the parties concerned consists only of "his mark" depend for their value upon the personality and reputation of the persons on the other side who are aware of the document that is being executed.'

The text of the Moffat Treaty, approved by Sir Hercules, was forwarded to the Colonial Office where, in due bureaucratic time, it received ratification. But Rhodes was impatient. Without even waiting for the outcome of Moffat's negotiating efforts, he had sent his own private man, a De Beers security officer named John Fry, to Bulawayo. The plan was simple. Even if Moffat succeeded in keeping the Boers out, somebody would still have to take the country over. Britain was unwilling; the Cabinet, and especially the Chancellor of the Exchequer, had no interest in assuming responsibility for tracts of uncharted wilderness. Moreover, even if Her Majesty's Government could be tricked into interceding, it would only bungle the job – as it had in Bechuanaland. Rhodes had decided he would do it himself, using the device which Metcalfe had already helpfully proposed: a chartered company. There was ample precedent for this tactic. The Hudson's Bay Company and the East India Company had been established as private ventures, and had resulted not only in profit for their backers, but in the addition of substantial holdings to the Crown. More recently in Africa itself, the Niger Company and the Imperial British East Africa Company had been created, and were doing well. Matabeleland, by all accounts, should be even more profitable. Everybody knew it was loaded with gold. The quartz samples which Carl Mauch brought back to the Royal Geographical Society had been assayed by the Bank of England, and the results duly published in *The Times* on September 11th, 1868: an incredible 1,185 ounces of gold to the ton. True, in the intervening years the massive gold reefs which had so impressed Mauch had not yet been found. But that was because people had looked in the wrong places – nibbling at the edges of Lobengula's country rather than going to its heart, where Mauch had travelled. Furthermore, Rhodes was known as a man with a magic touch when it came to extracting money from the ground. He was confident that all he needed to attract backers for his scheme, all that he had asked Fry to get for him, was an exclusive concession of mining rights in Lobengula's kingdom. Unfortunately, Fry had not succeeded. Desperately ill, he was forced to turn back to Kimberley, where he shortly died of cancer.*

Rhodes would gladly have gone to Bulawayo himself. The round trip involved some 1,600 miles of passage through largely uncharted country, and would have to be made without protection. An armed escort would defeat any hope of successful negotiation. Personal courage in the face of danger and hardship were not qualities which Rhodes lacked, as he was later to demonstrate, but there were too many matters in Kimberley which required his presence. In desperation, he asked his partner, Charles Rudd, to make the trip.

Rudd was then 44 years old, comfortably settled with his family on a pleasant plantation, and wealthy enough to turn down speculative ventures of this kind. Nevertheless, to please Rhodes, he agreed to go. In order to help him, especially with the natives, Rhodes provided an assistant, another former De Beers employee named Francis Robert Thompson.

Thompson had been born in Africa and raised on an outlying farm in Natal. When he was 17, he and his father were attacked by marauding Zulus. Thompson, although wounded, had managed to escape, but his father had not been as fortunate. When his body was found, he had been scalped, his arms and legs chopped off, and a ramrod thrust down his throat until its point came out in the middle of his back. The farm had been burned to the ground, and the stock driven off. Thompson first met Rhodes in 1884 and went to work for him as 'secretary-guide-interpreter'. In this capacity, he was put in charge of organizing the compounds for native labourers at the Kimberley mines. When Rhodes proposed the idea of the trip, Thompson at first refused. The notion of placing himself among natives, not cooped up in cages but free and armed, evoked painful memories. He tried to put Rhodes off by saying he would have to ask his wife's permission. Rhodes pulled a letter from his pocket: 'I knew you would say that. Here is her written consent.'

There was also to be a third member of the party, an old Oxford acquaintance of Rhodes named Rochfort Maguire. The two men had little in common; Maguire was a friendly, extrovert Irishman who excelled at his studies, taking two Firsts on his way to becoming a Fellow of All Souls College. They had not seen each other for ten years when they chanced to be fellow passengers on a steamer to Cape Town – Rhodes was returning from a quick business trip to London; Maguire, who had been called to the bar in 1883 but did not need to practise, was on a pleasure trip. Lawyers, Rhodes remembered, were useful in negotiations, so he impulsively asked Maguire whether he would like to go along. Equally impulsively, Maguire agreed. Upon being told of this added starter, Thompson grumbled about

---

* Rhodes's comment on the attempt was: 'Never have anything to do with a failure.'

dragging novices through dangerous country. Rhodes replied that Maguire would take care of himself, and moreover could give private lessons during the long evenings. He knew that Thompson was ashamed of his lack of a formal education.

The trio, accompanied by two wagons drawn by six mules each, started out from Kimberley on August 15th, 1888. All three men wrote accounts of the journey, on which the history of southern Africa was to turn. The best and probably most truthful, since it was written in the form of a personal diary, with no expectation of publication, is Rudd's. The first entry reads: 'We started at 2 p.m. on Wednesday. I lunched with Rhodes at the Club, and then I went round to the Bank and got the specie – £5,000. ... When we got an hour out of camp Thompson found that he had left behind the map and some other things, so we sent a boy back on Maguire's pony to look for them. ... '

After noting this doubtful start, Rudd goes on to describe a fairly uneventful, not unpleasant trip, typical of the country and the period. The day began at six o'clock, with two or three of the men riding ahead on horseback. They would try their hand at hunting, partridges and an occasional hare, and stop around eleven and have a second breakfast, waiting for the wagons to catch up. Two or three times a day, they had to outspan in order to give the mules some food and rest. The evening stop came around six. Having covered some thirty miles, they would have dinner, then read, write letters, occasionally play chess or backgammon, and turn in by ten o'clock. (If there were any private lessons, Rudd does not mention them.)

The monotony was dispelled by letters from Rhodes, dispatched by post riders and containing afterthoughts and suggestions. On September 10th, he wrote: 'My Kimberley work in all ... will take three months. ... As to Lobengula ... go on the lines of becoming his Gold Commissioner and working for him.'

He closed with some helpful advice: 'Your most valuable man will be Moffat – he is thoroughly with you. ... Stick to Home Rule and Matabeleland for the Matabele, I am sure it is the ticket.'

If Rhodes was thinking in political terms, it may have been because an important part of his unfinished 'Kimberley work' was the need to stand for re-election to his seat in the Cape Parliament. He had already done well by his constituents, but now he could promise them even more. During a stump speech on September 28th, 1888, he told them: 'We should state by our own policy that we are prepared to take the administration right through to the Zambesi. ... You are miners by birth, by education and by profession, and I believe you are as capable of developing the far interior as you have been the alluvial wealth of the Vaal river.'

In earlier campaigns, they had been cattlemen, but times had changed.

Gold was in the air, and Rhodes could as easily wave it before the voters of Barkly West as he planned to before investment-minded gentlemen in the City.

Meanwhile, Rudd and company had entered the most difficult part of their trip, a passage across a corner of the Kalahari Desert. One of the mules died, another ran away. Water became scarce; the rivers, which would turn into torrents when the rains arrived in November, were broad hollows of hard clay and rock which shook the wagons to pieces, and caused repeated stops for repairs. Thompson, on whom the work fell, grumbled about Maguire's skill at 'playing the part of the onlooker well'. Game, which had been plentiful, vanished. Rudd's entry for September 8th reads: 'We had rather short commons for dinner – our last bit of tough goat and some rice.' The scenery was hardly more inspiring: 'The whole place is a mass of red sand and filth, and about the ugliest place all around one could well see.'

The following day, they were reminded of something they had known all along: that another British group, taking advantage of the Moffat Treaty, was also trying to extract a concession out of Lobengula. Rudd notes: 'We reached water and found four wagons of the Bechuanaland Exploration Company. ... They gave us information about the King ... and also some bread and meal, of which we were very short.'

Talking about Lobengula reminded Rudd that, treaty or not, the ancient prohibition against white men entering his country without permission was still in force. He sent a message to Moffat in Bulawayo, asking him to 'arrange that we not be detained longer than necessary'.

Protocol demanded two days, after which the visitors were allowed to cross and see for themselves the attractions of Matabeleland. As they climbed from the desert's floor, the scenery changed. 'Appearance of country improving,' Rudd wrote, 'broken kopjes and better class of trees.' From the top of the pass, he could see 'beautiful country – grand flats broken with huge masses of granite 100 to 200 feet high, and in the far distance ranges of broken blue hills.' After another day's travel, they arrived at Bulawayo. The King, however, was not there but at his private residence near the Umgazi River, about two miles away. With him, Rudd was told, were his court, his wives, his sacred cattle, and 'all the white people'.

The residence turned out to be two ox-wagons, stationed in the middle of a small kraal. Surrounding it, 'dotted about under the trees', were tents and about eight or ten wagons. 'All the white people' were thirty men, sticking to Lobengula like leeches and representing the interests of eleven different concession seekers. Some were legitimate – to the extent that they were interested in looking for gold. Many were simply traders who had lived in Matabeleland for years, swapping lengths of calico for whatever they could find of value. They had neither plans nor means to go into mining, but appreciated that Lobengula's mark on any bit of paper would be highly negotiable, and counted on their acquaintance with the King to earn them preferred treatment.

Rudd, who had not expected any such competition, had little time to plot strategy. Before he could finish setting up camp, an interpreter – a missionary named C. D. Helm who was to play a crucial role in the events which followed – arrived to announce that Lobengula wished to see them. They went at once. 'The King', Rudd writes, 'climbed up on his wagon and sat on the box while we squatted below. I explained through the interpreter who we were, and said that we had come on a friendly visit and begged of him to accept our present of £100, which I then presented to him and asked his leave to visit him while we stayed there.'

Later that night, Rudd set down his first impressions of Lobengula:

> The King is just what I expected to find him – a very fine man, only very fat, but with a beautiful skin and well-proportioned. ... He spends a great deal of the day in the kraal, where he makes medicine. He has a curious face; he looks partly worried, partly good natured and partly cruel; he has a very pleasant smile. ... He had his dinner brought up while we were there. ... He lay down with his head and arms on the front of the box of the wagon, and a great mass of meat – like the pieces they give lions at the zoo, only as if it had been thrown into a big fire – was put before him, and some kind of bread. He told the slave boy who brought the meat to turn it over, and then began to tear pieces off with a kind of stick. Altogether very much like a wild beast.

For the next six weeks, the 'wild beast' carried on protracted negotiations with the Cambridge man and the Oxford don, and very much held his own. Rudd's nightly summaries give an account of the talks. The King temporized, promising to think over the proposal and asking seemingly ingenuous questions. Was it true that the white men had no interest in his land, and only wanted to dig holes in it? Where would the holes be, and how many men would be sent to do the digging?

In bargaining style, Rudd began threatening to leave: 'We told the King that another of our horses was sick and that I was very anxious to get away, etc. The King replied that we had surely not understood him: that he would send to our wagons when he was ready to talk business. We then said that as the King was praying for rain, we hoped he would pray for our horse also.'

Lobengula's reply to this request, according to Rudd, was 'I am not a missionary – you should go to Helm for that.'

When they were not hanging around the kraal waiting for a private talk with Lobengula, the white men held endless discussions among themselves. Some of the traders withdrew their own candidacy and began offering their services to the highest bidder. Everybody tried to bribe the lesser Matabele chiefs. Moffat recalls: 'There is a perfect avalanche of present-giving.

Every Tom, Dick and Harry who goes to camp comes away more or less clothed – horses and saddles are given to indunas, full suits to the next of rank, cloth and beads galore to the plebs.'

Taking Rhodes's advice, Rudd pressed Moffat to intercede. Moffat, more than willing to help, urged patience, Maguire, for want of anything else to do, sat down and wrote drafts of a proposed agreement. No progress had been made, however, when word arrived on October 14th that Sir Sidney Shippard, Her Majesty's Administrator for Bechuanaland, was coming for a visit.

Sir Sidney was neither liked nor trusted by the Matabeles, whose nickname for him was *Marana Maka* – 'father of lies'. But he did represent the authority of a powerful nation – an authority which he casually brought along with him in the person of a detachment of sixteen armed troopers of the Bechuanaland Police. For himself, he chose a uniform more appropriate to his mission: a full-dress frock coat with the Star of the Order of St Michael and St George glittering over his breast. Thus attired, he strode across the dung-strewn ground in front of Lobengula's wagon and began the first of a series of private discussions which were to last a week.

No one knows for certain what was said during these talks. Lobengula's side did not issue communiqués. Sir Sidney later explained that 'I gave the King to understand that the concession-seekers ... were not in any way connected or authorized by Her Majesty's Government, and that any private concession-seeker who professed to represent the British Government was trying to deceive him by false representations.'

But apparently Sir Sidney said more than this, because after his departure indunas from far-away kraals were sent for. Moffat was called in to answer questions, as was Helm. On October 30th, Lobengula indicated that he would sign the concession, and asked that it be brought to him. Rudd writes:

> We all went in and found the old King on a brandy-case in a corner of the kraal. He said good morning very good-temperedly, but appeared much hustled and anxious. To cut a long story short, he absolutely declined to sign for half an hour, saying that he never signed his name. I had almost made up my mind to try the clearing-out business again when he suddenly said 'Hellem lete lapa' (Helm, give it to me) and there and then he signed it.

Maguire had earned his keep. The concession which Lobengula signed consisted of a single sentence, 496 words long. In it, Lobengula granted

> the complete and exclusive charge over all metals and minerals situated and contained in my Kingdom, Principalities and dominions together with full power to do all things ... necessary to win and procure the same and to hold, collect or enjoy the profits and revenue if any derivable from the said metals and minerals. ...

That seemed ironclad enough, but Maguire had added another thought:

> ... whereas I Lobengula have been much molested of late by divers persons seeking ... rights in my territories, I do hereby authorize the said grantees ... to take all necessary and lawful steps to exclude from my Kingdom ... all persons seeking land, metals or mining rights therein, and I do hereby undertake to render them such needful assistance that they may from time to time require for the exclusion of such persons. ...

Thus, again, Lobengula was putting his troops – the same arrogant impis which he had so long restrained – at the disposal of the whites. That the latter spoke English rather than Dutch, one supposes, made the arrangement less unthinkable.

In exchange for all this, Lobengula was to receive 'One Hundred Pounds sterling British Currency paid on the first of every lunar month' and 'one thousand Martini-Henry breech-loading Rifles together with one hundred thousand rounds of suitable ball cartridge'.

In order to dispel any doubts about the legality of the document, Maguire insisted that Helm endorse it. This the missionary did, certifying that it 'has been fully interpreted and explained by me to Chief Lobengula ... and that all the Constitutional usages of the Matabele Nation had been complied with prior to his executing same.'

What Helm did not explain to Lobengula is that he was, in fact, secretly working for Rhodes. Rudd wrote in his Journal that he had offered Helm a retainer of £200 a year to act on behalf of the Rhodes group in dealing with Lobengula. In his own account, Thompson confirms the offer – indeed, takes the credit for making it. Obviously, no receipts or cancelled checks have ever been found, but in the latest, 'definitive' biography of Cecil Rhodes (*Rhodes*, by J. G. Lockhart and C. M. Woodhouse, published in 1963) – a work whose overall tone ranges from hearty approval to outright admiration – the authors make reference, without amplification, to the fact that Lobengula was 'unaware that Helm had become Rhodes's man'.

The post-signing formalities were brief. Maguire said, with great prescience, 'Thompson, this is the epoch of our lives.' Rudd recalls: 'I told the King good-bye. He took my hand and held it some time and said "Are you really off so soon, and when will you come back?" I told him I would be back in March with the guns.'

Rushing home, Rudd overtook the leisurely-moving Shippard, who expressed surprise at his good fortune. Then, trying to take a short-cut through the desert, he lost his way and nearly died of thirst. He buried the precious paper in an ant hill, pinned a note on a tree explaining what he had done, and collapsed in delirium. Fortunately a group of Bushmen found him and gave him water. He retrieved the concession and travelled on, covering the last 260 miles to Kimberley in 45 hours. Rhodes joined him and together they took the express train to Cape Town, where the document was presented to Sir Hercules Robinson.

Sir Hercules congratulated them warmly, and sent it up to London with his own endorsement: 'I trust that the effect of this concession to a gentleman of character and financial standing will be to check the inroad of adventurers, as well as to secure the continuous development of the country with a proper consideration for the feelings and prejudices of the natives.'

The Colonial Office, too, was pleased by the turn of events, but expressed reservation about the Martini-Henry rifles. Peddling rusty flintlocks was one thing, but traffic of this kind was not only unwise, but could create international complications as well. Ever helpful, Sir Sidney Shippard had an answer:

> A Matabele warrior unaccustomed to the use of firearms, with only a rifle in his hands would, in my opinion be far less formidable than when, assegai in hand, he stalks his victims as at present. The experience of all those who have fought the native wars in South Africa proves that bloodshed is decreased in proportion as the native discards the stabbing assegai and takes to missiles or firearms.

The last statement was in reference to the belief that natives, untrained in the use of modern rifles, habitually raised the gunsights as high as they would go in the belief that this made the bullets travel faster. True or not, the explanation satisfied the Colonial Office, and earned Shippard a pat on the back from Rhodes. Writing to Maguire, who was holding the fort in Bulawayo, he said: 'Getting guns through has been no joke. Shippard has behaved like a brick.'

The news found Maguire with his hands full. In order to discourage new gold-seekers, Rhodes had announced the signing of his concession to the Cape newspapers. The disappointed suitors in Bulawayo seized on these stories, which described the generous terms of the concession, as proof of Rhodes's perfidy. Again, the missionaries were summoned to the kraal and asked questions, more pointed this time. Did the paper give Rhodes the right to dig holes anywhere? Even near the royal kraal? How many men could Rhodes send? How long would they stay?

The interrogation occasioned a *crise de conscience* among God's workers in Matabeleland. The Reverend W. A. Elliot described one interview to his superiors at the London Missionary Society: 'We went to the Chief and I read the paper to him. ... A good deal of conversation followed, in the course of which the Regent Unhalaba asked me if the mining rights of a like tract of country could be bought anywhere else for a similar sum. Only one answer is possible to that question, and we gave it – "No!"'

Helm, too, had something he wanted to get off his chest: 'The Grantees (Rudd, Maguire, and Thompson) promised that they would not bring more than 10 white men to work in his country, and that they would not dig anywhere near towns, etc., and that their people would abide by the laws of the country, and in fact be as his people. But in fact these promises were not put in the concession.'

As soon as he realized that they had not been put in, that Helm had lied to him, Lobengula sent his own statement to the newspapers – to the *Bechuanaland News* and the *Malmani Chronicle*: 'I hear it is published in the newspapers that I have granted a concession in all my country to Charles Dunell Rudd, Rochfort Maguire and Francis Robert Thompson. As there is a great deal of misunderstanding about this, all action in respect of the said concession is hereby suspended, pending an investigation to be made by me in my country.'

The notice was dated 'Royal Kraal, Matabeleland. 18th January, 1889', stamped with the royal seal, and witnessed by three of the white traders in Bulawayo. Then, confused, angry at having been tricked, fearful of the reaction of his hot-blooded young soldiers when they learned the truth, Lobengula, sitting in his fly-blown kraal in the centre of Africa, conceived an extraordinary notion. As the reigning sovereign of an independent state, he would address himself directly to the reigning sovereign of another state. One of the unsuccessful concession-seekers, representing the Bechuanaland Exploring Company, was a man named E. A. Maund who had been to Bulawayo before as a lieutenant with the Border Police. Lobengula wished to send two ambassadors bearing a letter. Would Maund accompany them, and bring back a reply? The letter was addressed to the White Queen, and read: 'Lobengula desires, if there is a Queen, to ask her to advise and help him, as he is much troubled by white men who come into his country and ask to dig for gold. There is no one with him upon whom he can trust, and he asks that the Queen will send someone from herself.'

For ambassadors, Lobengula chose two of his indunas: Umshete, a powerful chief who had the reputation of being a great orator, and Babjaan, lower in rank but gifted with a celebrated memory. As befitted a head of state, he also insisted on paying his envoys' way, and asked Maund what the trip might cost. Maund guessed £600; Lobengula gave it to him in golden sovereigns, carefully counted out and tied in a large red cotton cloth.

The trip, aboard 'a great kraal which pushed through the water', was uneventful. From London a special train took them to Windsor, where the royal carriage awaited them. Picked men of the 2nd Life Guards lined the approaches to St George's Hall. Babjaan thought they were stuffed, until he saw one of them move his eyes. In the Audience Chamber, the party was seated on gilt *fauteuils* before the throne. Maund relates that, while they waited for the Queen, 'an awkward contretemps occurred such as often happens to excited children,' so the chiefs were presented to Her Majesty in the Distinguished Visitors' Gallery.

They delivered Lobengula's letter and made polite talk. 'You have come a long way to see me. I hope it was made a pleasant journey, and that you do not suffer from the cold.'

It had been raining steadily since their arrival, but silver-tongued Umshete was ready. 'How should we feel cold,' he replied, 'in the presence of the Great White Queen?'

Luncheon was a state affair complete with toasts. Perrier Jouet '75 was considered too risky for the envoys' heads, so lemonade was secretly substituted in their goblets. Afterwards they were given a tour of the Castle and its historic sights, including the assegai which had belonged to the great Cetewayo, last of the kings in Chaka's line. Later, at Aldershot, they were treated to a sham battle involving 10,000 troops commanded by Lieutenant-General Sir Evelyn Wood, who had personally collected the trophy after taking Cetewayo prisoner.

Before leaving England, they spent three heady weeks in London. South Africa was very much in fashion during the season of 1889, and the envoys attended a round of parties. Of all of the glittering ladies, they later recalled that the most beautiful was Lady Randolph Churchill. They went to the ballet, and visited the London Zoo. Babjaan tried to attack a caged lion with his umbrella, and could not understand why he was restrained from finishing him off. They were shown a telephone and were duly impressed, though they doubted that it could be taught to speak their language. On a visit to the Bank of England, the White Queen's treasure house, Umshete offered the information that when any distinguished visitor was received by Lobengula and shown the royal flocks, he was also presented with the fattest ox as a gift. The hint was not taken up.

Finally, exhausted and enlightened, they boarded the *Grantually Castle* and headed home. Once ashore in Cape Town, Maund says, ' ... they began to be afraid of wearing the English clothes which they loved so well. First one garment disappeared then another. When we got to the frontier and were going to be doctored with the mystic rites, Umshete appeared with nothing but his monkey tails around his loins.' Babjaan retained his waistcoat as a keepsake.

Restless and concerned about the turn of events in Bulawayo, Rhodes decided he could not afford to wait any longer for the colonial bureaucracy to approve his proposed charter. He had tried, unsuccessfully for once, to intercept the indunas, and could only imagine what stories they were telling the White Queen and her ministers. 'Our enemies', he told Rudd, 'may bowl us out if I do not go at once to headquarters. Our concession is so gigantic it is like giving a man the whole of Australia.'

Before he could leave, however, there was one detail to attend to – the first delivery of rifles to Lobengula. Rudd flatly refused to go. Rhodes asked his closest friend Leander Starr Jameson to make the trip.

Jameson was a small, bird-like man, quick-witted, urbane, impulsive – 'mercurial', a novelist of the day would have said. He was a physician – a brilliant one, according to the record. At the age of 25, he had been appointed Resident Medical Officer of University College in London, but the work proved too tame, for in 1878 he saw and answered an advertisement offering to share a practice in Kimberley. Soon after his arrival, his senior partner, a Dr Prince, was obliged to depart hurriedly because of a misunderstanding with a lady patient, leaving Jameson as the chief local medical practitioner. In this capacity, he was able to do Rhodes an enormous favour. Smallpox – or, more precisely, a disease diagnosed as smallpox by a Dr Hans Sauer, the other ranking doctor in Kimberley – had broken out. This was not an uncommon event in frontier towns, and would normally have been handled by draconian measures of quarantine, which would have caused work in the diamond mines to stop. Jameson examined one of the victims and pronounced that it was not smallpox at all, but 'a bulbous disease of the skin allied to pemphigus', an obscure ailment characterized by unsightly blobs, but neither contagious nor fatal. This difference in medical opinion led to a public debate which culminated in dual libel actions. The Court, in a display of even-handedness, found both parties guilty and awarded equal damages. Meanwhile, digging at the mines had not been interrupted.

After this, Jameson and Rhodes became good friends, and eventually housemates. One morning, Rhodes showed up with all his belongings at Jameson's doorstep and asked if he could move in. The doctor agreed.

It was impossible to spend an afternoon with Rhodes, much less live with him, without becoming aware of his preoccupation with 'the North'. Jameson was not eager to go. Nor did he take seriously Rhodes's suggestion that the trip to Matabeleland would be a pleasant vacation. But there was no one else so, like Rudd before him, he finally consented.

Rhodes was now free to rush to London, where he arrived in March 1889 – just as the indunas were leaving, and under far less promising auspices than they had enjoyed. Lord Knutsford, the Colonial Secretary, considered him an Africa-firster, dangerously cosy with the Boers. At Number 10, he was known as the political benefactor of Charles Parnell, to whose Irish nationalists he had contributed £10,000. Whether this had been done to buy votes, or because of his belief in the justice of home rule, it was not the sort of gesture to make him popular with Lord Salisbury and his Tory government. Despite these obstacles, Rhodes set to work at once. In an orgy of 'squaring', and using tactics which one biographer described as 'more American than British', he proceeded to buy off every one of his unsuccessful rivals. Those with good political connections, like the Bechuanaland Exploring Company, received bigger shares, but there was something for everyone. An itinerant painter named Thomas Baines produced a concession which he claimed Lobengula had granted him in 1871, and which had been gathering dust ever since. Rhodes bought it. Another man, Sir Joseph Shipton, had a concession to mine gold in the Tati region, whose jurisdiction was contested between Lobengula and Khama, his neighbour to the south. Sold. For five days, the corridor outside Rhodes's suite of rooms at the Westminster Palace Hotel was crowded with a procession of colourful old Africa hands. One of them was a tall, handsome, blond-bearded and blue-eyed man named Frederick Courtenay Selous, whom Rhodes and everyone in Africa knew as the most famous hunter of his day, the hero of a thousand miraculous escapes, and the model for Rider Haggard's *Allan Quatermain*. Obviously ill at ease in the world of commerce, Selous launched upon a long story, the point of which seemed to be that Lobengula, whom he knew well, had once made some sort of verbal promise to him about sharing in any future gold rights. Rhodes barely heard him out and pressed him to accept £2,000. He had special plans in mind for Selous.

With obstacles melting under the heat of Rhodes's largesse, the Charter quickly found appropriate sponsors: the Duke of Fife, son-in-law of the Prince of Wales; the Duke of Abercorn, among whose sixteen titles were Lord of the Bedchamber and Groom of the Stole; Albert Grey, heir-presumptive to Earl Grey, the former Secretary of State for the Colonies. All this of course helped, but under the ermine was the hard-headed realization that Rhodes was offering an opportunity to do some colonizing on the cheap. This was the biggest, most ambitious 'squaring' of all; by proposing to pick up the bills, Rhodes was bribing Great Britain into letting him have his way.

It worked. On July 5th, Salisbury gave his all-important consent, and a petition was forwarded to 'The Queen's Most Excellent Majesty in Council', humbly praying that Her Majesty would 'be graciously pleased to grant ... a Royal Charter of Incorporation, by name or title of the "British South Africa Company" ... with limited liability, and with such other powers and privileges as to Your Majesty may see fit.'

The proposed Charter spelled out some of these powers and privileges. They included

> ... the right to make and maintain roads, railways, telegraphs, har-bours; to carry on mining and other industries; to carry on lawful commerce; to settle territories and promote immigration; to establish or authorize banking companies; to develop, improve, clear, plant and irrigate land; to establish and maintain agencies in Our Colonies and Possessions, and elsewhere; to grant lands for terms of years or in perpetuity. ...

Barring a few prerogatives, the Charter was a full licence to own and operate an independent country. Interestingly, though it was extremely explicit in other details, running to well more than 5,000 words, not a single mention was made of the northern boundary of the territory which it covered. Rhodes saw to that.

Meanwhile, in Bulawayo, clouds were gathering. Jameson and the rifles had arrived at a propitious time: Lobengula was suffering from an attack of gout. One look at the patient and a quick review of his habits – a diet rich in meat and beer, and near-total lack of exercise – enabled the doctor to make an easy diagnosis and relieve the painful symptoms, something which Lobengula's corps of private physicians had never been able to do. (In fairness, they had never heard of morphine.) Lobengula was understandably grateful, and intrigued by this cheerful white man who, for once, wanted nothing from him. For his part, Jameson enjoyed his gun-running hugely – so much so that he never did go back to his practice, but instead undertook other diplomatic missions for Rhodes, not all with this initial success.

When Jameson left, pleading that other patients required his attention, Maguire went with him. Eight months of half-cooked beef, available but unappetizing female company, and what passed for conversation among the whites at the kraal was as much as any man who had brought his own *eau de cologne* to Bulawayo could be expected to endure.

This left Thompson alone. From London Rhodes tried his best to appeal to the man's sense of history or, failing that, his greed. 'Dear Thompson,' he wrote,

> Stick to it. I trust to you alone. Upon you depends the whole thing. ... I ask you, is there a better chance in the world for you? Besides being one of the richest men in the Colony you will have the *kudos*. Napoleon was prepared to share the world as long as he got Europe. Work on those lines. Can't you give the whites who are in the country something? Yours,
>
> C. J. RHODES

It was not the whites who were worrying Thompson, but the blacks – and particularly the young warriors who made no secret of what they planned to do to him as soon as Lobengula gave them permission. In an earlier letter, Rhodes had agreed upon a simple code: as soon as the Charter was signed, and Thompson could therefore leave, Rhodes would send him a one-word message – 'Runnymede'. He had been living from day to day, sticking close to the missionaries and waiting for the word to come.

Instead, it was Umshete and Babjaan who arrived. Days were spent while they described everything they had seen – the crowded streets, the metal boxes which carried people and rolled of their own accord, the soldiers – the white men did have impis. Then came the reading of the letter which the Queen had sent in reply to Lobengula:

The Queen advises Lobengula not to grant hastily concessions of land, or leave to dig, but to consider all applications very carefully.

It is not wise to put too much power into the hands of the men who come first, and to exclude other deserving men. A King gives a stranger an ox, not his whole herd of cattle, otherwise what would other strangers arriving have to eat?

On hearing this, Lobengula asked Thompson for an explanation. The best he could do, still working within the metaphor selected by the White Queen, was to point out that it was possible to give away the contents of a bowl of milk without giving up the bowl itself.

The King was unimpressed. He understood now that he had been deceived. Partly out of anger, and partly as a calculated gesture to satisfy the militants, he called a council meeting at which he bitterly reproached one of the indunas for having advised him to sign the concession. This was equivalent to a death sentence; the old man was led outside the kraal and clubbed to pieces. For good measure, his entire household – more than 300 men, women and children – was rounded up and butchered.

Thompson was hiding at the mission house when news of the execution reached him. His feeling, as he recalled, was that 'if Lobengula could bring himself to sacrifice so trusted a counsellor ... he could not be expected to feel unduly anxious about me. Indeed, so far as he was concerned, I could do him no better service than to disappear until the storm blew over.'

Of such reasons autobiographies are made. More likely, Thompson suddenly and horrifyingly relived the death of his father. He rushed out of the mission house and cut the fastest horse from its traces. Not stopping for food, water, or even a hat, he galloped off. By sundown, he reached the desert and spent the night in a tree, for fear of lions. The next day, his horse foundered and Thompson abandoned it, continuing on foot until he met a trader with a mule-drawn wagon who gave him a lift part of the way to Mafeking where he stopped, exhausted and shaking.

No inducement would get him to go back, so he never did receive his long-awaited 'Runnymede' – news that on October 29th, 1889, the Queen, despite her own advice to Lobengula, had signed the Charter.

Rhodes returned to Africa in August 1889, as soon as the signing was assured. He had already placed an order for 250 miles of telegraph line, Siemens No. 8, and the required quantity of poles, and was told that the matter would receive immediate attention, but did he mind waiting until the British South Africa Company – the purchaser – actually became a reality? On the day it did, he signed an agreement to extend the railroad northward from Kimberley to Vryburg and Mafeking. Metcalfe had already done the surveying work, and Pauling's crews were at work within the week.

Across the Limpopo, and now entrusted to his care, lay an empire as large as that of the Habsburgs and Hohenzollerns combined. But one difficulty remained. Whatever the Directors had been told, or the enthusiastic shareholders allowed to imagine, Rhodes was well aware that it was not the tsetse fly alone which barred him from crossing the river. Lobengula had not been 'squared', nor were prospects likely that he could be. On the contrary, the King had by every means at his command made it clear that he had repudiated the Concession. Rhodes took his problem to Frank Johnson.

At 23, Johnson was known in Kimberley as a bright young lad, self-assured and enterprising. He had run away to sea at 16, landed at the Cape and worked his way up-country, doing some trading, prospecting, and soldiering with the Bechuanaland Border Police. For a time, he had been general manager of the Exploring Company, Rhodes's old rival. He even knew Lobengula; the King had thrown him out two years earlier for illegally digging for gold. After some private discussions, the two men signed a contract on December 7th, 1889, whereby Johnson, in return for £150,000 and the right to 100,000 acres of land, agreed to raise a force adequate ' ... to carry by sudden assault all the principal strongholds of the Matabele nation ... and to reduce the country to such a condition as to enable the prospecting, mining, and commercial staff of the British South Africa Company to conduct their operations in peace and safety.'

Johnson's plan, as he later described it himself, was to introduce a number of innocent-looking prospecting parties into the country just south of Lobengula's border. Then, ' ... with Rhodes supplying the money, I would gradually and unostentatiously bring these "prospecting" parties up to a total of five hundred men, all trained ex-members of South African forces. ... A day's halt to get one's breath, and I was to make the spring on a moonlight night. ... '

As to what would happen next, Johnson was not certain: 'I had an open mind as to procedure after securing the king ... whether to make a complete job of it by killing Lobengula (he might conceivably try to escape); ... or ... dig myself in at Bulawayo with Lobengula and his entourage as hostages, and open negotiations.'

If Rhodes had a preference, he did not get a chance to voice it. Before Johnson could organize his parties, word of the scheme reached Sir Sidney Shippard. (The game was given away by Johnson's partner, an Irishman named Maurice Heany who got drunk and bragged about the plan to a missionary.) Much as he admired Rhodes and wished to help, Shippard could not 'be a brick' in this instance; Queen Victoria had recognized Lobengula as the legitimate ruler of Matabeleland. Johnson was called on the carpet, not by Shippard but by Rhodes:

> I was summoned in frantic haste to Rhodes's office to hear that
> he had just come back from seeing the High Commissioner and

Administrator. He had denied all knowledge of what I was doing, and
I was taken to Government House to corroborate his innocence. ...
When I got away, I had a bad half-hour with Rhodes, whose anger
was as violent as his command of language was surprising. ...

Although this story, signed by Johnson, was published in the *Cape Times*
on September 12th, 1930, and has not been denied, it does not appear in
most subsequent accounts of Rhodes's life – a strange oversight, since it
helps to round out a complex character. Nor is it taught to Rhodesian
schoolchildren.

The version which they learn, and which has a charm of its own, has the
same cast of characters, but a different plot. It opens on a morning just
before Christmas in 1889, with a perplexed Cecil Rhodes, still looking for a
solution to his problem, walking into the Kimberley Club for breakfast.

Rhodes hated to eat alone. Seeing the familiar face of Frank Johnson in
the room, he lumbered over and sat down across from him. As Johnson
recalls the meeting: 'Without saying good morning or asking where I had
come from, Rhodes plunged straight into his troubles. "Carrington wants
to be made a major-general at my expense," he almost screamed. "Now you
know the interior. How many men do you think are wanted?" '

Carrington was Colonel Sir Francis Carrington, commander of the
Bechuanaland Border Police. Rhodes had asked him what kind of force
would be required to assure the safety of a pioneering expedition, and had
been told that it would take 2,500 men. The cost of such a force would just
about have wiped out the Company's entire working capital of £1 million.

Johnson scoffed at Carrington's estimate: '2,500 men? Nonsense. Why,
with 250 men I would go anywhere in Africa.'

Rhodes continued to eat his ham and eggs for a minute. 'Then', Johnson
writes, 'the practical financier spoke. What would a force of 250 men cost?
I replied that I had not the remotest idea, but ... if he gave me the use of a
room, with plenty of foolscap, I could tell him by lunch-time.'

At the appointed hour, Johnson produced his figure: £94,000.

'That's splendid,' Rhodes boomed, 'you are quite right. I will not make
Carrington a major-general. I appoint you to command the expedition.
When will you start?'

That was a little hasty, for some details still had to be ironed out, but in
the end Johnson brought the project in under budget. As Rhodes reported
to the Company's Board of Directors fifteen months later, the cost to the
Company of the expedition was £89,285 10s. 0d.

The plan was to avoid a confrontation with Lobengula by skirting Matabeleland and striking instead for the eastern part of the country, populated
by gentler Mashona tribes. This would necessitate cutting a road through
virtually unknown territory, much of it low-lying swampland, before reaching the upper veld. But Rhodes was confident that Frederick Selous could

do it. Not only did he know the country as well as any European, but he was just the kind of settler Rhodes had in mind for his new country: young, idealistic, able to take care of himself in a corner, and the son of the president of the London Stock Exchange.

Rhodes had given much thought to the question of settlers. He wished that, among them, all trades, professions and walks of life be represented, so that once established in their new home they could immediately start functioning as a nation in miniature. (The one oversight – the exclusion of women – probably did not occur to him.) With a large number of volunteers to choose from – more than 2,000 had flocked to Cape Town, attracted from as far away as Canada and Australia – the condition presented no problems. The Pioneer Column included lawyers, engineers, builders, bakers, butchers, bankers, sailors, printers, farmers, clergymen, and at least two physicians in addition to Dr Jameson, who was to go along with them. Among the 196 men who were finally chosen, there were English, Dutch, Germans, and at least two Americans. It so happened that the U.S.S. *Pensacola* was lying at anchor in Table Bay, preparing to make observations of a solar eclipse. Two members of its crew, a photographer named C. A. Orr and William H. Brown, a naturalist, asked permission to go along, having been assured by the American Consul that they did not risk losing their citizenship because Mr Rhodes's venture was a purely private affair, in no way connected with the Queen. Their pay, like that of the other pioneers, was to be seven shillings and sixpence a day – six times that of a private in the British army. In addition they received uniforms – brown corduroy tunic and trousers, leather leggings and a Buffalo Bill hat with the brim pinned up on the left side to add a dashing note. As bonus, they were also to receive 3,000-acre farms and the right to stake fifteen gold-mining claims.

Miffed at losing his chance at a star, Colonel Carrington nevertheless managed to salvage something. At his insistence, the High Commissioner refused to permit the Column to move without some kind of military protection. After some grumbling, Rhodes agreed to pay for an additional force of 500 Bechuanaland Police, under the command of Colonel E. G. Pennefather of the Inniskilling Dragoons, a leather-tough veteran of the Zulu wars. With great high spirits and, for a secret expedition, considerable fanfare, the men – Pioneers and escort – gathered at a training site north of Mafeking, which was immediately christened Camp Cecil. On June 27th, 1890, Major General Methuen, the deputy acting Adjutant of the Cape Command, arrived, inspected the troops, and pronounced them fit to march into the teeth of some twenty or thirty thousand blood-thirsty Matabeles. There was just the matter of their orders:

'Gentlemen, have you got maps?'
'Yes, sir.'

'And pencils?'

'Yes, sir.'

'Well, gentlemen, your destination is Mount Hampden. You go to a place called Siboutsi. I do not know whether Siboutsi is a man or a mountain. Mr Selous, I understand, is of the opinion that it is a man; but we will pass by that. ... Mr Selous is of opinion that Mount Hampden is placed ten miles too far to the west. You had better correct that; but perhaps on second thoughts, better not. Because you might be placing it ten miles too far to the east. Now, good morning, gentlemen.'

After these stirring words, the Pioneers and their escort saluted smartly and took off. The trip to Mount Hampden, wherever it might be, was long – 460 miles – and tedious – 13 weeks – but every mile and every day is recorded in Rhodesian legend. In addition to the Pioneers and troops, the column included 100 natives to help with the road-building and the pushing and goading of 3,000 oxen dragging 117 wagons. Together they resembled an articulated snake 2½ miles long, wriggling through the dense bush. Road-cutters worked in pairs, one man chopping while the other held the horses and kept a sharp eye out. At night, the snake would break into several tight pieces – squares formed by laagered wagons – and its eye would brighten with a piercing beam. The pioneers had borrowed a 10,000-candlepower searchlight from the naval depot at Simonstown; it was turned on at night-fall to frighten or discourage Matabeles who, it was reputed, preferred to attack just before dawn's first light.

Three times the column paused to establish way-stations: Forts Tuli, Charter and Victoria. Each morning, Selous rode ahead to scout the road; Ellerton Fry, an expert from the Cape observatory, corrected the route by observations of the sun – though it is hard to see what he corrected it against, since the maps which he carried were largely fanciful. Towards the end of July, the bush began thinning and giving way to granite terraces which succeeded each other like a monumental staircase, straining the patience of the men and the endurance of the oxen. On August 3rd, Selous, who had been gone for two days, galloped back as the column was just getting started. He had found a pass through the mountains. Beyond it lay their goal, miles upon miles of grassy rolling plain, dotted with solitary clumps of trees and strange, almost perfectly conical hills which rose sharply out of the flat ground, like a child's drawing of a mountain.

If Rhodes had wished to infuse his country with the spirit of Britain, he had done well: when the main body of the column reached the crest of the pass – Providential Pass, it was named – they found that the forward party which had preceded them had broken ranks and picked up sides for a cricket match.

In part, their exuberance was caused by relief. Once in open country, the threat of surprise attack by the Matabeles vanished, if indeed it ever existed. Not a shot had been fired, not a man injured. Commenting on this good fortune, Major H. L. Leonard of the Police, who had been left behind to take care of supplies, noted: 'It does not seem to be within the bounds of common sense to suppose that a nation of ferocious savages whose all-pervading instinct is blood and rapine, will allow us quietly to take possession of a country which is virtually theirs by right of conquest without in any way resenting it. To imagine it even is a direct insult.'

It has now been established that Lobengula had given strict orders that the column not be attacked. Nor was it the searchlight which provided the principal deterrent. The Matabeles would have willingly stormed it; or they could have ambushed the column in a dozen different places; or picked it to pieces. That they did none of these was not due to neighbourliness on Lobengula's part, but to regard for self-preservation. He had, through the eyes of his indunas, seen the future.

The column trudged along for another four weeks, stopping finally near a substantial hill they took to be Mount Hampden. (Not that it mattered, but they were wrong; the real Mount Hampden was twelve miles away.) Because no one had remembered to bring along the Company's own flag, Lieutenant Tyndale Biscoe hoisted the Union Jack on the straightest tree they could find. Canon Balfour said a prayer; three cheers were raised to the Queen; the Orders of the Day – September 12th, 1890 – were read: 'It is notified that the Column, having arrived at its destination, will halt.'

A fort was started and named Salisbury, after the Prime Minister who had speeded the Charter on its way. A courier service was established and the first letter, appropriately, sent to Rhodes announcing the expedition's safe arrival. His comment on receiving it was, 'I do not think there was a happier man in the country than myself.'

On September 30th, when the fort was finished, the Pioneers fell out in formation for the last time, were issued three months' rations, 100 rounds of ammunition, and at the command, 'Dismiss,' disappeared as a military body and became the entire civil population of a country. A few set about preparing to practise the skills or professions for which they had been chosen, but by far the greater number elected instead to become prospectors, and scattered out to search for the gold which, they were convinced, lay all around them.

It was a year almost to the day before Rhodes himself visited the country which some people had already started calling by his name.* He had wanted to go along with the Column, but was prevented from doing so by a

---

* The official choice of Rhodesia was not made until 1895, but it was probably first used in an article in the *Cape Argus* in 1891. Other names considered were Rhodesland and Cecilia.

political crisis in Cape Town – a crisis which he resolved by taking on the job of Prime Minister of Cape Colony himself. In that capacity, he had journeyed north as far as Fort Tuli, and cast an eye towards what he referred to as 'my protectorate'. One of the witnesses to the scene wrote:

> I saw a substantial organism, slow in his movements, deliberate in his manner and phlegmatic in his temperament. A big, heavy-looking man, not unlike a Dutch farmer, with an awkward slouching figure and a dull, rather expressionless face. ... But I am beginning to think he is very deep. For under that dull exterior which is but a mask, he is continually taking in all around and about him.

Major H. L. Leonard, the author of this passage, was as perceptive about empire builders as he was about the behaviour of Matabeles.

In September 1891, Rhodes decided the time had come for a proper visit. Spurning the long overland route, he went instead by way of Beira, on the coast of Portuguese Mozambique.

Salisbury, which he reached on October 16th, may have been something of a disappointment. It was a sprawling, uneven collection of straw-roofed mud huts spaced out along what could at one time have been conceived as streets. The 400 inhabitants were mainly traders and speculators, and nearly every one of them had a grievance to register with the Managing Director. To put it charitably, things had not worked out as anticipated. The plan had been that columns of supplies would follow the Pioneers as soon as the road was secured. But bureaucratic delay had interfered, compounded with unusual weather – the worst rainy season within memory. More than 50 inches had fallen in four months, turning first the road and then the entire veld into an impassable sea of mud. There was no hope of sending a wagon through; even dispatch riders stopped trying to make the trip. The supplies – food, tools, building materials – lay piled up in Tuli while in Salisbury prices for the few available objects climbed out of reason. A pot of jam, which cost 6d in London, fetched £3; whisky, if it could be found, was 10 shillings for a small tot.

Too busy prospecting to bother with their farms, the Pioneers had run out of food, and averted starvation only by buying pumpkins and mealies from the Mashonas. Without tools, it had been impossible to build anything more elaborate than mud-and-stick huts, which often as not disintegrated under the daily deluges. The random aspect of Salisbury's town planning was due, in large part, to the fact that the men tired of rebuilding and simply left the ruins of one hut to put up another one somewhere else. In the interest of speed, changes of clothing had been left behind, to come with the supplies. Pioneers were obliged to live in their soaked uniforms; when boots wore out, their owners went barefoot. For diversion, there was absolutely nothing to do. The community's literary resources consisted of some prayer books, almanacs and a text of elementary arithmetic. A few men had had the foresight to bring along packs of cards; they rented them out in exchange for part of the winnings.

Rhodes had set down a policy that all proceeds from mining would be divided on a half-and-half basis with the Company – better than most, he knew that a bonanza could reward its finders without at the same time enriching the community. The formula was resented as being iniquitous and piratical. But even more galling than the prospect of sharing was the fact that there was virtually nothing to share. Having ridden off with shovels and sacks in which to collect nuggets, the Pioneers had discovered that if any gold did exist in the country it was locked into massive quartz formations from which it could only be extracted with heavy stamping machinery. To frustrate them further, all around lay the traces of the mines whose output presumably had added glitter to the Queen of Sheba's dowry. There were the burnt tips of quartz reef – the miners of the day had heated the rock, then poured cold water over it to break it up. They also found huge, saucer-shaped granite pans in which the quartz had been pulverized by hand. But these were the techniques of savages, not the means to get rich fast.

Nevertheless, Rhodes was in great spirits, admiring everything in sight. When shown a vacant plot and told that it was to be the site of a synagogue, he was especially impressed: 'Ah, if the Jews are coming, my country is all right.' He had an answer for every complaint. The rains had been unexpected, but better transport was being organized; he himself had just traced the course of a railway which would solve the problem. As for food, it would be plentiful if only they would plant the seeds they had brought with them. The other amenities? A telegraph line was being strung, and the rest would follow. The most pressing need, a wagon-load of whisky, was already under way. They were, after all, pioneers, and had to expect to put up with some discomfort. As pioneers, they were bringing into being a great new country which soon ... and here Rhodes would go off on his descriptions of sprawling townships and shiny cities. Many of his listeners seemed satisfied, even heartened, but one who had made the long trip to Salisbury from Scotland voiced a growing sentiment: 'I would have ye know, Mr Rhodes, that we dinna come here for posterity.'

During Rhodes's stay in Salisbury, a distinguished visitor arrived from London: Lord Randolph Churchill, former Leader of the House of Commons and Chancellor of the Exchequer, husband of the lady whom Umshete and Babjaan had so extravagantly admired, and father of a young cadet just entering Sandhurst. The reason for his visit, as he explained in the first of a series of dispatches he sent back to the *Daily Graphic*, was that he believed ' ... that the day might not be distant when it might be useful and beneficial that a member of Parliament might be able to offer to the House of Commons observations, opinions and arguments based upon personal inspection, actual experience of those localities.'

More candidly, since everyone in England knew that degenerative disease had already placed parliamentary usefulness behind him, he added: 'The attractions of travel, of the chase, and especially of seeing gold for oneself, or acquiring gold mines or shares in gold mines, contributed also to decide me on the enterprise.'

He was already a shareholder in the British South Africa Company, but he brought along 'an American mining expert of great eminence', Henry Cleveland Perkins, to help with the acquisitions. For the chase, he rounded up three white servants, two Cape boys, four grooms, two cooks each with native boys to assist, two donkey herders, 14 native drivers, and Hans Lee, 'a well-known and most successful hunter'. The group, travelling in seven wagons drawn by 103 oxen, carried 40,000 pounds of supplies, including saddlery, furniture, trading goods, an arsenal of weapons and about 10,000 rounds of ammunition.

Moving leisurely, Churchill made great inroads in native herds, but still found time for some useful observations: that horse sickness seemed to carry off 80 per cent of the animals, and that 'scientific investigation ... carried on patiently would make discoveries of value'; that Fort Victoria was adequately defended, but Fort Charter could be taken by a determined rush and should be fortified by the erection of *chevaux de frise*; that in general 'the Company should cause posts and notices to be erected along the road where water is near.'

As for the gold fields, Churchill and Perkins were appalled by what they found:

> Many parties of *soi-disant* prospectors have been fitted out and maintained by syndicates, whose idea of their duty appears to be that they are to stick to the main routes, lie under their wagons most of the day ... and from time to time offer a blanket to some native who will guide them to an old working, where claims can be pegged out.

Eschewing the main roads himself, Churchill did come across a site promising enough to warrant the investment of £2,000. But his overall judgment was equivocal: 'It cannot be denied that the high hopes which were entertained by so many and various competent authorities as to the great mineral and agricultural wealth of Mashonaland have not hitherto been justified or nearly justified. ... Mashonaland so far as is known, and much is known, is neither an Arcadia nor an El Dorado.'

Despite this discouraging note, hundreds of newcomers poured into the country – veterans of other gold rushes, amateurs with little more than a one-way ticket in their pocket, scholars who were convinced they had deduced the true location of the legendary Ophir. None of them found anything. The Company remained officially optimistic, and even helped circulate a story that Lobengula himself had requested and been granted claims of his own. What possible use he had for more gold is hard to imagine; the 100 sovereigns which arrived regularly at the start of every lunar month piled up untouched in the back of his ox-wagon.

To maintain law and order required a police force of 700 men out of a total European population of less than 3,000 – surely a record – and an annual expenditure of £250,000. Jameson was appointed administrator and immediately reduced expenses to £30,000 by cutting the police to 150 men, and strengthening them with volunteer patrols. As a further economy measure, he was told that 'Mr Rhodes would like you to sweep away entirely the military regime; give each Magistrate 10 policemen, and let them run the show as civil administration, pure and simple.'

Jameson complied, thereby putting the machinery of justice into the hands of men not likely to be either impartial or gentle when dealing with the minor grievances – cattle thefts, refusal to work – which had begun to mark relations between white and black. Surrounded and hopelessly outnumbered, the settlers quickly learned that their surest shield was respect – earned by the promise of stinging punishment. (The city of Salisbury's motto, adopted in 1897, is *Discrimine Salus*, 'In discrimination there is safety.') One of the Pioneers – the American naturalist, Brown – had wandered widely around the country and gave it as his opinion that the Mashonas could not conceive of bravery unsupported by power: 'When one or two [white] men present a bold front, these natives will often desist from violence, believing that a large force may be lying in the bushes near at hand.'

Far from dispelling such belief, magistrates tried to confirm it by every means. When Mashonas failed to show up for work, entire kraals were set to the torch; when some goods were stolen from a settler named Bennett, Police Captain Charles Lendy arrived with a band of volunteers, and when refused – by his account – the right to search the hut of a suspect, proceeded to kill him, his son and 21 other natives. For good measure, he confiscated and took away the slain man's 47 head of cattle. The Colonial Office complained that Lendy had acted with 'recklessness and undue harshness', and that 'the punishment inflicted ... appears utterly disproportionate to the original offence.' It also pointedly observed that 'the Natives of Mashonaland are not British subjects or subjects of the British South Africa Company,' and consequently could not be considered to have risen in insurrection – the excuse given by the Company for Lendy's actions. But that was just Grandmamma talking; Rhodes, writing to Jameson, said, 'I am glad to hear that you are maintaining the dignity of the law.' For his part in the affair, Lendy was promoted to Magistrate of Fort Victoria.

Meanwhile, shares in the Company, which had gone from £1 to £3¾, fell to below par on the London Stock Exchange. Told that 'the Bank will not advance another shilling,' Rhodes began to sell off huge tracts of land in order to raise money. That he was able to do so was the result of still another of his enterprising ventures. Even if it was valid, the Rudd

Concession had only given him rights to look for minerals, but no right to the land itself; Lobengula would never have consented to that. The point had come up, casually, during the discussions over the Charter. Joseph Chamberlain, then an influential Liberal M.P., told Rhodes: 'Well, you have got the gold of the whole country ... but I should like you to get some territorial acknowledgment from Lobengula, further strengthening your claim as a whole.'

The opportunity arose in April 1891, when Edward Lippert, one of the original suitors at Lobengula's court, suddenly appeared brandishing a new concession which he claimed Lobengula had just signed, and which conferred 'exclusive right, power and privilege for a full term of 100 years to lay out, grant or lease ... farms, townships, building plots ... to impose and levy rents, licences and taxes thereon ... ' and so forth. If valid, this concession was in effect a title deed to Lobengula's kingdom. Rhodes's first reaction had been to challenge its validity and, for good measure, order the arrest of the agent who had brought it from Bulawayo. But reflection suggested a better idea. Lobengula could only have granted this new concession – Rhodes never doubted its validity, for it was far too brazen a bluff for Lippert to try – because he thought it might invalidate his own. Very well, let him think he had succeeded.

Privately, Rhodes made a deal with Lippert, whose own business practices had earned him the reputation of being 'the evil genius of the Transvaal'. If Lippert could get a new concession, duly certified by the British Resident in Bulawayo, Rhodes would not only acknowledge it, but he would buy it – for a price which one historian described as 'an exorbitant sum'. (Actually, it was £30,000, and 15,000 shares of B.S.A. stock, not an unreasonable price for an entire country.)

The British Resident in Bulawayo was, at the time, John Moffat. One would have supposed that he was by now well-schooled in extracting royal signatures, but the British High Commissioner in Cape Town, who was in on the scheme, nonetheless spelled the situation out for him: 'It will be undesirable that the fact of any agreement should become known until after the ratification of the concession by Lobengula, as it is likely that the King has granted [it] under the impression he is strengthening a corporation hostile to the Company, and thus dividing the white men amongst themselves.'

Moffat's response, somewhat belatedly, was a show of indignation. He wrote to Rhodes: 'I feel bound to tell you that I look on the whole plan as detestable, whether in the light of policy or morality.'

Still, he did as he was told, and for his service was rewarded with a cut in salary and removal to a less sensitive post. The new concession was hastily endorsed by Her Majesty's Government.

The game, dirty already, was to get much worse. Sales of land had not brought enough money into the treasury, and gold had not yet been found in any useful quantity when, on November 24th, 1892, Rhodes rose to address the shareholders of the British South Africa Company, assembled for their second annual meeting. As is common on such occasions, the Managing Director had a rosy picture to paint. To be sure, no dividends had been paid out yet, and the stock was still languishing at 10 or 12 shillings, but weren't they all in it for the long pull? On that basis, prospects were brighter than ever. The telegraph line from the Cape had reached Salisbury, and was already earning 4 per cent on capital. Half-jokingly, he told the shareholders that if each of them would send him £10, it could be extended as far as Uganda, 1,500 miles away. Beyond that, the Sudan was in revolt, but presented no problem. 'I do not propose to fight the Mahdi,' Rhodes explained, 'but to "deal" with him. I have never met anyone in my life whom it was not as easy to deal with as to fight.' The railway, he reported, was coming along. As for another problem which had been mentioned in the press, that was nothing to worry about, either. 'We are', Rhodes said, 'on the most friendly terms with Lobengula. ... I have not the least fear of any trouble in the future from [him].'

The second part of the statement may have been true; the first was an outright lie. Far from being friendly, relations with Lobengula were deteriorating as rapidly as the Company's agents could manage to strain them. Lobengula did not want war; he had made that plain in a dozen ways which must have been painful to his pride, and possibly risky to his tenure as monarch. But from the beginning, from the abortive conspiracy with Frank Johnson, Rhodes had determined to destroy the Matabeles and take over the entire country. In 1891, he promised a group of prospective settlers, 'As soon as they interfere with our rights, I shall end their game, and when it is all over, I shall grant farms to those who assisted me.'

Though he had now been duped into giving away rights to his land as well as to its resources, Lobengula still maintained jurisdiction over the natives who inhabited it. Of this there was no question, as the Colonial Office repeatedly reminded Jameson. Ever since the founding of the Matabele nation, a function of this jurisdiction had been the right of person over the Mashonas – the right to their women as prizes of war, and to their cattle and grain as taxes. These rights were rigorously enforced, and outside the scope of any possible commercial agreement with white men. Every year, after the rains, Lobengula sent out a dozen tax collectors, each accompanied by a party of warriors, who fanned out and simultaneously called on the principal Mashona chiefs. If any of them dared refuse to pay, the collector had only to dispatch a messenger and all the warriors could quickly be gathered to deal with the offender. This method had been effective for as long as anyone could remember, but in 1892 a Mashona chief named Mazorodze refused to pay his tribute. It is fair to assume that he had been emboldened to resist, and possibly promised protection, by the whites.

This concern on their part did not stem from any new-found sense of justice. From the beginning, the settlers had discovered that 3,000-acre farms and fifteen gold claims were totally useless without cheap hands to work them. Traditionally, the Mashonas did not work – not in the settlers' sense of the word. They were friendly, inquisitive people. The explorer François Coillard, who had travelled among them in the early 1870s, reported that

> We caught sight of black figures ... who cast furtive glances at us and disappeared like shadows. Others, growing bolder, approached us little by little, and before evening brought us flour, peas, groundnuts, rice, etc. ... From this moment our wagons were besieged by natives from far and near, who escorted us by day and bivouacked beside us at night, to satisfy their curiosity.

Mashonas fashioned pottery, among the most graceful to be found in Central Africa; they wove cloth of ancient, symbolic designs; they performed on musical instruments of their own creation. They, or rather their women, planted and tended what little food they required. As among many African cultures, work was at best a means to an immediate end. A man might raise a few extra goats or chickens as instruments of trade, but that was the extent of it. One of the Company's first acts had been to eliminate this trade as a wasteful diversion. In April 1891, Colonel Pennefather reported, 'All the natives who have been accustomed to trade with the Portuguese are protesting loudly that we have no stuff to barter with them, and that as we have driven the Portuguese out of the country they cannot now do any trade.'

The Matabeles, when they came to collect taxes, scrupulously avoided touching whites or – with very rare and inadvertent exceptions – their property. Nevertheless, their appearance was a source of irritation to the settlers because the Mashona's instant reaction to the sight of a Matabele warrior was to drop the pick or shovel that had been forced into his hands and scurry into the bush. It would take days, and the threat of physical punishment, to round him up again.

This – the settlers' discovery of their total dependence on the natives – determined the one-sided relationship between white and black. The Matabeles had to be destroyed not because they threatened the white man's safety, but because they interfered with the integrity of his labour supply. But for a white man to say that a bloody Kaffir refused to work for him because he was afraid of another Kaffir was an admission of failure, or at least inferiority. So white men skirted the issue, as the British South Africa Company did when it asked the Colonial Office for the right to impose a hut tax on the Mashonas: 'One of the principal difficulties in dealing with African races is of teaching them habits of settled industry and ... in a country with a considerable demand for native labour, the necessity of paying this small tax would furnish an incentive to labour.'

Lobengula did not descend to such rationalization. His national economy, too, was based on the Mashonas – as indeed was the psychological under-pinning of Matabele society. The Mashonas and the lesser tribes that lived to the east were *maholis* – slaves – to be plundered at will. Their subser-vience validated the superiority of his own warriors, who were far above such menial chores as planting grain or tending cattle. Any interference with the exercise of his rights was therefore not only an economic nuisance, but an open act of *lèse majesté*. The raid against the recalcitrant Mazorodze, and others like it, were simply a way of serving notice that the coming of the white man had not affected the ancient order of tribal life.

The whites did not see it that way. On August 27th, 1892, the *Rhodesian Chronicle* reported 'increasing insolence' on the part of the Matabeles: 'The ostensible object of these impis which regularly roam about Mashonaland ... is to collect tribute from the Mashonas. ... It is, we contend, a disgrace to the Chartered Company to allow these raids on natives whom they have taken under their protection.'

Picking up the cue, settlers in Salisbury drafted and published a resolu-tion stating that 'in the event of the Company not taking the initiative, a very large proportion of the inhabitants are determined to take the matter into their own hands.' This was, in plain terms, the familiar frontier call to vigilantism, and it was not lost on Jameson. Still, provocation would be helpful. The Matabeles, however, did not seem ready to provide it. On the contrary, as Dr Rutherfoord Harris, the Company's Secretary in Cape Town, reported to the home office in London: 'The position of the Mata-bele today seems quite the reverse of what it was two years ago – *now* they fear an attack from us. Their apprehension is that the whites will enter Matabeleland and evidently they have quite abandoned any idea of offen-sive action. ... '

This assessment was dated April 12th, 1893, and was proved almost immediately wrong. Early in May, 500 yards of the freshly-strung copper telegraph wire to Salisbury were cut and stolen. The culprit, a petty Mashona chieftain named Gomalla, was readily traced because the evidence of his theft appeared as necklaces and bracelets on the ample bodies of some of his wives and concubines. Faced with a choice between punishment or a fine, Gomalla willingly chose the fine and handed over some cattle. The choice had been easy, for it turned out that the cattle were not his, but belonged to Lobengula, for whom he had been tending them.

Because of the special significance of royal cattle, this was not just another Mashona trick, but a direct challenge to Lobengula's authority as king. Advising Jameson of his intention, and again assuring him that the whites had no reason to be alarmed, he sent a punitive expedition to Fort Victoria, where the guilty Mashonas had taken refuge.

Matabele warriors ordered to teach their slaves a lesson do not travel on tiptoe. The impi which arrived at the gates of Fort Victoria on July 9th left behind a trail of smouldering huts, women ripped and impaled, and men and children roasted alive like meat. Still, three days later Harris cabled to London: 'The incident, Mr Rhodes says, is greatly to be regretted, but it has afforded strong proof of Lobengula's determination not to come into collision with the white man.'

Jameson, in Salisbury, concurred: the description of burning kraals and Mashonas killed was 'of course very harrowing, but that was at first blush'. Nevertheless, he decided he had better ride down to Fort Victoria and see for himself.

Somewhere along the 188-mile trip he changed his mind, for his first cable from Fort Victoria said that 'The labour question is the serious one. There is no danger to the whites, but ... there have been so many cases of Mashona labourers killed even in the presence of the white masters that the natives will have no confidence in the protection of the whites, unless we actually drive the Matabele out.'

The sight of Fort Victoria confirmed this view. The second largest settlement in the country, it consisted of a hollow rectangular structure – offices, police quarters, a jail and court-house, stables for horses, all linked by a wall and surrounding a large courtyard. At one corner rose a square wooden tower on which was mounted a single machine gun which could sweep the flat countryside in every direction. When Jameson arrived, on July 17th, the magistrate's office had been converted into a field hospital; women and children, some ninety in all, had been huddled into the sturdiest buildings; the courtyard was a mob-scene of refugees, white settlers from outlying farms and Mashonas frightened out of their wits. Because there was no room inside the fort for everybody, a laager of wagons had been formed outside the south wall. The Matabeles were nowhere in sight.

Jameson briskly took charge, ordering the Matabele leader sent for, and announcing his own plan of action to Harris: 'I intend to treat them like dogs and order the whole impi out of the country. Then if they do not go, send Lendy out with 50 mounted men to fire into them.'

Hans Sauer, Jameson's old adversary in the smallpox controversy, but now a good friend, was present at Fort Victoria. He relates that Manyao, the Matabele chief, requested that the culprits be turned over to him, pointing out in a calm voice that Mashonaland was still a province of the Matabele kingdom, that Lobengula had never ceded governing rights, and that these rights included the settlement of disputes and the appointment or removal of Mashona chiefs. Under these rights, he asked Jameson for permission to carry out his order. Sauer's comment, in describing the episode, was that 'From a legal point of view, there was no answer to him.'

Jameson was not prepared for legal niceties. The Matabeles were told to clear out, and warned that they would be fired upon if they were not out of the country by a certain time. Soon after, Lendy – the same Lendy who had gone to look for Mr Bennett's stolen goods – was sent to see whether they were gone. They were not, and a fight ensued – a one-sided fight in which nine Matabeles were killed, although not one of Lendy's troopers was hurt. Because the Fort Victoria incident was soon to assume greater importance – in fact, to serve exactly the purpose intended – it eventually became the subject of an Inquiry. What, exactly, had been Jameson's ultimatum? How much time did he give the Matabeles? How soon did Lendy charge off after them? What happened when they met? The findings did not quite answer these questions, but 'clearly exonerated Dr Jameson and the officers of the B.S.A. Company from all blame' – a judgment which must be viewed in the light of the fact that the man who rendered it, F. J. Newton, shortly thereafter accepted appointment as Treasurer of the B.S.A. Company.

But that came later. Having sent Lendy off, Jameson still had work to do. Rhodes was in Cape Town, where Parliament was sitting. Unfortunately, there is no record of the telegram which Jameson sent to him, but the reply was to appear in every book ever written about Cecil Rhodes. 'Read Luke XIV, 31,' he wired back to his friend. (The verse, not one of the better-known, reads: 'Or what king, going to make war against another king, sitteth not down first, and consulteth whether he be able with ten thousand to meet him that cometh against him with twenty thousand?')

Before replying, Jameson made a request of Dr Sauer. 'There are some Dutchmen in the town. Go and ask them how many men they think it would take to fight the Matabele nation.' Sauer came back and reported, 'Eight hundred to one thousand men.' Then Jameson sent Rhodes his answer: he had read St Luke, and it was all right.

Jameson made additional use of the new telegraphic facilities. On July 19th, the day after the incident, he suggested to Harris: 'We have the excuse for a row over murdered women and children now, and the getting of Matabeleland open would give us a tremendous lift in shares, and everything else.'

To the High Commissioner, he proposed on July 21st: 'Should you not prohibit it, we could from Mashonaland settle the question finally.'

Obviously the Commissioner did prohibit it, and also warned his superiors in London of what was being planned, for on September 1st, Rhodes received this message from one of the Directors of the Company in London:

Ripon [Lord Ripon, the new Colonial Secretary] sent for us the other day, and told us we might protect ourselves if attacked, but that we must in no case be in any way aggressive. ... I gather it is your intention to find some way round the Governor's prohibition and settle the Matabele question this September once and for all. We are in darkness as to your plans but I have the fullest confidence in any move which you and Jameson agree in there. ... We will support you, whatever the issue.

The Board of Directors of the British South Africa Company had approved the expansion programme of their resident Managing Director in Cape Town, and of his deputy in Fort Victoria. The rest was purely a matter of implementation.

In fact, the deputy had already set the programme in motion. Now the time had come for vigilantism, but better than pure vigilantism was vigilantism plus 5 per cent or even more. On August 14th, Jameson instructed Captain Allan Wilson of the Company's police to recruit some men. The letter, which did not come to light until 1914 when another, more searching inquiry was made into the Company's affairs by the Privy Council, started out by stating: 'The following are the conditions of service for members of the Victoria Force for Matabeleland,' and then spelled out in ten clauses the rewards offered to volunteers: 6,000 acres of land in any part of Matabeleland, 20 gold claims, and so forth. Clause 7 read: 'The loot shall be divided one half to the B.S.A. and the remainder to officers and men in equal shares.' The word loot was an odd term to use in official correspondence – the letter was signed 'L. S. Jameson, for the British South Africa Company' – but it had the virtue of leaving little to the imagination. Lobengula owned gold, rifles, mounds of presents brought by the concession-seekers; he was reputed to possess buckets of diamonds, smuggled out and presented to him by Mashonas who had worked a term in the Kimberley mines. But even without all this, there were his cattle. They alone would be worth at least £1,000 – a colossal sum – for each member of the Victoria Force in Matabeland. Quickly, 672 volunteers signed up and were issued weapons. They could not start out just yet because of a shortage of mounts, but Rhodes was taking care of that, buying up every available horse in the Cape Colony and sending them north.

Under the terms of the Charter, Her Majesty's Government clearly retained the responsibility to mediate in differences which might arise between native chiefs and the Company. In the spirit of discharging this responsibility, the High Commissioner sent a note to Lobengula on August 16th – two days after Jameson had started organizing his vigilantes: 'Let there be peace between you and the white men. I understand that you intend to send two of your indunas to speak to me. I shall be glad to receive them. ... '

The statesman-like tone may well have been lost on Lobengula. For five years, he had watched the inexorable intrusion of the white men. First they had come bearing gifts and begging favours. Then they had tricked him again and again. 'There is a wall around the word of a king,' he had once told Moffat when his friend, the son of his father's friend, had asked him to put his mark on a piece of paper. What weight did the paper carry, compared to a solemn, verbal promise?

Still, he would try one more time. To one of the indunas whom he sent to see the Commissioner he gave a letter, again addressed to the Great White Queen. It began:

> I have the honour to respectfully write and state that I am still keeping your advice, laid before me some time ago, that if any trouble happens in my country between me and the white men, I must let you know. I dispatched an army for my cattle, stolen by Mashonas. My impi was told to leave their arms behind, coming into the camp, which they did. The white men, after holding a meeting with them, shot my people without cause. ...

Lobengula went on to summarize his relations with Rhodes and Jameson. And he ended: 'Your Majesty! What I want to know from you is, why do your people kill me?'

The letter never reached its destination. Indeed, the only mention of its existence, at the time, is a passing reference in a report from Cape Town to London: 'The induna Umshete, who was in England, is on his way here. ... He is the bearer of a letter to the Queen, written ... in an illiterate style and containing nothing of importance.'

Early in October, Lobengula made a final attempt to avert war. On the basis of a safe-conduct from the High Commissioner, he sent his own brother and two other envoys down to Tati, the nearest white emplacement. They arrived in the midst of hectic preparations. Troops of the Bechuanaland Border Police, rushed north by way of the railway, were being assembled, rations and ammunitions distributed, orders circulated. In the confusion, the three Matabeles were arrested as spies. Before explanations could be made, two of them were killed and the third forced to flee. Whatever message they carried was not delivered.

At approximately the same time, Cecil Rhodes, Prime Minister of the Cape Colony and Managing Director of the British South Africa Company, decided that the season was appropriate for some upland shooting. Accompanied by several friends, he sailed from Cape Town to Beira and started inland towards Salisbury. Halfway, the party wandered off the trail and made camp in the wilds, where Rhodes seemed determined to destroy every pheasant in sight. Finally, a trooper rode in with a message from Salisbury which put an end to the exercise. Jameson and his volunteers were beyond the range of recall, on their way towards Bulawayo.

The Matabele War – if that is the correct term – consisted of two engagements lasting little more than an hour each, and was adequately summed up as a military history by Hilaire Belloc's famous couplet:

> Whatever happens, we have got
> The Maxim gun and they have not.

Jameson had five Maxim guns, only recently perfected by their inventor in his London garage-workshop, as well as three other machine guns, two seven-pound field pieces, some 1,000 mounted troops, and a gaggle of Mashonas who tagged along to retrieve their missing sisters and daughters. The Matabeles fielded against them approximately 18,000 men, few of whom got to within stabbing range of the attackers. After the second exercise in target practice, Sir John Willoughby, a former Guards officer serving with the Company's forces, extended himself in praise: 'I cannot speak too highly of the pluck of these regiments. I believe that no civilized troops could have withstood the terrific fire they did for at most half as long.'

The taking of the enemy's capital was a fitting end to the conflict: Bulawayo, which the victors entered on November 4th, was a smouldering ruin, deserted of all life except for two white traders, long-time residents who had accepted Lobengula's promise of safety. Jameson's men found them sitting peaceably on a half-burned roof. Nevertheless, all the trappings were observed: bagpipes, flag-raising, thanksgiving services. As one of the participants noted, ' "Onward, Christian Soldiers" was sung again, for we had not yet captured Lobengula, with his cattle, diamonds and gold.'

Nor did they. After ordering his town destroyed, the King had hitched up the ox-wagon which served as his palace and moved north, towards the Zambesi. Four hundred soldiers were sent off in pursuit, but Lobengula was never found, alive or dead. It is supposed that he succumbed to fever, or possibly to wounds; another version has it that he committed suicide by taking poison. For a number of years, a story persisted that he had somehow managed to have himself buried in a secret cave and, like Mzilikazi, surrounded by his treasure. No search has ever uncovered it. Nor did anyone come forward to claim his throne.

For Rhodes – and for Her Majesty's Government – the fight against Lobengula had been only a prelude, an episode whose outcome they had both discounted. Four days before the first shot had been fired, the Colonial Office warned the Company that 'all negotiations with Lobengula are to be conducted by the High Commissioner and under his complete control.' Rhodes's immediate reply was that 'the idea is so monstrous that I cannot believe it.' Not a nice way to talk to Grandmama, but necessary: the Government had not been over concerned about the welfare of the Matabeles, but they might yet draw the line somewhere short of 'loot', and 6,000-acre farms freely handed out. Empire-building was serious business, and should be left to the man on the spot.

This was also the view, forcibly expressed, of the Cape Town newspapers. On October 26th – still before Bulawayo had fallen – the *Cape Times* warned of a plot to 'weaken the energies of our fellow colonists by holding up some spectre of a settlement in which neither they nor Mr Rhodes shall have any controlling voice or even any concern.'

The *Cape Argus* contributed a thought, under the headline CRIMINAL IMPERIALISM: 'Instead of allowing its subjects in this part of the world a chance of driving monsters like Lobengula over the Zambesi, Britain comes in on these wrong principles and seems to be willing to protect a powerful Kaffir in the execution of his murders.'

With wealth had come diversification; among other properties, Rhodes owned the *Times*, and was a major shareholder in the *Argus*. But he could still speak for himself, too. On December 19th, he showed up in Bulawayo to address his victorious volunteers: 'You have been called free-looting marauders, blood-thirsty murderers and so on. ... I am as loyal an Englishman as anyone can be, but I cannot help saying that it is such conduct that alienates colonists from the mother-country. We ask for nothing ... and still a certain portion vilify us. In the same spirit it was that the mother-country lost America.'

In the face of such eloquence, supported by steady pressure from influential members of the Board, Grandmama conceded. Under the circumstances – 'the success achieved by the forces of the British South Africa Company' – the Government was prepared to accept 'terms agreed by Mr Rhodes'.

The terms were very simple: a free hand to do exactly as he wished. Appearances were preserved by the creation of a Land Commission which was charged with safeguarding 'land sufficient and suitable' for Matabele needs. In practice, before the Commission could be appointed, little was left to safeguard. Speculators, some of them accompanied by their own personal surveyors, arrived to buy up unwanted claims and assemble county-sized estates. The land was good – 'The Matabeles were no fools,' one of the volunteers conceded – and prices moved briskly. Hans Sauer recalls in his autobiography that he bought up a block of several thousand acres which ran from Bulawayo into the Matopo Hills. He paid £500 for it, and sold it a few months later for £20,000 to Cecil Rhodes himself.

Rhodes could easily afford it. The double conquest of Matabeleland marked the climax of a decade of uninterrupted success, financial as well as political. De Beers, while engaging in the wide range of its other activities, now controlled nine-tenths of the world's diamond supply. The railway had reached as far as Mafeking, and was already referred to as the 'trunk' line to Cairo. Shares in the Chartered Company, which had begun to climb with the first rumble of war, soared to £8. A new public issue of one million shares was quickly taken up, filling the coffers for new enterprises. On a visit to England in the winter of 1894, Rhodes was accorded the rare privilege of a private dinner at Windsor. 'What', asked the Queen conversationally, 'have you been doing since our last meeting?' 'Madam,' he replied, 'I have added two new provinces to your possessions.'

At home in Cape Town, Rhodes was beyond criticism. The offer of the Premiership, made to him in 1890, might have posed irreconcilable conflicts of interest to a lesser man, but he did not see it that way: 'I thought of the position [I] occupied in De Beers and Chartered Company, and I concluded that one could be worked with the other, and each to the benefit of all.'

And so it had worked out. After five continuous years in office, Rhodes commanded 58 out of 76 seats in the House. Diamonds and gold had brought prosperity to South Africa – diamonds alone accounted for £4 million out of the colony's annual £6 million exports. But still, Rhodes did not trust to luck. He bullied the Dutch farmers into inoculating their sheep against disease; he imported Arab stallions and pure Angora goats from Turkey to improve breeding stocks; he sent to America for experts on how to grow and package oranges, and how to protect groves against insect pests; he tried, unsuccessfully, to secure preferential treatment on the London market for the Cape's wines. But his pet project – his 'favourite child' – was the Glen Gray Act, which he pushed through in the face of strong objection from London. Its intention was the orderly development of South Africa's fundamental natural resource – a goal which it proposed to attain by creating native preserves, taking away the voting franchise of inhabitants herded into them, and substituting a token system of self-government. In order to stimulate the natives thus penned in to work – to 'train them in the arts of civilization', as Rhodes put it – it also imposed a fine or tax on anyone who did not find work outside his specified district. The Act proved effective in creating a virtually inexhaustible pool of docile labour, as well as the machinery to stock and breed it in perpetuity. As the operational basis of *apartheid*, it is working still.

Good fortune rubbed off on Rhodes's close associates, too. Charles Rudd, his lone field mission accomplished, returned to his ledgers. He also did well for himself in the gold fields and, in time, followed Rhodes into politics, representing Kimberley for five years. After the Boer War, he returned to England where he died peacefully in 1916, leaving 'considerable benefactions'.

Rochfort Maguire, his legal work done, went back to Britain where he twice stood successfully for Parliament, and under the pseudonym 'Imperialist' wrote a biography of Rhodes in which he gave himself high grades for 'keen and tactful diplomacy in securing the Rudd Concession'. In addition to his political and literary interests, he also closely followed the affairs of the British South Africa Company, becoming its Chairman in 1923.

Francis Thompson used the proceeds of his shares to pay for a belated college education – at Oxford of all places – and returned to South Africa where, by his own account, he was much in demand as an expert in native affairs, and an after-dinner storyteller.

Not everyone fared this well. Immediately after the war, John Moffat was transferred once more to a still more undesirable and meaningless post from which, since he would not take the hint, he was requested to retire.

In May 1894, while he was in Cape Town looking for a job, he sat down to write a letter to his son:

> The great Rhodes is prancing around. He has too much on his shoulders, and will probably end up by making a mess of it, but meanwhile everyone down here is bowing down and worshipping him as the wisest of men. The popular tide is with him. Great is success. I suppose there will be a crash some day – and men will suddenly recollect that there is still such a thing as justice even to niggers.

The 'niggers' are still waiting for justice, but for Rhodes the crash was not far off – just nineteen months away.

PART THREE

Bulawayo to Bukama

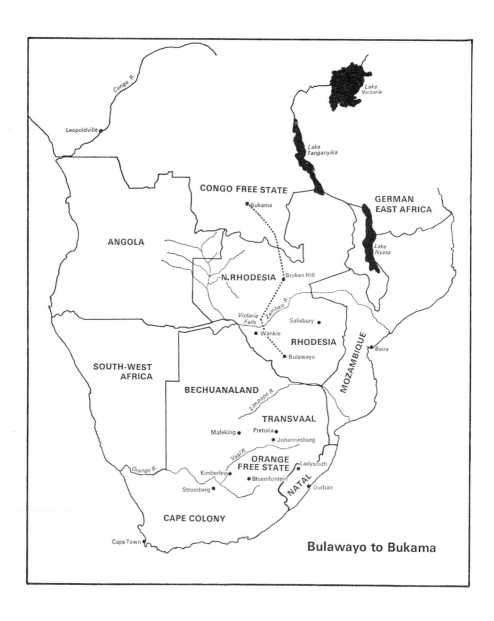

Bulawayo to Bukama

EVEN as he was taking his giant steps northwards, Rhodes was looking back over his shoulder at a chain of events which, to his mounting annoyance, was not at all going according to expectations. The Transvaal – the South African Republic, as it called itself – was doing very well indeed.

Having with poor grace restored to the Transvaal most of the independence it had sharply asserted on Majuba Hill in 1881, the majority of right-thinking Englishmen at the Cape – Rhodes among them – assumed that it was only a question of time until the state collapsed under its own weight. Boers were temperamentally unsuited to administration – most of the civil servants in Pretoria had been imported from Holland. The internal and foreign policies set down by President Kruger were derived, with only slight adaptation, from the Old Testament. And, to make matters certain, the country was an economic impossibility. Without any industry, without any exports, without even a harbour, it could not hope to survive. Annual receipts in 1885 had amounted to £186,000, hardly enough to pay for schoolteachers and land registry clerks. It was only a matter of time and patience until Kruger would be obliged to come back, his silly stovepipe hat in hand, to Cape Town.

But then, all this changed overnight. As Edmund Garrett, the editor of the *Cape Times*, noted: 'In all South Africa, in all the known world, there is only one gold field with the exact characteristics, as to extent and regularity, of the Witwatersrand. And the Witwatersrand must needs crop up in the Transvaal.'

By 1896, income of the Transvaal had risen to £4 million a year, and could be expected to rise even further, because the Rand was producing one quarter of the world's output of gold.

For most Englishmen – and most bitterly for Rhodes, who had not found any more paying gold reefs in Matabeleland than in Mashonaland – the irony was that the Boers were not interested in gold. The British writer James Bryce, who visited the Transvaal during this period, wrote:

Two centuries of solitary pastoral life have not only given them an aversion for commerce, for industrial pursuits, but an absolute incapacity for such pursuits; so that when gold was discovered they did not even attempt to work it, but were content to sell, usually for a price far below its value, the land where the gold reefs lay, and move off to resume their pastoral life elsewhere.

Paul Kruger was not this naive, for he knew that gold had its uses. But still, it also had its place. Under his rule, the corrosive effects of the yellow metal had been contained. With one glaring exception, the Transvaal of 1895 was the sort of place which Jehovah Himself – and, in humility, Kruger felt competent to interpret His wishes – would have approved.

The exception, of course, was Johannesburg. Rising suddenly out of the empty veld, hundreds of miles from the sea and 6,000 feet above its level, it was not only by virtue of its geography that it merited description as one of the Cities of the Plain. Johannesburg had the inevitable rows of corrugated iron shacks, but it also had eight-storey marble-fronted buildings. It had electric lights and trams, streets of 'gorgeous shops and gay music halls', a race course, a permanent circus and menagerie, 650 licensed bars, unnumbered brothels, and a Stock Exchange. All of this had happened in ten years, and constituted a self-contained community. As Colvin, Jameson's biographer, described it:

> ... at the top stood the several great mining and financial houses, whose heads and chief servants were the magnates and patricians of the place. Upon the main stem of the mining industry all manner of subsidiary activities contrived to exist – English accountants and bank clerks, German chemists and import agents, the British shopkeeper, Australian prospectors and mine managers, and a cosmopolitan crowd of stockbrokers and land agents, liquor-sellers, illicit gold-buyers, pimps and fried-fish shopkeepers, and the votaries of all nationalities of a hundred and one other trades and occupations, reputable and disreputable.

A few – the magnates and patricians – had complaints about the Boers. They did not like the excessive taxation – which, at two shillings to the pound, was in fact far lighter than that imposed on mining earnings by the British South Africa Company. They resented the system of concessions, granted by Kruger as much to maintain services as to generate income. In a Manifesto of protest, mine owners cried that 'No sooner does any commodity become absolutely essential to the community than some harpy endeavours to get a concession for its supply.'

Indeed, there was a Water Concession, an Electric Light Concession, a Bread and Jam Concession. But the most heartfelt abuse was reserved for the Dynamite Concession. Control of this commodity, essential to mining, rested with Rhodes's former business associate, Edward Lippert. As the state's sole licensed importer, he paid 30 shillings a case and sold it for 90 shillings, pocketing a profit of some £600,000 a year. In order to make their complaints appear less self-serving, the Chamber of Mines in 1894 collected some 13,000 signatures on a petition demanding the right to vote. (As foreigners, the *Uitlanders*, who outnumbered Transvaalers in Johannesburg by more than seven to one, were naturally denied the franchise.) The petition was brushed aside by Kruger. 'If we give them the franchise to-morrow,' he told the *Volksraad*, 'we may as well give up the Republic.'

As he fully expected, the population of Johannesburg hardly looked up from its principal occupation – making enough money to get out – to voice a protest. Flora Shaw, the *Times* colonial expert, wrote: 'Johannesburg at present has no politics. It is too busy with material problems, luxury with-out order, sensual enjoyment without art, riches without refinement, display without dignity.'

Perversely, the gold fields showed no signs of petering out; the deeper men dug, the more they found. Meanwhile, the wealth of the land of Ophir remained as legendary as ever. Seeking to redress the balance, Rhodes hired John Hays Hammond, an American mining engineer who was reputed to be the world's greatest expert on gold fields.* Together, the two men, accompanied by Jameson, made a prospecting voyage through Matabele-land in the autumn of 1894. The findings, as ever, were discouraging. In the evenings, talk around the campfire turned to the Rand, which of course Hammond knew well. He reported to Rhodes on the *Uitlanders'* grievances, and gave it as his opinion that 'Unless changes are made, there will be a rising of the people.'

Hammond knew gold, but Rhodes knew politics and people, including his fellow mine owners. He doubted seriously that anything short of out-right expropriation would stir them. Still, it was the only thing he had to work with. Though they did not yet know it, the oppressed *Uitlanders* had gained a formidable ally.

There was going to be, just as Hammond had predicted, an uprising in Johannesburg. Outraged and abused beyond endurance, their lives in danger, the *Uitlanders* were going to throw off the yoke of Boer oppression and stand for freedom. As they rose, they would send a cry for help. The cry would be heeded and that help, in the form of an armed column of troops, would swiftly appear.

But in order to be able to do so, the troops needed a place conveniently near by where they could wait for the call. Rhodesia was too far; Cape Colony was too public – the presence of several hundred armed, mounted men poised at the border might raise questions. Bechuanaland was ideal. It was virtually empty, and only 170 miles – three days' hard ride – from Johannesburg.

The Colonial Office, to whom Rhodes proposed this scenario, was not unwilling to co-operate. The new Secretary was Joseph Chamberlain –

---

* A Californian, Hammond had been brought to the Rand by Barney Barnato who, like many Kimberley tycoons, had moved over to Johannesburg. To secure his services, Barnato had paid the unheard-of fee of $1,000 a week. 'Just wait', he said, 'until Rhodes hears about this.' Rhodes did hear, and bought Hammond off by offering him $1,500.

'Pushful Joe' to his colleagues. A successful businessman, he had been mayor of Birmingham and President of the Board of Trade. As an important M.P., he had had his choice of Cabinet posts, and selected the Colonies because, as he wrote to a friend in America, he suspected that was where the action was going to be. Talks between Chamberlain and Rhodes's agents had passed beyond basic agreement and were at the haggling stage when an unexpected snag developed. Khama, paramount chief of the Bechuanas, had heard about the proposed arrangement and rushed to London. Having seen what happened to tribes such as the Mashonas and Matabeles who were entrusted to the care of Mr Rhodes he understandably preferred to remain under the Queen's direct tutelage.

The awkward problem was that Khama was not just another native chief, but the Colonial Office's very model of a native chief – the one they trotted out for inspection by other chiefs, and by other nations' Colonial Offices. He had embraced Christianity, he ruled wisely – which is to say he did what the Resident Commissioner told him to do – and he even put on a hat and tie to have his photograph taken. Finally, a compromise was reached: Khama would remain a subject of the Queen; the British South Africa Company would be allowed to purchase a strip of territory along the Transvaal border, ostensibly to build their railway. It was a likely reason, and also would help to explain the sudden appearance, this close to Johannesburg, of a large military force. In case anyone asked, they were there to protect the working crews. As a further concession to Khama, the B.S.A. Company was required to set aside some of the land it bought as a native preserve. Rhodes was furious at this. It was a 'scandal' that so much territory should be given in perpetuity to 60,000 of 'the laziest rascals in the world', he wrote to his fellow Director, the Duke of Fife.

While these details were being worked out, Jameson was in Johannesburg, organizing the spontaneous uprising. His 'cry for help' was to be a letter, which read in part:

> The position of matters in this State has been so critical, that at no distant period there will be a conflict between the Government and the Uitlander population. ... Thousands of unarmed men, women and children of our own race will be at the mercy of well-armed Boers. ... We cannot but believe that you and the men under you will not fail to come to the rescue of the people who would be so situated.

The letter was signed by five leading citizens, including Hammond, the American mining engineer, two mining magnates, and Cecil Rhodes's brother Frank, a colonel in the British Army temporarily on leave. It was, of course, for the moment left undated.

To make certain that the 'men of our race' were not quite as unarmed as the letter claimed, Rhodes had purchased 5,000 rifles and a million rounds of ammunition, which Hammond undertook to smuggle in. With these, the insurgents were to take and hold Johannesburg until Jameson and his men could gallop in. Together, they would then race to Pretoria and capture the lightly defended arsenal, which was supposed to contain another 10,000 rifles and 12 million rounds – the Boers' entire military equipment. What would happen next was not exactly clear. There would be a plebiscite, or just a spontaneous call for English rule; Kruger would be deposed, taken prisoner or allowed to choose exile. In any case, the South African Republic would cease to exist.

In keeping with Johannesburg's abiding interest, a transparent code was devised in which the plot was a 'flotation', the chief actors 'subscribers', the High Commissioner – he, too, was involved – the 'Chairman'. Telegraphs clattered *en clair*: there must be 'absolutely no departure from plan, as many subscribers have agreed to take shares on this assurance'; 'Chairman starts immediately flotation takes place.'

Meanwhile, the conspirators themselves scurried between Cape Town, Johannesburg and London. Not everything went smoothly: during one surreptitious visit to Johannesburg to confirm last-minute arrangements with Colonel Frank Rhodes, who fancied himself a ladies' man, Jameson found the house empty and a note propped up on the mantelpiece: 'Dear Jimjams, sorry I can't see you this afternoon, have an appointment to teach Mrs X. the bike.'

The plan, in addition to being criminal, was idiotic. Even without such complications as Frank Rhodes's schedule of bicycle lessons, it had little to appeal to a man who, during his whole life, had refused to trust to luck. That Rhodes consented to it, much less participated in its development, has posed a problem for his biographers. Several point out that he was in poor health at the time. One states flatly that 'He was not himself. What part he took in the thing was simply due to the influenza.'

For a conspiracy which matured over fifteen months, this explanation is not only frivolous, but insulting to the reader's intelligence. Probably health had a great deal to do with Rhodes's decision – not a touch of flu, however, but the realization that, at 42, he did not have long to live. It is even more likely that arrogance, fed as Moffat had predicted by unalloyed success, played its part.

The plot reached its critical point in mid-December 1895, with Jameson's arrival at Pitsani, the relief party's jump-off point across the border in Bechuanaland. 'Dr Jim', as he was known across South Africa, had mustered 372 men of the Mashonaland Mounted Police, all employees of the British South Africa Company. Waiting in Mafeking for the signal to join them were 122 men of the Bechuanaland Border Police. They were employees of the Queen, but in the excitement of the moment the distinction was overlooked. Jameson read them the letter of invitation, stressing the passage about women and children. There were cheers.

Everything was ready. But Johannesburg could not make up its mind.

From the conspirators' headquarters came the message: 'It is absolutely necessary to delay flotation, as public will not subscribe one penny towards it.'

But for Jameson, the time for code had come and gone. On December 28th, he telegraphed to Rhodes in plain English: 'Unless I hear definitely to the contrary, shall leave tomorrow evening.' Remembering Fort Victoria, he added: 'And it will be all right.'

Fittingly for a plan which had thus far worked so smoothly, the telegram was delayed. It had been addressed to the Company's offices which, the day being Saturday, were closed. Having received no reply by nightfall, Dr Jim led his column across the border. The Jameson Raid was on.

Although Sir John Willoughby was in military command, it was Jameson who had planned the operation. To buoy up the sagging spirits of the Johannesburg insurgents, he had talked about drawing 'a zone of lead a mile wide on each side of the column'. What he had in mind, however, was a bold, clean thrust – a repetition drawn from the limited strategic repertory he had assembled in the successful Bulawayo campaign. Secret rendezvous points had been arranged; stores of food for the men and fodder for the horses had been hidden. To preserve the element of surprise, two troopers had been sent out ahead to cut the telegraph line to Pretoria.

It subsequently turned out that, confused and apparently drunk, they had cut some cattle fencing instead. The mistake was not decisive, however, because Kruger – and everyone in South Africa who read the newspapers – already knew what was happening. A Reuters dispatch from Johannesburg published on the day before the departure had reported that 'persistent rumours are afloat of secret arming ... and war-like preparations.' As to the exact route, it was simply a matter of back-tracking along the supply points, none of which proved hard to find.

By morning, Jameson's scouts reported that Boer commandos had been sighted on both flanks of the column, and also straight ahead across their line of march. Had they done a thorough job, they would also have noted that an even larger body of Boers had fallen in to their rear, cutting off the possibility of retreat. Paul Kruger had a strategic plan of his own. 'To kill a turtle,' he noted, 'you must wait until it sticks its head out.' Jameson was plunging forward – not exactly along the planned route, but by evasive zig-zags which led him, he discovered too late, into a narrowing defile. On Tuesday morning, January 2nd, having covered 169 miles in 86 hours, the column found its way blocked: ahead was a steep, rocky slope; on both sides, the ridges loomed above them. They had been rounded up and penned in like a herd of stray cattle, so tightly wedged that they could not use the eight Maxims and three field pieces they had dragged along. As they tried to reverse direction, rifle fire poured down from all sides. At nine fifteen, someone broke out a white flag, and Willoughby sent a message inquiring

about surrender terms. They were that ' ... if you will undertake to pay
the expense which you have caused the South African Republic ... then I
shall spare the life of you and your men. Please send me a reply to this in
30 minutes. P. A. Cronje, Commandant.'

Willoughby knew Piet Cronje by reputation – he had beaten and humiliated a British force during the Transvaal's war for independence in 1881.
The reply came back in fifteen minutes, accepting the terms and asking 'how
and where we are to lay down our arms'.

Rhodes's reaction when Jameson's telegram finally reached him around
noon on Sunday was to delay. He agreed to try to communicate with
Jameson and order him back, but instead cabled to the Company's Directors
in London that 'Johannesburg is united and strong on our side.' Only when
it became clear that this was wishful thinking did he try to blunt the
inevitable blow. 'We are 24 hours in front of public opinion,' he told F. H.
Hamilton, editor of the Johannesburg *Star*, who happened to be in Cape
Town. 'You must go round all the papers and get them to prepare the mind
of the public.' The letter of invitation was pulled out of the Company's
safe, dated December 28th, and made public. In London, where *The Times*
picked it up, public opinion swung sharply behind Jameson. But in
Johannesburg, where it counted, the effect was disastrous. There had, of
course, been no uprising. On the contrary, several of the same men who had
signed the letter weeks earlier were in the midst of negotiations with Kruger
for a peaceful settlement of their grievances. When their names became
known, all of them including the American engineer Hammond and Colonel
Frank Rhodes were arrested, tried for treason and sentenced to death. This
was immediately commuted to fines of £25,000 for the leaders, and lesser
amounts for the smaller fry – a total of £212,000. Rhodes immediately paid
£61,500 of it out of his own pocket. It was a small down-payment on what
the adventure would end up costing him.

When he knew that the Raid was going to fail, Rhodes retired to his
quarters to survey the ruins. He had submitted his resignation as Prime
Minister as soon as news of the attack – an unprovoked attempt to over-
throw a foreign country – reached Cape Town. To his surprise, he discovered that it would be accepted, and for five days tried desperately to
cling to office, even going to the extent of suggesting to the High Commissioner that the last thing he wished to do at this tense moment was to
precipitate a Cabinet crisis. Philip Jourdan, his private secretary at the
time, recalls: 'I do not think he slept a wink for five nights. Tony, his
personal servant told me, "The Baas walks up and down his bedroom, which
is locked, at all times of the night." '

Finally, looking more haggard and distracted than anyone had ever
remembered seeing him, he emerged. To anxious friends he confided: 'Old
Jameson has upset my apple-cart. Twenty years we have been friends, and
now he goes and ruins me.'

That was going to be the story. On January 15th, Rhodes left hurriedly
for London to rehearse its details in person with Chamberlain. There was
no nonsense about telegrams or 'flotations' now. The problem was to save
Rhodesia and the Charter.

Jameson, too, was on his way to London, but under different circumstances. After the surrender at Doornkop, only twenty miles from his goal
of Johannesburg, he had been taken to Pretoria and thrown into jail with the
rest of the column. An angry rumble immediately arose in Cape Town,
threatening Kruger with reprisals if any harm should befall the plucky Dr
Jim. In fact, now that he had played out the part of the turtle to perfection,
Kruger had no further use for him. Jameson, along with Willoughby and
the entire surviving personnel of the column – sixteen had been killed during the skirmishing – were put aboard two British steamers in Durban and
sent back to the Queen, to deal with as she saw fit.

The charge, when the prisoners were brought to Bow Street Police
Court in London, was that they had 'unlawfully prepared and fitted out a
military expedition against the dominion of a friendly state', in violation of
the Foreign Enlistment Act of 1870. The crowd in the courtroom did not
appear impressed with the severity of the offence. An observer noted that
'Loud cheers were raised and hats waved, and for several minutes the Court
was turned into a bear garden.'

A *Times* article had set the stage by painting the Raid as a spontaneous
chivalrous act, but even more helpful had been a telegram which Kaiser
Wilhelm II sent to President Kruger immediately after Jameson's arrest.
Brushing aside the counsel of his ministers, Wilhelm had conveyed his
hearty congratulations 'on the fact that you and your people, without
appealing to the aid of friendly Powers, have succeeded by your unaided
efforts in restoring peace and preserving the independence of your country
against the armed bands which broke into [it].'

It was a toss-up whether the Kaiser or Paul Kruger was more unpopular
in Britain. Grandmama – the real Grandmama – was once again not
amused. (She wrote to her impetuous grandson: 'My Dear Wilhelm: I
must now also touch upon a subject which causes me much pain and
astonishment. It is the Telegram which is considered very unfriendly towards this country – not that you intended it as such I am sure; but I
grieve to say it has made a most unfortunate impression here.' Wilhelm
replied promptly: 'Most beloved Grandmamma, Never was the telegram
intended as a step against England or your Government. I thought the
raiders were a mixed mob of gold diggers, the scum of all nations, never
suspecting that there were real Englishmen or Officers among them. ... ')
The Poet Laureate, Alfred Austin, rose to the occasion:

> Wrong! Is it wrong? Well may be,
> But I'm going boys, all the same.

Do they think me a Burgher's Baby
To be scared by a scolding name?

There are girls in the gold-reef city
There are mothers and children, too.
And they cry: 'Hurry up! For pity!'
So what can a brave man do?

So we forded and galloped forward
As hard as our beasts could pelt
First eastward, then trending northward
Right over the rolling veldt.

And so it ran for eight stanzas, which, in fairness to Austin's literary reputation, were composed in something less than six days.*

The prisoners were released on bail, with the admonition that 'for the
sake of the peace of this country, [they] keep away from any place where
their presence may cause public excitement.' The Lord Chief Justice of
England, before whom they finally came up for trial, took a sterner view.
Brushing aside a jury which clearly wanted to find a reason for exonerating
them, he sentenced Jameson and Willoughby to fifteen months in prison.

Meanwhile, Rhodes, his business in London quickly concluded, found
himself for the first time in fifteen years a simple, private citizen. (He was
still the Member for Barkly West, but prudently stayed away from the
Cape Assembly.) For appearances, he had resigned as Managing Director
of the British South Africa Company, although he confided to friends that
'For the time being, my chief work shall be the opening of the North.'
There was scarcely anything else open to him. A great number of questions
remained unanswered about the Raid. And, most intriguing of all, was *the*
question: who had been involved?

Joseph Chamberlain, after his chats with Rhodes, tried to lay ugly
rumour to rest by stating flatly: 'I say to the best of my knowledge and
belief that everybody, that Mr Rhodes, that the Chartered Company, that
the Reform Committee of Johannesburg, and the High Commissioner, were
equally ignorant of the intention or action of Dr Jameson.'

He only failed to mention himself and the Colonial Office among those
who were innocent because the finger of suspicion had not yet pointed in
their direction. That detail remained for historians to rectify. Still, a diversion was highly desirable. To his own superior, Lord Salisbury, Chamberlain proposed that the time was ripe for 'an act of vigour ... to soothe the
wounded vanity of the nation. It does not matter which of our numerous
foes we defy, but we ought to defy someone.'

Salisbury ignored the suggestion, and before Pushful Joe could pursue

* In further mitigation, it was his first outing as Poet Laureate.

its possibilities, the diversion presented itself, spontaneously and miraculously. It was nobody's fault that it was more than he, or Rhodes, could have wished for.

Although Lobengula had been destroyed, the Matabeles had not. They had been robbed of their land. Their cattle – estimates of their numbers ranged from 150,000 to 280,000 – had been taken away from them; part had gone to satisfy Jameson's promises of 'loot' for his volunteers; some were simply appropriated by arriving settlers as prizes of war; the rest, branded with a bold 'C.C.' – for 'Chartered Company' – were left to roam over the veld, which now also belonged to the whites. Stung by charges of high-handedness, the *Cape Times* noted – as if this was all that needed to be said – that most of the settlers were 'public school and university and army men of a well-known English type, not saints all, perhaps rough customers, but gentlemen, not brutes, not cowards, not liars.'

William Milton, the Chief Secretary of Rhodesia, and hardly a negrophilist, disagreed. Shortly after his arrival, he wrote to his wife: 'Everything official here is in an absolutely rotten condition, and will continue so until we can clear out the Honourable and military elements which are rampant everywhere. Lady Dudley's son, a youngster of the la-di-da class, has just been sent up here, probably with an expression of Jameson's wish that half a country may be given to him.'

Land had been set aside for the Matabeles – 6,500 square miles. It sounded very impressive, and looked generous on the maps which the Company provided in response to complaints by such meddlers as the Aborigines' Protection Society. In reality, it was scarcely habitable. Hugh Marshall Hole, the Company's own historian, later conceded that 'the bulk of it was waterless,' and the rest infested with tsetse flies.

But the Matabeles still existed – more than 100,000 of them, leaderless, landless, deprived of the great herds which had been not only the source of their sustenance, but the basis of their social organization. Frederick Selous, who had known them well for two decades, and now lived among them in peaceful retirement, wrote: 'They found themselves treated as a conquered people who had only been permitted to return to the country from which they had been driven under certain conditions, of which one was that all the able-bodied young men in the country be required to work for a certain number of months per annum at a fixed rate of pay.'

The rate, considered more than adequate to their needs, was ten shillings a month.

Bulawayo, easier to reach from the south, and the centre of a new prospecting boom, had quickly supplanted Salisbury as the country's leading city; Rhodes himself had a house here, built over the traces of Lobengula's old kraal. On March 24th, 1896, the shocking news arrived that a white man, a settler on an outlying farm, had been killed by a band of Matabeles. Other reports followed: a family of seven had been hacked to pieces; two prospectors had been bludgeoned to death, and their bodies speared to trees. Before the carnage was over, one tenth of the white population of Rhodesia was massacred.

Panic seized Bulawayo with the arrival of the first refugees. According to one Company officer, 'the gallant inhabitants lost their heads and scrambled and fought for what rifles were left in the Government Store. It was a disgraceful scene and the less said about it the better.' Black police, recruited and trained by the Company as an economical means of law enforcement, deserted and joined the rebels. (Lord Grey, who had replaced Jameson as Administrator and who *was* a gentleman, later said, 'I cannot help liking them for that. I should have done the same thing had I stood in their place.')

Rhodes, homeward bound, had just landed in Beira when news of the uprising reached him. He immediately threw himself into a frenzy of activity. Bulawayo was surrounded on three sides by marauding, blood-thirsty Matabeles; the nearest friendly haven to the south was Mafeking, 557 miles away. A relief column must be mounted in Salisbury and sent to the rescue. Other columns must be raised and thrown against the rebels' headquarters. At the same time, the safety of Salisbury itself must be assured, because in the midst of everything else the meek Mashonas had taken it into their heads to rise as well.

The formal aspects of the military operations were, again, superficial. As the armed columns fanned out, the Matabeles, without central command, retreated into the fastness of the Matopo hills. Here, within a day's walk of Bulawayo, were more than 1,000 square miles of great, jumbled granite boulders, ravines, caves, and narrow gorges overgrown with waist-high bush. It was country better suited to hunting than to warfare, and indeed the most vivid description of the war, Robert Baden-Powell's *The Matabele Campaign, 1896*, reads more like a book about sport than about battle. The author, who later turned his woodsman's skills to more peaceful ends, writes lovingly of 'spoors', of lessons in stalking to be learned from a broken twig or a bent blade of grass. Detailed descriptions of how to track 'niggers' are interspersed with accounts of bagging antelopes, kudus, and even a solitary lion. A dedicated sportsman, Baden-Powell sometimes makes little distinction between one kind of game and another:

Today, when out scouting by myself ... I saw a charming picture. ... There was a swish of the tall yellow grass, followed by the sudden apparition of a naked Matabele warrior standing glistening among the rocks within thirty yards of me. ... He stood for almost a minute perfectly motionless, like a statue cast in bronze, ... listening for any suspicious sound. Then, with a swift and easy movement, he laid his

arms and shield noiselessly upon the rocks, and, dropping on all fours
beside a pool, he dipped his muzzle down and drank. ... When at last
his frame could hold no more, he rose with evident reluctance [and]
disappeared as silently as he had come. I had been so taken with the
spectacle that I felt no desire to shoot at him – especially as he was
carrying no gun himself.

Baden-Powell had only Matabeles to worry about – and sporting instinct
to guide him. Complicating Rhodes's job was the necessity, once more, of
fighting off Imperial interference as well. He had managed to save the
Charter thus far, but another full-scale native war so close on the heels of
the first – and particularly a war in which hundreds of white people were
being slaughtered – could well be too much for Britain to swallow. There
was also the cost of waging what promised to be a prolonged, inconclusive
struggle. The Matabeles would have to be swept out of the hills; the durable
Sir Frederick Carrington, by now a General but always ready for another
promotion, was still at hand and willing to take charge. This time, the
asking price was 2,500 infantry, a detachment of engineers for blasting
operations, two to four mountain guns, and 2,000 native carriers. Moreover
– and this was the unkindest cut of all – the loyal Rhodesians were not being
quite as unanimously loyal as they could have been. One of them had said
publicly: 'I hope the Charter will go; it would be a blessing to get rid of
financial men as rulers.' Another had even trespassed into heresy: 'The
South African Republic have asked the Imperial forces to take over the
Charter, and for once we might agree with them.'
    It is against this background of complicated jeopardies that Rhodes rose
to what virtually every one of his chroniclers has called the finest achievement of his life. For weeks, the Matopo hills had echoed with deep rumb-
lings as the hunters, weary of following faint footsteps, had started dyna-
miting the Matabeles – women and children along with the men – out of
the caves in which they had taken refuge. Rhodes ordered the violence
stopped. Unarmed and accompanied only by an interpreter and two companions – the ubiquitous Dr Sauer, and Vere Stent, a correspondent for the
Cape Times – he walked into the hills and asked to talk to the rebel chiefs.
    The discussions stretched out over several weeks, and were largely one-
sided. One Matabele chief after another recited long lists of grievances that
went back to the first coming of the Pioneers. Some, in their dotage, even
recalled the glorious days of Mzilikazi. With patience and tact he had never
been able to summon in Cape Town, Kimberley or London, Rhodes
listened. Probably much of what he heard about – the whippings, the
humiliation, the taking by whites of Matabele girls on their wedding nights
– came as news to him. He had always looked at the large vista, and left the
details to others. For himself, he had little use for Mashonas, but 'great
sympathy for that fine upstanding fighting man, the Matabele, with his Zulu

blood and clean military antecedents'. He promised – with total sincerity – that the abuses would stop. The Matabeles believed him and agreed to lay down their arms. They even gave him a new title: *Lamula N'Kunzi*, Separator of the Fighting Bulls.

After this high point – 'one of the moments in life that make it worth living', Rhodes called it – it was back to business as usual. Sauer and Stent rushed to Bulawayo to telegraph orders to buy Chartered Company shares, which had tumbled with the outbreak of violence. Rhodes received word of Jameson's conviction and sentence, and a request for his own appearance at a Parliamentary Inquiry into the Raid. The severity of Jameson's punishment came as a surprise. It was, he told an audience, 'a tribute to the unctuous rectitude of my countrymen, who have "jumped" the whole world'. A reporter who was present helpfully offered to change 'unctuous' to 'anxious', but Rhodes brushed him off: 'No, let it stand.' As for the Inquiry, he had expected it, and was fully prepared to 'face the music'.

Much was made, at the time, about the Select Committee of the House of Commons which met in February 1897, with the charge to ' ... inquire into the origin and circumstances of the Incursion into the South African Republic by an Armed Force, and into the Administration of the British South Africa Company, and to report thereon. ... '

The presence of Cecil Rhodes alone – rumpled, self-confident, the wealthiest and most controversial Englishman of the moment – was enough to pack the galleries and jam the press tables. In addition, the Prince of Wales attended all the sessions, giving rise to speculation that Royalty was somehow involved, and leaving no doubt as to where its sympathies lay: at one point, His Royal Highness walked over to Rhodes and warmly shook his hand.

But even without such patronage, Rhodes had every reason for confidence. The music had all been orchestrated in advance. Much of the suspense disappeared when Joseph Chamberlain, who some whispered should have been in the dock, sat down at the judges' bench instead. Rhodes was the first witness, and his most serious problem was not with the Committee, but with his own lawyer, Bourchier Hawksley. In the course of preparing Jameson's defence – his services had been loaned to Dr Jim by Rhodes – Hawksley had come across a sheaf of telegrams exchanged between Cape Town and London which implicated Chamberlain 'up to the neck' in the preparations for the Raid. Rhodes had absolutely refused to permit the lawyer to use them, even though they would probably have gained Jameson an acquittal. The telegrams had a far more important role to play than keeping the good Doctor out of Holloway Gaol: in exchange for their non-appearance, there was to be no nasty report, and above all no suggestion of abolishing the Charter, which had been flagrantly violated.

Still, the charade played out. Rhodes did not deny that he had encouraged the aggrieved *Uitlanders*. On the contrary, they had received his full support: 'I hold, whatever people may say, that you will have no body of Englishmen in any place for any period without those men insisting upon their civil rights. I am sure of that.'

That, however, was not the issue. Pressed about possible complicity on the part of the High Commissioner, Rhodes taunted: 'You want an answer? I think you should get it from him.' That, by pre-arrangement, was impossible. The High Commissioner – the 'Chairman' of the telegrams and Rhodes's old friend, Sir Hercules Robinson – had been prevented by poor health and advancing years from making the long journey from Cape Town to testify before the Committee. Rhodes made a great show of taking the hearings seriously. The examiners adjourned for lengthy luncheons; he took his simple meal – a sandwich and a glass of porter – at his seat. As public opinion turned decisively in his favour, he managed to score a few points of his own. One of the members of the Committee was Henry Labouchère, editor of the militantly pro-democratic journal *Truth*, and a long-time critic of Rhodes and the B.S.A. In response to a question from him about the justification of using force to achieve desirable ends, Rhodes produced a clipping in which *Truth* had called for revolution in the corrupt Turkish empire. 'You have your warm feelings in this matter,' he said quietly, 'I have proved the warmth of mine by what I have risked and lost.' To another critic, Sir William Harcourt, he was more blunt: 'Anyway, Sir William, you have not had a country named after you.'*

The Inquiry dragged out for six months. Thirty-five sessions were held and 9,862 questions asked. Few, if any, elicited truthful answers, Rhodes completed his testimony early in March and made a mute comment on the proceedings by leaving England for a leisurely tour of Italy and Egypt. After two days of perfunctory debate in the Commons, Chamberlain announced that 'the Government do not intend to abolish the Charter.' The question, half of the purpose for the Inquiry, had not even been raised. As for Rhodes himself, he received a rebuke for incaution and the misuse of his official position as Prime Minister of the Cape. But even this slap on the wrist was mitigated by a much-relieved Chamberlain who reported that nothing which the Committee had heard 'compromised Mr Rhodes's position as a man of honour'.

Not everyone shared this conclusion. J. A. Spender, editor of the *Westminster Review*, discerned a 'stubborn, but extremely obscure duel going on between Chamberlain and Rhodes.' He wrote that 'witnesses were whisked out of the box just when their evidence seemed to be becoming

---

* Having this honour fall on him was seldom far from Rhodes's mind. On one occasion he asked a companion, 'They don't change the names of countries after you die, do they?' Unfortunately, they do. Northern Rhodesia is, of course, now Zambia. And if the vast majority of the inhabitants of the remaining Rhodesia ever have the opportunity to do so the name of that country will be changed, too – probably to Zimbabwe.

important; the public sittings were suddenly suspended when the scent seemed to be getting warm; and when the curtain was raised again, an entirely different branch of the inquiry was found to have been taken up.'

Arnold Morley, a Liberal wit, simply called the whole affair 'The Lying in State in Westminster'.

Cleared of a crime which, in the face of deteriorating relations with Kruger and the Boers, seemed to many Englishmen less of a crime and more of an act of premature patriotism, Rhodes returned to Cape Town as a conquering hero. No mark of esteem or affection was spared: torchlight parades, brass bands, delegations – all of them, if one cared to notice, English-speaking – from every corner of the Colony. Rhodes's carriage was unhitched and dragged through the streets by cheering crowds. He himself strolled into the House to take his old seat, for the first time since the Raid sixteen months earlier. It was merely a token gesture, for he had no interest for the present in the parochial squabbles of Cape politics. To his colleagues he declared, 'I am only starting my career.'

It would have to be, he knew, a brief one. The 'consumption' which had originally brought him to Africa had long since been diagnosed and confirmed as cardiac disease. He had reconciled himself to it, and even found consolation in his infirmity. 'At any rate,' he said to Jameson, 'death from the heart is clean and quick. There is nothing repulsive or lingering about it; it is a clean death, isn't it?' Nevertheless, he acceded to his physicians' urging that he take a long enforced rest at Inyanga, his model 100,000-acre farm high up on the plateau south-east of Salisbury.

It was for reasons of health, therefore, that Cecil Rhodes was not among the notables who gathered in Bulawayo on November 4th, 1897, to celebrate the greatest day in the city's brief, stormy history – the day the railway was to arrive. It had been long coming. First Jameson's impetuosity, then the Matabele uprising had set back construction. Then, Rhodes had become embroiled in a squabble with the British Government over financial and political arrangements. They were still unresolved when an epidemic of rinderpest, a disease harmless to man, had swept across the country and all but wiped out draft animals. With the cost of freight rising beyond all reason – the price of carting a ton of goods from Mafeking reached £200 – the ominous alliteration of 'Rhodes, Raid, Rebellion, Rinderpest,' began to be heard. Before setting out for the Inquiry, Rhodes had given in and told Pauling to put the rails through, regardless of cost. That was all the instructions the engineer needed; he completed the last 400 miles of track in less than 400 days.

The *Bulawayo Chronicle* greeted the arrival of the railway as 'the parting of the ways for Matabeleland, the beginning of civilization in its entirety'. It reassured its readers that ... 'The country has been well advertised all over the world. Bulawayo is as much a household word as London or Vienna, and the prospects of Matabeleland have been made known wherever the English language is spoken.'

Serious citizens criticized the Festivities Committee for placing too much emphasis, in planning their ten-day programme, on races, dances and athletics competitions. More appropriate, they felt, would have been to show the visitors something of the mining activities, 'to inspire in them a desire to invest their savings in the country'.

There had been no time to erect a proper station, but Pauling did agree to throw up a large, temporary pavilion which was decorated with the Royal coat of arms and a long streamer, the work of an anonymous wit, which read OUR TWO ROADS TO PROGRESS: RAILROADS AND CECIL RHODES. Four special trains had been scheduled to bring up the dignitaries. The first two arrived on time, but the third flew off the tracks – fortunately, no one was hurt – and blocked the line. Nevertheless, 'the largest concourse of White people ever assembled in Rhodesia' was on hand to hear His Excellency Sir Alfred Milner, the new High Commissioner, read messages from the Colonial Secretary and from the Queen, who, resting at Balmoral after the observances of her own Jubilee, took time to send her subjects in Bulawayo her good wishes for their future prosperity.

Although the most distinguished guest of all was not present in person, he was far from forgotten. In the course of one of the nightly banquets at the Palace Hotel a speaker noted that 'In the centuries there has always arisen from time to time among the civilized nations some one man, some giant among his fellows, who has striven to penetrate the heart of Africa and implant the national influence.'

Let them travel the land, the speaker continued, go where they would. They would find that no nation – not the French, the German, the Portuguese, nor the Dutch – none of them had been able to advance far enough from the coast to leave any permanent mark. What they had failed to accomplish had been achieved by one man. He had penetrated 1,400 miles into the heart of Africa; he had introduced the most potent factor for civilization the world had ever known.

Then Mr C. E. Prior, Justice of the Peace and Mayor of Beaconsfield, a suburb of Kimberley, rose and called for three cheers for the Right Honourable Cecil Rhodes. The request, it is recorded, was greeted with 'almost frenzied enthusiasm'. All was forgiven.

Rhodes had replied with a telegram of his own, inviting them all to another ceremony: 'I have made up my mind to go to the Zambesi. You must come and we shall meet there.' But his 'thought', as he liked to call it, had already crossed that river, and was plunging ahead. On April 21st, 1898, he was in London to address the shareholders of the British South Africa

Company. The meeting was held in the Cannon Street Hotel, the largest public hall in the City, but many had queued for three hours to be sure of getting a seat. This was their first opportunity to express themselves on the propriety of the Raid, which had been staged with their funds and on their behalf. They did so by re-electing Rhodes by acclamation. 'I have had two years of trial,' he told them, 'but it has made a better man out of me.'

To one of the spectators, John Verschoyle of the *Fortnightly Review*, he even looked like a different man: 'As he stood up there ... he looked less impassive and more human, more like a modern man ... who had known what failure and suffering mean, than like what he generally resembles, some old Roman emperor born with the single ambition to annex and administer the habitable world ... .'

But annexation was precisely what he had come to talk about:

> I want two million pounds to extend the railway to Lake Tanganyika –
> about 800 miles. ... Look at the matter. You get the railway to Lake
> Tanganyika, ... and ... you have Kitchener coming down from
> Khartoum ... it is not imaginative; it is practical. That gives you
> Africa – the whole of it ... the conquest of Africa by the English
> nation is a practical question now.

The financial details, as is often the case, were too intricate for most share-holders to follow. Rhodes proposed to ask the Government for a loan. In exchange, he would pledge the entire existing 579 miles of Rhodesian rail-way from Vryburg to Bulawayo, plus any further extensions, subject of course to provision for safeguarding the prior rights of holders of present debentures .... This was complicated stuff; but everyone knew where Cape Town was, and Cairo. The meeting ended with a standing ovation – and a second, off-the-cuff speech by Rhodes to those shareholders who had not been able to get in.

While in London Rhodes met an acquaintance from Kimberley, a young mining engineer named Robert Williams, who was convinced that there were valuable mineral deposits in northern Rhodesia. Such deposits, or their presumed existence, had served as a powerful magnet before. With little hesitation, Rhodes therefore agreed to grant Tanganyika Concessions, Williams's company ' ... a 2,000 square miles mineral concession, together with the right to locate a township at the southern end of Lake Tanganyika, to be the Rhodesian terminus of the Cape-to-Cairo railway.'

Having thus, in his mind at least, reached the lake, Rhodes turned to the next problem – a wholly unnecessary complication which had arisen out of Grandmama's usual lack of foresight. Through a series of treaties, Great Britain had recognized the territorial claims of Germany and the Congo Free State in Africa. On the map, their borders met to form a solid wall across the waist of the continent. Above, Egypt and the Sudan were reassuringly red; below, Rhodes himself had wielded the paint brush. But to connect the two, he would have to negotiate for passage of his railway with either the Kaiser or Leopold II of the Belgians. Neither prospect was appetizing.

He tackled Leopold first. A letter went to Sir Francis Plunkett, the British ambassador in Brussels, on January 23rd, 1899:

> A few years ago I received a message from the King of the Belgians saying he would like to see me. At that time I was unable to go to Brussels. The territories of the British South Africa Company and the Congo Free State being coterminous, there are many questions arising between the two territories which it would be desirable to discuss. ...

The appointment was quickly arranged, but what actually happened at the meeting is glossed over in the Rhodes biographies. The two neighbours did not get on. Rhodes left abruptly, muttering – according to one or another source – 'Satan, I tell you that man is Satan,' or 'I have just supped with the Devil,' or 'He haggles like an old Jew.'

Reading from the other side, it appears that Leopold made impossible demands – for instance, that Rhodes help him secure a port on the Nile. Rhodes countered with a merger offer: the amalgamation of their respective countries. When it became clear that the King was not interested in a deal of this sort, Rhodes turned surly. During luncheon, the King asked his opinion about the melons, grown in his private hothouses. Rhodes replied that he had better ones in his vegetable garden at home.

Rhodes himself reported the gist of the interview in a long, private letter to his friend the Prince of Wales: 'I found that the King of the Belgians was not in want of money. ... He has floated many companies for Congo development, in which he has a great many shares; in fact, there is quite a Congo exchange in Brussels. ... '

The trip to Brussels had been secret, in keeping with Leopold's preferred way of doing business; the one to Berlin was exuberantly public. To the small but growing colonial faction, which had just begun to reap the fruits of African adventure, he and his railway represented competition; to most Germans, who had sided in sympathy with the Boers, the Raid was just another example of British bully-boy tactics.

One of the Berlin newspapers wrote: 'We welcome our English guest in the sincere wish that he may turn his back on Berlin as soon as possible. The more unfavourable the impression he takes away with him, the more it will please us.'

Rhodes, however, rose to the occasion. He had several long meetings with the Kaiser, one of which Prince Bülow records in his memoirs:

> [Rhodes] gave His Majesty the broad outlines of an all-British Cape to Cairo railway. The Kaiser's eyes shone, for every largely conceived plan in any part of the earth fired his imagination. ... Those fine and

expressive eyes lit up still more brightly when Cecil Rhodes expressed the view that, while Germany had no vital interests in Africa, she was entitled to be compensated in Asia Minor. Mesopotamia, the Tigris and Euphrates, Bagdad, the City of the Caliphs – there lay her future.

To divert the Kaiser's attention away from Africa, Rhodes would cheerfully have agreed that he was entitled to the newly built Eiffel Tower, and even the Brooklyn Bridge. Lascelles, the British ambassador to Berlin, noted in his report to Salisbury: 'He might also have talked about eating apples in the Garden of Eden, but this thought does not seem to have occurred to him.'

In the aura of mutual good feeling, the outline of an agreement was quickly drafted, and *The Times* was able to tell its readers that

> When two such clever men as the German Emperor and Mr Rhodes meet with their minds made up to do business, the business is generally done with rapidity and smoothness. ... Such progress has been made towards an agreement in regard to the Cape-to-Cairo railway that the conclusion of a satisfactory arrangement is looked upon as certain.

For once, *The Times* was premature. An agreement was signed, and Rhodes publicly claimed that '[The Kaiser] is a big man ... he met me in the fairest way and gave me every assistance.' Later and privately, he complained that the contract was 'all ifs and buts'. For the time being, however, Teuton was made Anglo-Saxon by adoption: Rhodes specified to the lawyers who were then drawing up the complicated provisions of his newest Will that a number of German students be included in his Scholarship scheme.

His triumphal return to London was dampened somewhat by news that Sir Michael Hicks-Beach, the Chancellor of the Exchequer, had rejected his proposal for Imperial guarantee of a loan. This was not unexpected, but another development aroused his fury. The Directors of the De Beers Company, so long tractable, informed him that they did not think they could go along with the Tanganyika plan, as Rhodes had taken for granted that they would. Off went a letter to the Secretary of the De Beers Consolidated Mines Ltd, 62 Lombard Street:

> Dear Sir, I think it is my duty as Chairman of your company and as a personal holder of over 20,000 shares ... to place on record my protest against the persistent manner in which the whole of my policy in connection with De Beers has been opposed by the London Board almost since it has been created, and to point out the enormous injury that the company has suffered owing to their opposition to my proposals.

The letter then went on for 16 full pages – the longest Rhodes had written since describing Kimberley for his mother in 1871 – to recall every *coup*, financial and political, which Rhodes had managed since the creation of De Beers. It closed:

... If the Board continues this persistent opposition to myself, then I propose to submit the whole situation to my shareholders, and if they don't support me, to retire from the active management of De Beers and leave it in the hands of those whose wisdom in managing the affairs of the company I hope will prove as satisfactory as I claim my record has been.

The prospect of a proxy fight with Cecil Rhodes could only have filled the prosperous and comfortable Directors with dread. They deputized one of their number to patch things up:

My dear Rhodes, I think it right as an old friend and an admirer of your genius and policy, to send you a few remarks which I think you will receive in the same spirit as they are intended. I am one of those who has never opposed judicious investments by the De Beers Company, but as a man of business of some little experience, I am perfectly convinced that it would have been injudicious on the part of the De Beers Company to have made, or to make investments if, in order to carry out new undertakings, the Company might thereby have been placed in financial difficulties. ... I only hope as a friend of yours that you will reconsider that portion of your letter which intimates that under certain circumstances you are prepared to call a Meeting of the Shareholders. Believe me, yours faithfully.

                                                    ROTHSCHILD

Here, this particular correspondence ends. As usual, Rhodes got his way. Lord Rothschild privately raised some of the money; the loyal shareholders of the B.S.A. subscribed the rest.

To the pleasure of having forced his will on the most powerful banking house in Europe, Rhodes was also able, during a heady summer, to add the satisfaction of receiving recognition from one of its greatest universities – in his mind *the* greatest. In June 1899, Oxford expressed its intention to present one of its most successful alumni with an honorary degree. It was by no means a unanimous decision, for a protest bearing many signatures including that of the Master of Balliol appeared in *The Times* 'expressing regret that the name of Mr Rhodes is on the list of those who are to receive the degree of D.C.L. honoris causa'. Nevertheless, he made the most of it, taking particular pleasure in the fact that Lord Kitchener, who was being similarly honoured for his work in Khartoum, received a less noisy welcome. (He told friends: 'I went to Oxford with the great general on whom the eyes of the world were fixed. ... I can assure you, gentlemen, they gave me a greater ovation.')

Tired but happy, Rhodes returned to Africa. Within two days of his arrival, he made a speech in the Cape Parliament. His subject was the question which had been on everybody's mind for months. And as usual, his position was unequivocal: 'Nothing will make Kruger fire a shot. The notion of the Transvaal being able to trouble Great Britain at all is too ridiculous. ... There is not the slightest chance of war.'

Words like this from people in positions of power, an unhappy world has learned, usually mean that violence is imminent. This was to be no exception.

Often enough, Britain had stumbled into war. This time, there was to be no reliance on chance to bring it about. The stakes were too high and the game, if played honestly, too likely to end in defeat. It had been expected that when South Africa was ready for unification it would take place just as it had in Canada – with the articles of confederation written in English, and signed under fluttering Union Jacks. But the Raid had changed all that. Rhodes had not only lost his patience, his temper and, some said, his reason; he had also lost the support of the Dutch in the Cape Colony. The view of many of them was expressed by a promising 26-year-old attorney, Jan Christiaan Smuts, who had returned from Cambridge in 1895 to enter public life. His first speech had been in support of Rhodes; but then: 'How shall I describe the sensations with which I received the news on New Year's Day of 1896 of that fatal and perfidious venture? It became clear to me that the British connection was harmful to South Africa's best interests. ... ' Smuts gave up his British nationality and moved to the Transvaal.

With the allegiance of the Cape Colony uncertain, with Kruger gaining strength from the inexhaustible reefs of the Rand, the spectre began to haunt a few Englishmen that the ceremony, when it came, might not play out as they had imagined. In time, this fear would infect Salisbury and cause him to write to Queen Victoria, who so *hated* to send young men to war unless there was a *good* reason, that 'It is impossible to avoid believing that the Boers really aim at setting up a South African Republic, consisting of the Transvaal, the Orange Free State, and Your Majesty's Colony.' But before this message could be sent, some groundwork had to be done.

Rhodes, the logical man, was out of it. The best he could do was to buttonhole listeners, be they Cabinet ministers or newspaper editors, and assure them that Kruger was 'the biggest unpricked bubble in the world'.* But there were two other men singularly well placed to move matters along.

---

* The Rhodes-inspired press campaign both in London and in South Africa became so intense that Edmund Garrett, editor of the *Cape Times*, later felt constrained to explain that 'The Press of South Africa, being a thing of the towns and therefore English, did not need to be "bought". As for the public, it was already more Rhodesian than Rhodes.' It was this observation, or another like it, which prompted Humbert Wolfe's little rhyme:

> You cannot hope to bribe or twist
> Thank God! The British journalist.
> But seeing what the man will do
> Unbribed, there's no occasion to.

One was Joe Chamberlain, the Colonial Secretary, ambitious and arrogant as only a self-made millionaire can be. The other was Sir Alfred Milner, his hand-picked choice as High Commissioner for South Africa to replace the doddering Sir Hercules Robinson.

Milner was a man of impressive intellectual achievement – 'the finest flower of culture reared in the University of that generation'. German-born, he had come down from Oxford to try his hand at journalism, but shifted easily into the game of power, as private secretary to the Chancellor of the Exchequer, then financial adviser to Lord Cromer, the British pro-consul of Egypt, and finally as chairman of the Board of Inland Revenue. He believed in Imperialism as 'a great movement of the human spirit', with 'all the depth and comprehensiveness of a religious faith'. Concepts such as this had made his book, *England in Egypt*, an enormous success, and marked its author – in the eyes of readers such as Chamberlain – as a useful man. But it was neither tax rates nor lost Pharaonic glory which were on Milner's mind during the voyage that took him to his new duties in May 1897. His constant deck-chair companion was Machiavelli's *The Prince*.

On arrival, he toured the Colony and announced that 'It is the British race which built the Empire, and it is the undivided British race which can alone uphold it.' John Merriman, whose father had been Bishop of Grahamstown, and who himself had entered Cape politics before Rhodes had ever set foot in Africa, was moved to observe that the new High Commissioner meant to 'convert South Africa into another Ireland'.

Milner openly cast suspicion on Kruger's designs, and left no doubt of his own position regarding the late unpleasantness: he allowed the British South Africa Company to hold a ball in Cape Town, celebrating the second anniversary of the Jameson Raid. In February, his inspection completed, he wrote to Chamberlain: 'There is no way out of the political troubles in South Africa except reform in the Transvaal, or war.'

The likelihood of reform, whatever Milner meant by it, was all but eliminated because Paul Kruger, running under the slogan 'Beware of Rhodes, and keep your powder dry' won re-election to a five-year term as President of the Transvaal. This left only one course open, and Milner cabled Chamberlain, unnecessarily, that he was now 'inclined to work up a crisis'. The Colonial Secretary warned his subordinate that, for the present, 'grievances are not considered as sufficient to work up a *casus belli*.'

Milner did his best. He travelled to Graaff-Reinet, in the heart of the Dutch country, and made a provocative speech demanding that colonists choose sides. The cause of the persecuted *Uitlanders*, stranded in Johannesburg amid their piles of gold, their stock exchanges, saloons and fancy bordellos, was dusted off and trotted out again. A new petition, demanding the right to vote, was circulated; complaints were brought against the state's corruption and its support of the monopolies. This was old stuff, but Milner, with the advantages of a classical education, was able to bring to it an added fillip. He sent Chamberlain a long dispatch, transmitted secretly but intended for publication at any time the Secretary felt appropriate, reporting that 'The spectacle of thousands of British subjects kept permanently in the position of helots, constantly chafing with undoubted grievances, and calling vainly to Her Majesty's Government for redress, does steadily undermine the influence and reputation of Great Britain ... within its own dominions.'

He urged a long-suffering England to 'strike at the root of all these injustices'. The press co-operated with a campaign, in word and drawing, at once vilifying Kruger and ridiculing the Boers as oafish clods. Rudyard Kipling contributed a description of the Transvaal's President: 'Cruel in the shadow, crafty in the sun ... sloven, sullen, savage, secret, uncontrolled.'

Almost alone in dissent was W. T. Stead. Hardly a pacifist or Little Englander, he had been among Rhodes's earliest supporters during the campaign for the Charter, and was in fact one of the Trustees in his current Will. But this was too much. Stead's *Review of Reviews* warned: 'Of all the disreputable, contemptible and discreditable proceedings by which a nation has been jockeyed into war ... this is just about the worst.'

For his courage, he received a note from a colleague in Cape Town: 'You old women of Fleet Street, can't you even take a thousand-to-one chance of war?'

There were some important men who thought Pushful Joe was going too far. Arthur Balfour, then Leader of the House of Commons, counselled against treating 'the South African sore ... by the free application of irritants'. But Salisbury, a decent man nearing the end of a long, brilliant career, had lost control of his own government. On August 30th, 1899, he wrote in unfeigned sadness to Lord Lansdowne, the Minister of War and one of his few friends in the Cabinet: ' ... I see the necessity for considerable military effort – and all for people whom we despise, and for territory which will bring no profit and no power to England.'

But Chamberlain wanted more. On September 2nd, with a possible eye to historians, he wrote to Milner: 'The technical *casus belli* is a very weak one.'

It was strong enough for the *Uitlanders*, on whose behalf the Mother Country was girding. They began deserting Johannesburg, using trains, carts, wagons – every means of transport available. Within weeks, English-speaking newspapers suspended publication, for want of readers. More ominous, for nothing else could so surely presage Armageddon, the mines were shut down.

On September 8th, orders were given to move 10,000 troops from India to Natal. Military credits of £750,000 were voted. On October 2nd, Parliament sanctioned mobilization. On October 8th, the first fresh troops began landing in Durban. The following day, the Transvaal, which had ordered its own mobilization – thousands of farmers, many of them accompanied by their wives, and with bandoliers slung over their work clothes, converged on horseback toward Pretoria – handed the British a note asking that the troops be removed and that other units, then on the high seas, not be landed. According to his biographer, Chamberlain, wakened at six fifteen a.m. to receive the news, greeted it as a piece of 'almost unbelievable good fortune'. His own ultimatum had already been approved by the Cabinet but, history would note, the Boers had moved first. Her Majesty's Government, now ready to fight, branded Kruger's request as a 'peremptory demand, impossible to discuss', and at five thirty p.m. on October 11th, war began.

Not for the first or last time, it started badly for England. With the expiration of the ultimatum, Boer commandos had begun coming down through the mountain passes into Natal. Lieutenant-General Sir George White, commanding the freshly arrived troops, won some preliminary skirmishes, but then managed to get himself outflanked, lose most of his artillery and leave 1,000 men to be taken prisoner before he could extricate himself. One of the Boer leaders, a former butcher and potato farmer named Christian de Wet, whose name would appear frequently in London papers in the months to come, urged that the fleeing British be pursued, but his commander, Piet Joubert, refused. The Boers used scripture for strategy as well as statecraft, and Joubert's order of the day was: 'When God holds out a finger, don't take the whole hand.'

General White did his best to compensate for this restraint by taking his entire army into the village of Ladysmith, a rail junction so cunningly wedged between hills that, the British discovered later, it was the only place for miles around where 14,000 men could effectively be bottled up and encircled by an enemy force half their size.

The defeat of British troops by bearded farmers shocked England. 'Mournful Monday,' the papers called it. General White sportingly acknowledged his blunder – 'I framed the plan ... and am alone responsible. No blame whatever attaches to the troops. ... ' – and both the Queen and the press were quick to forgive him. The farmers had been lucky, that was all.

A more serious disaster, although it was not immediately recognized as such, was the arrival on the following day of the new supreme British commander, General Sir Redvers Buller, V.C. Over the centuries, British soldiers had been led into battle – pushed was often a more accurate verb – by an astounding collection of nincompoops. But for sheer idiocy, for the uncanny ability to size up a situation and pick out the single course of action which led unerringly to débâcle, few could match Redvers Henry Buller.

He was, of course, a career officer – a 'social' general. His father had been an M.P., his mother the niece of the Duke of Norfolk; he himself could trace his lineage directly back to Edward I. As a boy, he had been so awkward and accident-prone that his family gave him the nickname of Murad the Unlucky, and decided that the safest place for him was the Army. There, he spent 41 years, serving in India, China, Canada and Africa, where he earned his Victoria Cross by saving the lives of four comrades during one of the many reversals of the Zulu Wars. But he had never once commanded a large body of troops in battle, and furthermore the last eleven years of his career had been spent in the War Office, as Quartermaster-General and Adjutant-General. In these commands, his most intricate manœuvring had been to gain political favour with the object of succeeding Lord Wolseley upon his imminent retirement.

Field-Marshal Sir Garnet Wolseley was Commander-in-Chief of the Army, a title held for the previous four decades by the Duke of Cambridge, the fatuous, lisping cousin of the Queen, known in senior military circles as 'the Great German Sausage'. For years Wolseley had chafed under the Duke, whose guiding dictum was that change must only be made at the right time – which was to say when it no longer could possibly be avoided. (Once, Victoria had complained about Wolseley to Disraeli, her favourite Minister. He replied, 'It is quite true that he is an egoist and a braggart. So was Nelson.')

Now, with a real war on his hands at last, Wolseley had a problem selecting a suitable field commander. Britain was, regarding generals, between vintages. He could not very well appoint himself; he was too senior in rank and too old. This also ruled out Roberts – Field-Marshal Lord Roberts, former Commander-in-Chief of the Indian Army – and General Sir Evelyn Wood. The younger men, including the fast-moving Kitchener, were too junior for the honour. That left Buller. Militating against him was the verdict of Gladstone, that fine judge of military talent, who had said that 'Joshua couldn't hold a candle to Redvers Buller as a leader of men.' It was also known at the War Office that desk work had made him soft, and that he was too attached to good food and drink – especially champagne.

On the *Dunnottar Castle* which left Southampton on October 14th, Buller fraternized with the war correspondents aboard – L. S. Amery of *The Times* and Winston Churchill of the *Morning Post* – and tried to provide them with colourful copy. A few days before they were to arrive in Cape Town, they crossed path with the *Australasian*, homeward bound. She had chalked up a message on a long blackboard: THREE BATTLES. BOERS DEFEATED. SYMONS KILLED. Symons was Major-General Sir William Pen Symons. If officers of that rank were being lost, there must have been heavy fighting. Buller wondered aloud whether, by the time they landed, there would be enough Boers left to bother with.

If Wolseley had had any qualms about sending Redvers Buller to war, he could comfort himself with the knowledge that the plan which he had laid out for him was the soul of simplicity – even Murad the Unlucky could have handled it. All Buller was expected to do was to wait in Cape Town until his 48,800 troops – the largest army Britain had ever sent overseas –

arrived. Then he was to march them straight up to Pretoria, pausing en route only to capture Bloemfontein, the capital of the Orange Free State which had allied itself with the Transvaal.

The Boers even co-operated with this strategy. Instead of pouring all their forces into Natal, where they could make themselves thorou ;hly disagreeable, threaten the fat eastern part of Cape Colony, and probably win a negotiated truce, they chose instead to besiege Mafeking and Kimberley, both of which lay far to the west and had not the slightest strategic importance. (Kimberley at least offered an enticing prize of war – Cecil Rhodes – but Mafeking was totally irrelevant, even though its ultimate relief caused one of the noisiest celebrations in the history of Great Britain.)

While waiting for his army to arrive, Buller conceived the genial notion of raising the three sieges – including Ladysmith – not serially, but simultaneously. Such a thing had never been done before in the long history of British arms, and therefore ought, he reasoned, to add something to his name.

It was not done this time, either. Buller split his army into three parts and suffered three staggering defeats. What did add to his name is that he managed to do it all within a single week.

It opened at Stormberg, on the northern border of the Colony. The Boers had cut the railway line, and General Gatacre, who had distinguished himself in the Sudan campaign, decided to take it back. In his rush, he did not give his 3,000 troops enough rest after a forced advance. They took their positions – the wrong ones, it turned out – and fell asleep only to be wakened by their own artillery shells falling in their midst. In the confusion of retreat, 600 men were left behind to be taken prisoner.

That was on Sunday, December 10th. On Monday, it was the turn of General Lord Methuen, another 'social' general who considered it sporting to announce his strategy in advance to the newspapers. His assignment was the relief of Kimberley, a goal from which he was separated only by a single low line of hills – Magersfontein. He proposed to take them by direct assault. A suggestion from a staff officer that the position could be flanked was rejected with scorn: 'My dear fellow, I intend to put the fear of God in these people.' For an entire day, British artillery shells poured down on the tops of the hills, raising a curtain of smoke, dust and fragments of rock which obscured the sun. At six thirty p.m., Methuen ordered the bombardment stopped, convinced that nothing living remained on the hills.

Undoubtedly he was right. But the Boers had not been on top of the hills; they had dug themselves into trenches along their base – a tactic improvised by another of their commanders, de la Rey, whose name was also to become better known in Britain. The Highland Brigade, the proudest unit in the British Army, had been given the honour of leading the assault. They marched off in pitch darkness and advanced in perfect order. A belt of yard-high mimosa scrub which caught and tore at their kilts slowed them down a little, so they were still some 150 yards away from the hill – point-blank range for Boer marksmen – when the first light rose.

That was as far as they reached, and where they left the body of their commander, General 'Andy' Wauchope, killed by the first volley. The Highland Brigade – Black Watch, Seaforths, Argyll and Sutherland, Highland Light Infantry – had 746 casualties that day, almost one quarter of its total strength, not counting hundreds of men who lay under the withering heat all day, and suffered sun-blisters on the backs of their knees.

That still left General Buller to be heard from – which happened on Friday, December 15th. Although he was in command of the entire theatre of operations, he had decided to take a personal hand in the relief of Lady-smith, the most widely publicized of the sieges.

More subtle than Methuen, he elected to try a wide turning movement to take the little village of Colenso on the Tugela River, behind which some 5,000 Boers under General Louis Botha had dug themselves in. A great believer in adequate preparation, Buller took five days to dispose his forces, which included 21,000 troops and artillery reinforced with a battery of naval guns dismounted from warships at Durban and hauled into position. With so much to worry about, it is perfectly understandable that Buller should change his mind about the tricky turning movement, and decide instead on a frontal attack. Less understandable is his failure to notify Major-General Barton, in charge of the artillery brigade, of his change in plan.

Even now, it is impossible to provide a coherent account of the battle of Colenso. The most professional description – in the full report on the South African War prepared by the Historical Section of the German General Staff – struggles manfully with the problem, then simply states, 'The causes of the English want of success at Colenso are first of all to be sought in the lack of sufficient force of character in the General in command.'

Shortly after the start Buller remembered that his artillery was not only pulverizing an area of the battlefield far from the action, but had itself been left totally unprotected. In his anxiety to retrieve the threatened guns, he issued a string of self-contradictory orders. Regiments which had clawed their way to high ground were ordered down again; others which found themselves pinned down were forgotten. When it was over – Buller did remember how to call for a general withdrawal – the British had lost 1,000 men to the Boers' 6 killed and 21 wounded. The guns fell intact into the enemy's hands, along with nine wagons full of ammunition.*

Black Week stunned England and Scotland – Princes Street was in mourning for months – in a manner that would not be matched by the

---

* Buller completed his day by heliographing to General White, still besieged in Lady-smith: 'Burn your cipher and code books, fire away as much ammunition as you can, and make best terms you can.' He even added, 'How many days can you give me to take up defensive positions?' During the understandable brouhaha which followed the publication of this message after the war, White said he ignored it because he believed it had been sent, as a ruse or taunt, by the Boers.

immeasurably greater losses of Passchendaele or by the far more imminent danger of Dunkirk. It was not even grief so much as plain shock. These were the finest regiments in the world – the Highlanders, the Coldstreams, the Grenadiers, the Connaught Rangers, the Royal Fusiliers. Every school-boy in Britain believed they were invincible, and so had every chancellery in Europe. Yet they had been cut to ribbons, all in one week, and all by a band of outlaw civilians – they could hardly be called an army because they had neither uniforms nor officers – who ducked from behind rocks and trees, and whose sum knowledge of military procedure was how to aim and fire their clip-loaded Mauser rifles.

After the impact of Black Week, Field-Marshal Roberts was rushed to Africa. He arrived on January 10th, 1900, bringing Kitchener along as his Chief of Staff, and immediately brought a touch of sanity to the proceedings. First he put his soldiers on horseback – all Europe and most of the Americas were combed to provide the 550,000 mounts which the British army eventually used up. Then he grouped them together and marched on Pretoria, as Buller had been instructed to do.*

The entire process took less than five months. There were no major engagements. Bloemfontein greeted the victors as casually as if they were militia, back from summer training. Pretoria, which Roberts entered on June 5th, was empty. Kruger had fled, first to Mozambique and eventually to Holland; Botha, de Wet, de la Rey, Smuts and the other commanders simply pulled back into the hills to see what would happen.

At first nothing did. The war was over, and Roberts returned to London where an enormously relieved nation presented him with an Earldom, the Garter, and a grant of £100,000. The Queen received him, but it was the last time she would greet a general who had conquered in her name. On January 21st, 1901, after a brief illness and a reign which had begun in 1837, she died peacefully.

Kitchener had been left behind to mop up. It was not a job to his liking – he had hoped to receive Roberts's old command in India – but he set about doing it with his customary thoroughness and attention to detail. Some Boers had refused to surrender, and continued to snipe at British positions. Clearly, they were receiving aid and comfort from the populace. It was Kitchener's attempt to interdict this aid which inaugurated the unsightly aspects of the Boer War, and earned it distinction as the first truly modern war. Within the next two years, much of the Transvaal and Orange Free State had been burned, looted, and criss-crossed with a web of barbed wire commanded by 8,000 fortified blockhouses. Most of the spaces between the lines of barbed wire were empty, except for British patrols. But into 46

---

* Despite his performance, Buller was not relieved of his command, but allowed to continue independent operations in Natal. The War Office considered that the recall of a senior commander was bad for morale, and an admission of failure on its own part. Buller obliged them with one more defeat, the worst of the entire war, at Spion Kop.

of them a total of some 110,000 human beings were penned. The action was described as humanitarian in motive: with so many farmhouses destroyed, there was danger that women and children might suffer from cold or hunger on the open veld. How serious such suffering would have been is a matter of conjecture. In the comfort and safety of the camps, a little more than 20,000 of them died, including 16,000 children.

In time, all madness must stop. Peace at last was signed, at Vereeniging on May 31st, 1902. Smuts, Botha, de Wet, who had humiliated the British by evading capture while raiding deep into Cape Colony, were there. So too was Milner and, in spirit, Chamberlain and Rhodes. They had gained their triumph: the Republics no longer existed. The price for their extinction had been higher than expected – far higher than the £750,000 which had originally been voted. By the end of May 1902, the South African War had cost Great Britain £223,000,000 – enough to build a railway to Cairo and back several times.

For the first time since the Great Trek, South Africa had been united – and under the Union Jack. It remained under it for 59 years – until May 31st, 1961 (the day and month were hardly a coincidence) when, still united, it again became a republic and severed its ties with the Commonwealth.

Rhodes had passed a moderately comfortable, enervating, but profitable war. Early in October 1899, when the only remaining question regarding hostilities was where they would begin, he had excused himself during a dinner party at Groote Schuur, his house in Cape Town, and, according to one of his guests, 'entrained at a wayside station without being observed'. His destination was Kimberley, and the need for secrecy was occasioned not so much by the presence of possible Boer spies as by the concern of his friends there. One of them had written to him on October 1st: 'I hear you are thinking of coming to Kimberley. ... Is it wise to run any unnecessary risk? ... Everything that we can will be done to protect the Company's property.'

The letter had no effect, because five days later the Mayor of Kimberley himself telegraphed: 'Under all circumstances would ask you kindly to postpone coming. Citizens generally feel your presence here would serve to entice rush.'

Rhodes arrived in Kimberley on the day before the Boers surrounded it. Through the next four months, he carried on business as usual, with the added self-imposed burden of directing a military campaign. The Army had provided Kimberley with a commander – Lieutenant-Colonel R. G. Kekewich – and with troops – four reinforced companies of the Loyal North Lancashires – but in Rhodes's view they were, respectively, incompetent and insufficient. He undertook to supervise the defence of the town himself, and urge greater vigour on the part of its deliverers. Among his dozens of messages, alternately pleading desperation and threatening reprisal, was one addressed to Lord Roberts: 'Your troops have been more than two months within a distance of little over 20 miles from Kimberley.' Then, cruelly, because he knew what had happened to the Highland Brigade, he added, 'If the hills are too strong for them, there is an easy approach over a level flat.'

In fact, Kimberley was never in serious danger. There were plenty of able-bodied men in the town, and a surfeit of arms and ammunition – 750,000 rounds, six machine guns and 442 rifles, all left over from the supplies accumulated in anticipation of the Raid. Nevertheless, Rhodes insisted that one of his mining engineers – an American named George Labram – put together a home-made cannon. 'Long Cecil,' as it was naturally christened, was built in 24 days and could propel a 28-pound shell through its 4·1-inch bore. There is no record of it inflicting any damage on the Boers.

Food was adequate for the whites – most of the natives, once the siege began, had been sent out through the Boer lines to shift for themselves. Some of the children suffered, but there was enough of one thing or another to eat so that there was no need to hunt down the cats and dogs. And, when the siege was finally raised on February 15, 1900 – in a spirited cavalry dash led by Lieutenant-General John French* – the De Beers larders and cellars yielded enough champagne and delicacies to permit Rhodes to welcome his guests in style. In the ensuing rounds of mutual congratulations, Rhodes happily said that 'We have done our best to preserve that which is the best commercial asset in the world, the protection of Her Majesty's flag.'

While Colonel Kekewich, a mere soldier, had been obliged to use the heliograph to communicate with the outside world, Rhodes had maintained a personal courier service of native runners during the siege. In addition to his military correspondence, they carried orders to buy and sell blocks of stock, and other business details. Among the incoming mail had been a letter, dated January 12th, from Robert Williams:

> Dear Mr Rhodes, It is with much pleasure that I have to inform you that my expedition has discovered a new gold field in Northern Rhodesia, ... In this particular old working, the natives seem to have worked for copper. ... I believe you will now have to reconsider the direction in which your railway will be extended.

What Williams had stumbled across were the Kansanshi copper mines. Neither he nor Rhodes could have had any idea of how enormous they would turn out to be, but Rhodes was in any case ready to consider a new route. By now, his friend Charles Metcalfe had had a chance to survey the country from Bulawayo to the lake, and had found it to present enormous

* Later Field-Marshal French, Earl of Ypres and commander-in-chief of the British Expeditionary Force in France in 1914.

natural difficulties. Williams's letter, plus the additional discovery of coal deposits near Wankie, far to the west, suggested a more desirable alternative. As Metcalfe later was to write, 'No part of the railway was made for sentimental reasons.'

Because this particular corner of Rhodesia was little known in England, and therefore not likely to stimulate the interest of investors, Rhodes approached an old gold-mining colleague, Abe Bailey, with a proposal to 'dramatize the territory'. Bailey thought the idea splendid, agreed to undertake an extended trip, and even suggested bringing along 'someone who would be capable of writing up the country, and giving in detail the beneficence to be derived by opening [it] up.' He even had a specific candidate in mind, as this letter shows:

> My dear Mr Rhodes, Abe Bailey has spoken to me about a plan to send a small private expedition from Capetown ... and has suggested my coming with him. Of course I must think first of all of getting into the House of Commons, but I dare say the general election will be over before the expedition would start and were that the case I dare say I could get away.
>
> I should personally like very much to take part in such an interesting venture, and as I have to make my own living it would be a great advantage to me to do so, for what with a series of letters to a London newspaper and a good sized book to be published later, I should be able to earn a good deal of money. Now it seems to me that this writing would help to attract public attention to the Cape to Cairo route and stimulate the interest taken in your railway scheme: so that perhaps you will think that our roads lie for some small distance in the same direction. ... I am sorry not to have seen you in South Africa, but the Boers interfered with most people's arrangements.

The writer of the letter – Winston Churchill – did stand for election. One reason he may have been in a hurry is that the General Election of 1900 – the Khaki election – offered unusually good prospects. The Government's slogan was 'Every vote for the Liberals is a vote for the Boers,' and it proved persuasive enough to win election for Churchill as Member for Oldham, a seat he had tried for and lost a year earlier. Parliamentary duties evidently pushed the job offer from his mind, for the Cape-to-Cairo railway – to its profound detriment – never had his services as a paid publicist.

Rhodes himself, however, in one of the very rare published pieces to bear his name, explained what part the railway was intended to play in his plans. Shortly after the raising of the siege, he had received a letter from a young man named Ewart Grogan asking Rhodes to provide an introduction for a book describing a journey he had just completed, largely on foot, from Beira to Cairo. The trip, which Grogan made in 1899 with a fellow student named A. H. Sharp, had been purely a lark – an extended holiday hunting expedition with no political, scientific or economic motives. But it caught Rhodes's fancy, and he acceded to the request:

My dear Grogan:

You ask me to write a short introduction for your book, but I am sorry to say that literary composition is not one of my gifts, my correspondence and replies being conducted by telegrams.

I must say I envy you. ... The amusement of the whole thing is that a youth from Cambridge, during his vacation, should have succeeded in doing that which the ponderous explorers of the world have failed to accomplish. There is a distinct humour in the whole thing. It makes me the more certain that we shall complete the tele-graph and railway, for surely I am not going to be beaten by the legs of a Cambridge undergraduate.

... Everyone supposes that the railway is being built with the only object that a human being may be able to get in at Cairo and get out at Cape Town.

This is, of course, ridiculous. The object is to cut Africa through the centre, and the railway will pick up trade all along the route. The junctions to the east and west coasts, which will occur in the future, will be outlets for the traffic obtained along the route of the line as it passes through the centre of Africa. ... We propose now to go on and cross the Zambesi just below Victoria Falls. I should like to have the spray of the water over the carriages.

Yours, c. j. rhodes

The Zambesi was crossed, and for this one occasion Metcalfe's rule was violated. As H. F. Varian, one of the engineers who built the bridge, wrote: 'The choice of its site was more for sentiment than for practical reasons. ... A simpler crossing could have been achieved 6 miles further up, where the longest span need only have been 150 feet.'

But the place chosen was a deep gorge cut through red-brown rock by the thundering water immediately after it spilled over the escarpment of the Falls – a curtain of white foam measuring a full mile across and whipping, as commanded, into the faces of onlookers. The engineering was relatively simple; Sir Ralph Freeman, who did the preliminary calculations, had far less trouble than with the Sydney Harbour bridge, which was also his creation. It was the concept that was bold, to the point of arrogance: to build a modern steel bridge supported by a single slender span here, in the middle of deserted jungle. No human soul lived within sixty miles of the Falls; out of superstition, the natives shunned their everlasting roar and rising columns of mist. Only fifty years earlier, David Livingstone had been the first European to describe them, 'creeping with awe to the verge', and even now a simple visit to behold their grandeur required a carefully planned expedition. Even counting missionaries and curious officials, it is doubtful that more than a hundred or so white men had ever seen them. And this was not just a bridge, but the highest bridge of its kind in the world. The gorge measured 650 feet across; at low-water mark the tracery of steel which was made to reach out from its two sides hung 400 feet above the river.

Rhodes, ill and resting at Salsomaggiore in the Apennines, had written to Williams on October 18th, 1901, that he expected the railway to be at the Falls within two years. He was out by six months. The tracks reached the south bank of the river on April 24th, 1904, and the bridge was finished and dedicated on September 12th, 1905. Again, notables from all over Africa and distinguished visitors from London gathered, and again Rhodes was not there. He had died on March 26th, 1902.

It had not been the clean death he had hoped for. Early in the year, when he returned from his annual visit to England, his appearance had shocked even those who had seen him a few months earlier. His face was almost unrecognizably bloated, his skin was not pale but mottled an almost solid purple. The massive aneurysm which pressed on his heart and lungs made breathing painful and at times almost impossible. He could not lie down, he could not move comfortably, he could hardly talk. The air, during this south African summer, was oppressively hot and still, so they took him away from Groote Schuur, down to the cottage he maintained at Muizenberg, on the water's edge. Great holes were torn in the walls to catch the breeze, and ice packed under the tin roof of the simple house to cool the air. Still he could not breathe. A special cabin was built aboard the boat deck of the *Saxon* to take him back to England, but he was too weak to be moved, and died on the day the ship was to sail. He was 49 years old.

Rhodes had left explicit instructions for his funeral. 'I desire', he wrote in his final Will, ' ... to be buried in the Matopos on the hill which I used to visit and which I called the "View of the World," in a square to be cut in the rock on top of the Hill, covered with a plain brass plate with these words thereon: "Here lie the remains of Cecil John Rhodes". ... '

He had discovered the hill, a barren rise topped by an uneven crown of boulders, during the Matabele rebellion – so barren and wind-swept was it that when the Bishop of Mashonaland, intoning the final prayer, reached the words 'Earth to earth', the mourners were obliged to pick up chips of granite and drop them into the open grave. From the ground, it was almost undistinguishable from others around it. One day, trying to show it to Metcalfe, Rhodes had difficulty finding it. But from the top of this particular hill, through a cleft in the distant mountains, there was an unobstructed line of sight all the way to the northern horizon.

The funeral was gaudy, heroic, far too much and yet too little – entirely appropriate. Rhodes's body lay in state at Groote Schuur, then in Parliament, then in St George's Cathedral in Cape Town. It was taken by special train through the Drakenstein valley where he owned another model farm, one million acres of orchards; to Beaufort West, where General French and his staff came aboard to pay respects; to Kimberley, where Njuba, a son of Lobengula now employed by the De Beers Company, was noted among the 15,000 who filed past the funeral car. In Bulawayo, the body lay in the Drill Hall where detachments of the Pioneers of 1890, the Column of 1893, the B.S.A. Police, the Rhodesian Volunteers, the Chamber of Mines, came to deposit wreaths. For the final leg of the journey, the coffin was placed on a gun carriage and drawn by straining mules over a rough track which had been cut only a few days earlier. Behind it walked Jameson, Metcalfe, Michell, Smart, Milton, Rhodes's brothers Frank and Arthur, and two former secretaries, Jourdan and Gordon Le Sueur. An elegy by Rudyard Kipling was read over the grave.

In the two weeks the ceremonies lasted, over the 1,500 miles across which they trailed, there had been few Dutch names or faces. Rhodes had often said that he could never achieve anything lasting in South Africa without the Dutch. Some of them would not come to his funeral; some who may have wanted to could not. The war which he had predicted would never happen was still going on.

Even before the great bridge was completed, construction of the railway had started north of the Zambesi. The objective was Broken Hill, 350 miles away, where more minerals had been found – zinc and lead, this time. The going was easy, and Pauling felt like doing a bit of showing off. One day, Charles Metcalfe arrived at the camp with a colleague, a visiting French engineer. How much track, he asked conversationally, could they lay in a day? Half a mile? One mile? Pauling said he wasn't sure, but he'd see what his men could do. Properly alerted, they put down $5\frac{3}{4}$ miles in one ten-hour working shift. Later, with the terminal in sight, they put on their own show for the boss: yanking the rails and sleepers from the open wagons of a slowly-moving train, they raced forward and bolted them together so fast that the locomotive was able to travel over the newly-made track without stopping or slowing down. A Pathé cinematographer, probably the first to venture into northern Rhodesia, recorded the event for posterity.

That was on January 11th, 1906, and here, just past the siding which fed the mines, work stopped. H. F. Varian, one of Pauling's chief field engineers, wrote: 'The Cape-to-Cairo Railway came to an end in the middle of a burnt-out *vlei*, without even a buffer-stop at the rail terminus. Beside it stood a solitary telegraph pole, and in this atmosphere of desolation, it languished. ... '

North of the railhead, 116 miles away, lay the frontier of the Congo Free State. Neither colony nor independent nation, it was a creation of convenience, the personal property of Leopold II, King of the Belgians.

The story of the Congo is a familiar tale, not very savoury even by

1. Cape Town railway terminus, 1878

2. Market Square, Kimberley, 1880

3. Kimberley Mine, showing aerial winding gear

4. Kimberley Mine shaft

5. Sorting for diamonds, Kimberley

6. Diamond sorters, De Beers Mine, Kimberley

7. (*left*) Lord Cromer

8. (*centre*) Paul Kruger

9. (*centre*) Barney Barnato

10. (*right*) Lobengula

11. (*left*) Dr Leander Starr Jameson

12. (*centre*) Henry Morton Stanley

13. Rhodes as a boy

14. Rhodes at Oxford

15. Rhodes with his family and household staff, 1877

16. Rhodes in the bush

17. Rhodes (*at left, front row, fourth from camera*) in the South African Parliament

18. Rhodes with the army

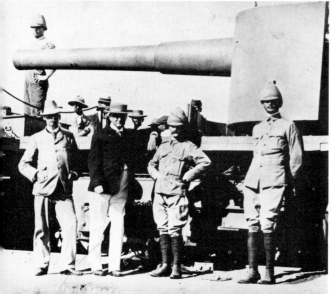

19. Rhodes on a picnic near Kimberley

20. Rhodes with Kitchener

21. Rhodes in retirement

22. Rebels in Rhodesia, 1896

23. The first train into Rhodesia, 1897

24. British troops at Durban on their way to the front, 1900

25. Canadian troops in action in the Boer War

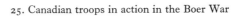

26. (*above*) A Boer 'Long Tom' at Mafeking
27. (*below*) Artillery crossing the Zand River Drift

28. Colenso station

29. (*above*) British artillery position, Battle of Colenso
30. (*below*) British troops digging in at Elandslaagte

31. A train blown up by Boers, 1900

32. The Victoria Falls Bridge under construction, 1905

33. The first train crossing the Zambesi on the Victoria Falls Bridge, 1905

34. Stanley's first house in the Congo, showing railway-building equipment

35. Track-laying in the Upper Congo

36. The first train into Elizabethville

37. Railway construction in the Sudan desert

38. Sudan railway scene, 1898

39. The defences of Alexandria after the bombardment, 1882

40. Scottish soldiers in Egypt, c. 1890

accepted standards of colonization. Leopold, ambitious out of all proportion to his own insignificant country, had played his powerful European neighbours off against each other and confounded them into granting him title to nearly one million square miles in the heart of Africa. He had hired Henry Morton Stanley to explore and secure this enormous estate, and then, under the guise of opening it to progress and civilization, had proceeded to bleed it dry and methodically work to death five or possibly ten million of its unfortunate inhabitants.

This was the man Rhodes had described as 'Satan'. His own humanitarian instincts may in this instance have been coloured by the recollection of how Leopold had snatched Katanga away from him, and further intensified by the disappointment of not getting what he wanted from the monarch. For his part, Leopold, a ferocious bargainer, had for once overplayed his hand. Katanga proved to be rich beyond anyone's expectations. Robert Williams, one of the first men to explore it methodically, had found more than 100 separate copper deposits in less than two years. And there was more. As Williams wrote, 'All one needed to prospect copper in the district was a good pair of field glasses. In any hill that was bare of brush or scrub, one was sure to find [it].'

In addition to copper, Williams and his geologists also found tin, silver, gold, some diamonds, and even an ore which yielded infinitesimal but still priceless quantities of a new element called radium.

All this, however, was paper wealth, worthless unless it could be brought out to the sea. For years, Leopold had talked about building a railway into Katanga. Its logical route would have been from the south, connecting with the Cape-to-Cairo, but Leopold had little faith in the British, and none whatever in Rhodes. Instead, he sent relays of engineers and surveyors to map a course which would travel through his own territory. 'It is', he commanded, 'by the North, not the South, that Katanga must be attached to our national activity.' But the task proved to be beyond their ability. One proposal, which would have used the course of the Congo itself for a long part of the distance, had to be rejected because the engineers had not anticipated that a river which was demonstrably navigable for native canoes, or even small flat-bottomed steamers, was not necessarily navigable for barges loaded with minerals.

In the end, pride bowed to profit. For three years, Leopold haggled with Williams and his Tanganyika Concessions, Ltd, each side knowing that the other needed it, and holding out to get the best of the bargain. For a time, even the British South Africa Company, by now gilt-edged and irreproachably mantled in near-imperial ermine, showed interest, but at the last moment fastidiously backed away. Finally, it was old George Pauling himself who saved the day. He would put his own money into the scheme – what was another few hundred miles of table-flat track to a man who had pulled the Cape-to-Cairo through Kimberley, Vryburg, Mafeking,

Bulawayo, and across the Zambesi itself? There was one condition, however; Pauling was damned if, after all that, he was expected to put locomotives on someone else's rails. He would go along, but only if he could do the whole job, and not be compelled to stop at the border and let a clumsy lot of Belgians take over.

With this proviso, the contracts were drawn up, and on December 11th, 1909, 2,156 miles from its starting point, the Cape-to-Cairo railway left English soil for the first time. The site was a clearing in the woods near the Congolese border town of Sakania. Here in the highlands, the weather was perennially balmy, and the countryside – lush but sparse trees, and beyond them open grass and a thin horizon line of gentle hills – looked more like Dorset than the centre of Africa. Adding to the illusion was the presence, unprecedented in this part of the continent, of some two dozen ladies who had ridden up from Rhodesia and the Cape for the occasion. Photographs show them, in full-length bustled summer frocks and parasols, inspecting the rustic triumphal arch which had been fashioned out of foliage and decorated with the Belgian, British and Congolese flags. In the foreground, two freshly-planted signs proclaimed, impartially, FRONTIÈRE and BORDER.

As such affairs do, the day opened with a small, symbolic ceremony: two pairs of hands, unused to labour, tightened the last bolt, after which a locomotive rode up ponderously to crush a pair of champagne bottles laid on the tracks. Then came lunch, and speeches in which the names of Cecil Rhodes and Leopold were linked in wholly imaginary co-operation. Dinner, set for 150 and interrupted frequently by toasts, turned out to be a disaster; Pauling's men, given unexpected access to large quantities of alcohol, took full advantage of it.

The following day they were back at work. It was still 150 miles to the *Étoile du Congo* mine, where a clutch of administrative buildings had been thrown up and christened, in honour of Belgium's reigning Queen, Elizabethville. Here, in front of a makeshift railway station, the first locomotive pulled up on September 27th, 1910.

This time, no ceremonies had been planned. Instead, there was a small mountain of 6,000 tons of copper ore which had piled up waiting for the arrival of the rails – the first instalment of a supply which, more than sixty years later, shows no sign of impoverishment.

Drawn by the further wealth in its path, the railway continued to move north. By World War I, its terminal had reached Bukama, on the Congo river – 2,700 miles from Cape Town, and almost halfway to its destination. Meanwhile, work had also been going on at the other end. It had started in the 1840s as a small, purely local project – a convenience for India-bound English travellers. But soon, and for a variety of reasons, the rails turned south to follow the ancient valley of the Nile.

PART FOUR

Cairo to Aswan

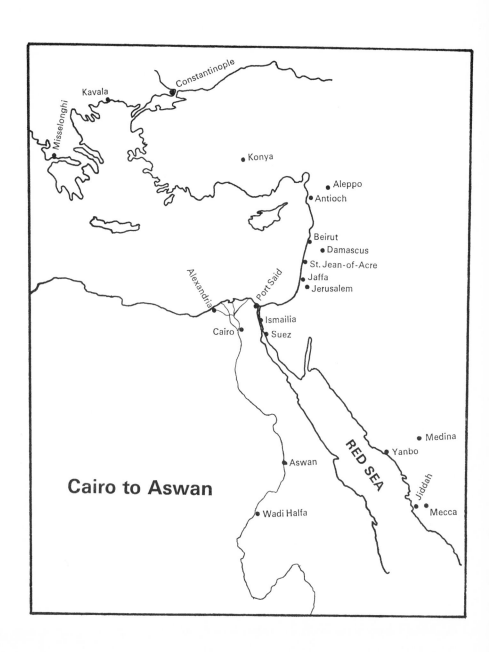

Constantinople

Kavala

Misselonghi

Konya

Aleppo
Antioch

Beirut
Damascus
St. Jean-of-Acre
Jaffa
Jerusalem

Alexandria

Port Said

Ismailia
Cairo
Suez

Medina
Yanbo

Aswan

RED SEA

Jiddah
Mecca

Cairo to Aswan

Wadi Halfa

PERHAPS the greatest misfortune which befell Africans – and the term in this context is not a euphemism for blacks, but includes Arabs, Copts, Malays, Boers, British settlers, French *pieds noirs* and all other inhabitants of the continent – is that virtually all the important decisions which affected them were made by European Powers motivated principally by European political considerations. Nowhere is this more evident than in the valley of the Nile. The simplest, if not the only intelligible way to reconstruct what took place there during the nineteenth century is in terms of the unyielding, vindictive rivalry of two of those Powers – Britain and France.

It began with a bang and ended with a whimper. In between, it engaged the full panoply of classical diplomacy – lying, deceit, bluff, back-stabbing, provocation, the naked threat of world war – and brought to the stage a company of actors to unglaze the eyes of the most torpid audience: unbelievably brave and inexcusably cowardly generals; wild-eyed religious fanatics; dim *éminences grises* from the great financial houses of the world; cynical soldiers of fortune and gentle, innocent dreamers; a beautiful, real-life Empress; the 'greatest engineer of his century', who knew nothing whatever about engineering; an Anatolian tobacco merchant who, on horseback, carved out an empire half the size of Europe; a gentle, scholarly Englishman who trained himself to think and act like an Arab thug; an obscure French soldier who became a national hero overnight through an impossible feat which had the unexpected consequence of nearly tearing his country apart.

When it was all over, when the last actor had left the stage – some survived the carnage to play roles elsewhere – France's dream of a trans-African empire lay shattered for ever, the entire upper right-hand quarter of the continent was in British hands, and the Cape-to-Cairo railway was closer to reality by 1,360 miles of solidly laid track.

The bang which started off the proceedings was fired by the French in 1798. Hoping to sever Britain's route to India and thus deprive her of the principal source of her wealth, the post-revolutionary Directoire elaborately faked a cross-Channel invasion but, instead, attacked Egypt.

Egypt was then, and had been since 1517, a vassal state of the tottering Ottoman Empire, nominally ruled by a Turkish governor appointed by the Sultan of Constantinople. In practice, authority had long since passed into

the hands of a self-perpetuating order of white slave-warriors, the Mamelukes. Originally brought to Egypt in the twelfth century by Saladin the Great
and trained to become the core of his army, they had managed to retain
their racial purity through more than 600 years, and had gradually taken
over control of the country's institutions – its army, its civil administration,
its cultural life. This had been done not against the wishes of the land-
owning Turkish pashas, but with their encouragement. With all onerous
matters of state taken from their hands, they were free to indulge in the
pleasures which their station permitted them. As for the native *fellahin*, they
simply paid their taxes and marked off the seasons by the rise and fall of the
Nile, as they had since the time of the Pharaohs. No one had ever bothered
even counting how many of them there were – estimates ranged from two
to three million – and it would be a long time, if indeed it has yet arrived,
before anyone would think of them as anything other than two-legged beasts
of burden and occasional cannon fodder.

For the invading French, led by a promising 29-year-old officer named
Bonaparte, the first taste of Egypt turned out to be a bitter disappointment.
Alexandria, behind its crumbling walls, was a dirty, dun-coloured village of
some 7,000 inhabitants, with no trace left of its ancient glory. Instead of
pleasure palaces and soothing gardens, there was sullen silence, blinding
– and, for troops dressed to force their way across Alpine passes – suffocat-
ing heat. But they were good soldiers and fought well. The name of Pyra-
mides is inscribed along with Iéna, Wagram and Austerlitz around the
victor's tomb, although the engagement could have given him only slight
professional satisfaction: the last time the Mamelukes had faced a European
army was in 1249, during the Ninth Crusade.

Peace was hardly more rewarding. After a year during which he lost his
navy to Admiral Nelson and much of his army to the fleshpots of Cairo,
Bonaparte sailed home in stealth, leaving Kléber, his deputy, to be assassinated by a religious fanatic. The British arrived to clean up what was left,
and then in March 1803 themselves departed. Beyond keeping it out of
French hands, Britain had for the moment no interest in Egypt.

Of all the categories of historical figures, the most exclusive belongs to
those few who can, with justice, be called 'father of his country'. As
aspirants have discovered, there are no generalized qualifications for the
title, no helpful models to emulate, no handy parallels of training or preparation. Even if there were, they would have to be elastic in the extreme to
include the unprepossessing, slightly bandy-legged figure who, as the last
British soldier boarded ship in Alexandria, set about seizing Egypt and,
during a reign that was to last 45 years, single-handedly moulding it into the
semblance of a modern sovereign state.

Mohammed Ali was born in 1769 in Kavala, a small seaport in Macedonia. This made him a subject of the Sultan, though his nationality was in all probability Albanian. Virtually nothing is known about the first thirty years of his life, except that he was orphaned early and brought up by first an uncle and then a family friend who found him a wife and set him up in the tobacco trade. He had become the father of three sons and was on his way to a moderately comfortable life when, in 1799, Kavala was ordered to provide 300 soldiers to help fight the French invaders in Egypt. Mohammed Ali was not only selected but, because of his station, appointed second-in-command of the small detachment. Its military history was brief: they were thrown back into the sea, attempting to land at Aboukir.

For the next four years he vanished, to reappear at the head of a few thousand Albanian mercenaries, still nominally in the service of the Sultan but now in his own pay and at his personal command. Politically, Egypt was worse than in chaos; it simply did not exist. Rival factions roamed the streets of the two principal cities and took turns looting the countryside. Free-booting commanders looked hopefully towards Constantinople and tried to gain the Sultan's favour in terms they knew were close to his heart: the size of the tribute they were willing to pay for recognition. Mohammed Ali's army continued to grow; soon he commanded 15,000 men, and his offer dwarfed all the rest. On May 12th, 1805, he was formally proclaimed Pasha – viceroy – of Egypt.

The title was expensive and largely honorary; his unsuccessful rivals paid obeisance to their new governor, but continued to rob and plunder as they chose. Chateaubriand, who visited Egypt in 1806, recalled meeting one of them, a huge, ferocious-looking giant named Abdellah. On closer acquaintance, it turned out that his real name was Dorau, that he had once been a cobbler in Toulouse, and that most of his men were, like himself, deserters from Bonaparte's army who had set themselves up in business. But the biggest threat to Mohammed Ali was the Mamelukes, who had regrouped and resumed their ancient way of life. For six years he bided his time, paying his tribute, building his army and tolerating their disdain with elaborate courtesy.

On March 1st, 1811, he was at last ready. He had just appointed his second son, Toussoun, commander of the army and was about to send him on a campaign in Arabia, across the Red Sea. To celebrate the departure, he formally invited the principal Mameluke chiefs, some 500 in all, to a ceremony in the Citadel, the official residence of the viceroy.

The Citadel, actually a walled city measuring 1,000 yards by 800 and containing palaces, mosques, barracks and arsenals, sat on one of the hills which overlook Cairo and the Nile. Its approach was a long, narrow defile commanded by heavy gates at either end. The Mamelukes had agreed to attend the ceremony only because Mohammed Ali had asked, not ordered them, and of course they had decked themselves and their horses in all the finery of their rank. Slowly the procession moved through the streets of

Cairo and into the defile. As soon as the last man passed through, the lower gate slammed shut, then the upper one. From the walls on either side, gunfire opened at point-blank range. Legend has it that one Mameluke managed to escape – by blindfolding his horse and forcing him to vault over a parapet – but that Mohammed Ali had him hounded to his death by thirst in the desert. Whatever his fate, that of the other Mamelukes is better documented. Thousands were butchered in Cairo that night, along with their families and servants. Others, by prearrangement, were attacked in outlying villages. By morning, Mohammed Ali was the uncontested ruler of Egypt. He was 42 years old, illiterate, and all his glory lay ahead of him.

Toussoun, who was then 15 years old, went off on his Arabian campaign as planned. Its objective was to recapture the holy cities of Mecca and Medina, which had fallen into the hands of the Wahhabis, a fundamentalist sect of desert Arabs whose religious zeal was matched by their fierce military efficiency. The Sultan had been asking Mohammed Ali since 1807 to dislodge them, not only because their possession of the holiest sites of the Moslem world tarnished his prestige as the terrestrial representative of the Prophet, but because he felt keenly the loss of revenue from the long files of faithful who made their pilgrimage to the two cities. Mohammed Ali had demurred as long as he could; he did not feel himself strong enough at home, and furthermore, as loyal liege, he was expected to pay the full costs of the expedition. There was, however, the nagging knowledge that as Pasha of Egypt he was only a middle-sized fish in a very large ocean. There were other Pashas, far wealthier and more important, in Damascus and Baghdad, to say nothing of those who ruled over the Sultan's European possessions. Liberating the holy cities would add enormously to his prestige.

Unfortunately, the campaign did not go well. The Wahhabis did not fight the same kind of war as the French, the Turks, and certainly the Mamelukes. You went out into the desert to find them, and instead they found you, appearing from nowhere to strike and vanish; pursue them and suddenly they appeared at your rear, massacring your wounded and setting fire to your stores. For two years the game continued while Mohammed Ali sat in Cairo and listened as Toussoun's petulant reports were read to him. Finally he lost his patience; on August 28th, 1813, he boarded a ship in Suez and, in three days, was in Jiddah, the port city of Mecca. Instinctively he fastened on the one effective strategy: instead of trying to destroy the Wahhabis in set battle, he moved slowly inland, capturing or destroying the oases which they relied on for support. Within a year he had taken both Mecca and Medina.

The conquest of Arabia gained Mohammed Ali the anticipated stature among his peers, but it also cost him virtually all of his treasury, with the result that even before his army could be brought home he had already begun planning his next campaign. The objective this time was the Sudan, the almost unknown region which lay to the south and which each year miraculously gave birth to the cresting Nile flood. A few white men – traders and eccentrics looking for the source of the river – had wandered here, and brought back stories of jet-black peoples (Sudan is the plural of the Arabic word for black), and the inevitable tales of gold, copper and precious ebony. Mohammed Ali's orders to the expedition were simple: to bring back all the gold and treasure it could find.

The treasure turned out to be more geographic than negotiable. There were great forests and mountains, and animals and vegetation such as had never been seen before. Even the Nile, it appeared, was not one river but two. At the point where they came together, there was an insignificant fishing village. Recognizing its strategic importance, Mohammed Ali ordered it knocked down and replaced by a small fortress. Because the merged river formed a wide loop which resembled an elephant's trunk it was given the Arabic name for that appendage: Khartoum.

Other campaigns followed. Ibrahim, Mohammed Ali's eldest son, led an army which captured Greece, only to be forced to relinquish it by a hastily convoked alliance of the Great Powers – Britain, France, Prussia, Austria, Russia. They had paid no attention while Mohammed Ali exerted himself in Arabia and the Sudan – one brigand or another always ruled such places. But Greece was something else; though it belonged nominally to the weak, corrupt Sultan of Constantinople, it was part of Europe. Frustrated, Mohammed Ali next turned against the Sultan himself, sending Ibrahim marching up through the Holy Land and over the Taurus mountains into Anatolia. His victorious troops had reached Konieh, within marching distance of the golden domes and lacy minarets on the Bosphorus, when again the Powers intervened. Each, for complicated reasons of its own, wished to keep the Sultan on his shaky throne.

Again Mohammed Ali was obliged to withdraw, but this time he was able to extract from the Sultan a concession which had lain close to his heart. It had been the rule throughout the Ottoman Empire that upon the death or removal of a Pasha, the Sultan had the right to appoint his successor. Egypt was to be the exception; it would remain the hereditary possession of Mohammed Ali's family. The decree granting this right was signed in July 1841, and marked for Mohammed Ali, now 72 years old, the end of four decades of nearly continuous war. He could now turn his full attention to the other goal which preoccupied him: the creation of Egypt.

The list of what he had already accomplished was staggering. Egypt had never had any public schools, except for religious institutions which taught the Koran, rudiments of arithmetic and, to advanced students, cosmology based on the pre-Copernican model. The literacy rate at the time of Bonaparte's invasion was perhaps 1 per cent for males, and one in 10,000 for females. Mohammed Ali had ordered the establishment of an educational system, based on fifty free primary schools. Only five were located in Cairo and Alexandria; the rest were scattered in the provinces, which civilization had barely brushed. For the students who successfully completed this course of studies, there were special institutes for languages, polytechnic studies, civil administration, applied geometry and geography. As early as 1826, Mohammed Ali had also begun the practice, which still prevails, of sending the most promising graduates to complete their specialized studies in France – whether in the Faculty of Law in Paris or in the silk mills of Lyons. For the others he provided libraries, ordering eight new printing presses to replace those the French had brought with them and had taken back. Gradually, on paper imported from Italy, a modest flow of books had begun to appear: grammars and manuals, histories and Arabic translations of European works.

There had never existed in Egypt a single hospital or public health facility of any kind. Cholera, dysentery, typhoid fever were endemic; more than 60,000 people died yearly of smallpox, and the periodic outbreaks of plague which wiped out entire communities were considered a natural aspect of life. Medical care, to the extent it existed, had slipped badly from the level it had attained in the Middle Ages under Avicenna. A few self-styled physicians with European training maintained practices, but limited them to the wealthiest and highest-born families; all others were abandoned to barbers, charlatans and, for medication, to the unguents compounded by village sorcerers. In 1825, Mohammed Ali was able to hire a promising 31-year-old French physician, Antoine-Barthélémy Clot, who agreed to come for a period of five years and stayed on for a quarter of a century. Clot began his herculean task by setting up rudimentary dispensaries; within two years he had established a medical school which numbered 215 students, and a school of pharmacy. He instituted a system of quarantine, patterned after that in force in Marseilles, and the beginnings of preventive medicine, which he introduced by publicly inoculating himself against plague. Every one of his new proposals was fought bitterly by the religious establishment, because they defied predestination, the will of Allah. In most instances, Mohammed Ali simply listened to Clot and issued new laws specifying punishment for their contravention. Occasionally, however, a touch of delicacy was required: when Clot complained that village women were refusing to be examined by male physicians, Mohammed Ali decreed that an adequate number of eunuchs be released from other duties and instructed in medical practice.

As for public works, Mohammed Ali had only to look around at his impoverished country and tick off its needs on his fingers. The Mahmoudieh Canal, connecting Alexandria with the Nile, had originally been dug by the Pharaohs; before silting up in the seventeenth century, it had provided not only a means of transportation, but a secure source of fresh water for the city. Mohammed Ali ordered it restored, and set 300,000 men to work on it; 20,000 of them died, but the project – 48 miles long, 90 feet wide and deep enough to accommodate barges – was completed in three months. A new lighthouse, visible for twenty miles out at sea, was built in Alexandria, as well as docks, shipyards and sturdy fortifications. A regular steamer service was started on the Nile, and a semaphore erected between Alexandria and Cairo, which also became one of the first cities outside Europe to boast of gas illumination in its streets. The road from Cairo to Suez, an uncertain 85-mile desert track, was widened and paved.

To overcome the resistance which his innovations caused among the Turkish pashas, Mohammed Ali chose the simple expedient of expropriating every landowner and putting all of Egypt in his own name. He then doled out the land back to the *fellahin* in parcels of three to five acres, dictating precisely what should be planted on every plot. The Nile, on which all life in Egypt depended, was destructively contemptuous of its bounty, offering it in an uncontrolled annual flood; Mohammed Ali determined to tame it, to channel and conserve its water so that it could be put to work the year round. Millions of cubic feet of sand were excavated, much of it with bare hands; hundreds of canals were dug, and more than 38,000 mechanical water-wheels installed. The most ambitious project of all, begun in 1835 under the supervision of Linant de Bellefonds, was a massive barrage which was to hold back the Nile just below the point where it split off into its two seaward branches and, when finished, would provide enough water to irrigate the entire area of the Delta.

As a result of all this back-breaking work, summer crops could, for the first time in history, be grown in Egypt. With an eye to world markets, Mohammed Ali specified which ones they would be: rice, sugar, indigo, linen, tobacco, hemp, even poppies – for opium was then expensive and not yet illegal. In 1820, a French horticulturist named Jumel brought to his attention a new variety of cotton. The first experimental crop yielded two bales of fibre; three years later, production had arisen to 259,426 bales, and long-staple cotton was on its way to becoming Egypt's most valuable resource.

It had not occurred to anyone who ever ruled Egypt – Romans, Arabs, Turks, Mamelukes or Frenchmen – that the passive, shiftless *fellahin* were good for anything more demanding than tilling the soil. There had been manufacturing of sorts in Egypt: silversmiths, parchment makers, rug weavers, potters. To equip his army, however, Mohammed Ali needed arsenals, metal-working shops, textile mills. He could, and did, hire foreigners to design them for him, but these establishments could not be made to run themselves; so he determined that the *fellahin* should be taught how to do it. Recruiting and training workmen for his new factories proved as difficult and frustrating as filling the ranks of his new regiments, but Mohammed Ali was determined to do it, and with the best teachers he could find. To start his first weaving mill, he sent to Florence for skilled artisans; a Cypriot Greek was put in charge of olive oil production. Upon being told that sugar cane could profitably be distilled into rum, he sent a mission to the British Antilles to learn how.

As with the land, all the new industries were in Mohammed Ali's name; he exercised complete monopoly over the country's economy. His agents in Marseilles, Leghorn, Trieste, even as far away as Stockholm, were empowered to take orders for anything Egypt might produce. And, like the shrewd trader that he was, he turned a good profit. The national budget of Egypt for the fiscal year 1833 would have satisfied Calvin Coolidge: receipts of 63 million francs, expenditures of 50 million francs – and this was at the height of his costly military adventures.

Mohammed Ali's inclination was to think in large terms – when he decided that he wanted a silk industry, he ordered 17 million mulberry trees planted; when he built a navy, he insisted that its flagship, the *Misr*, carry 136 guns – but he also found time for details. One of his ordinances required that all houses in Cairo be numbered and all streets clearly marked; another imposed fines against anyone in front of whose house was found a dead dog or cat. Some things, however, were beyond him, partly because there was no time, partly because the need was not clearly apparent. He did virtually nothing about the administration of justice, or about providing for even the most elementary form of representative government. Perhaps because of this, a number of modern historians have been harsh in their judgment of him, going so far as to suggest that everything he accomplished was for the sole purpose of creating and supporting a modern army. Possibly this was indeed his motive, but it could hardly have made any difference to his subjects, for whom the massive doors of ignorance, poverty and disease opened for the first time – if only to let in a tiny crack of light. And even his sternest critics must grant Mohammed Ali this much credit: what he accomplished he did alone, without the aid of a government or ministers, and without anyone he could wholly trust – except for his own sons and his Armenian interpreter, Borghes, who served him faithfully until the very end.

Stories and personal accounts of Mohammed Ali abound, for throughout his career he was willing to see and listen to almost every foreign visitor to Egypt. Some were merely curious, most had something to sell; but even if they did not succeed, they did not leave empty-handed, for they could dine out for weeks on stories of this strange potentate who was unfailingly courteous and gracious, but whose slightest whim was law in that large part of the world which stretched from the Libyan desert to the far side of the Persian Gulf, and from Crete to the unknown reaches of central Africa.

Mohammed Ali himself was under no illusion about his visitors' motives.

He told one of them: 'I know that among 50 men who come from Europe to offer me their services, 49 are only to be compared to false stones. Without testing them, however, I cannot discover the only genuine diamond that may be among them. I begin by buying them all and when I discover the one, he often repays me by a hundred-fold for the loss I have incurred by the others.'

To another, the Frenchman Mimault who once chided him for his grandiose schemes, he said: 'You must understand we are only children, but growing children; it is necessary that we make our clothes too large for our present size.'

And to still another, the Englishman Bewring, who had written a highly disparaging report about the living conditions of the *fellahin*: 'Do not judge me by the standards of your knowledge. I do not expect to do what you are able to do. I have never seen countries more civilized than my own.'

He was keenly conscious, too, of what it had taken to bring him to power in Egypt, and keep him there. Referring to those early days in a conversation with the German writer-traveller Prince Pückler-Muskau in 1837, he admitted: 'I do not love this period of my life, and what would the world profit by the recital of this interminable tissue of combat and misery, cunning and bloodshed to which circumstances imperatively compelled me? My history shall not commence until the period when, free from all restraint, I could arouse this land from the sleep of ages.'

Always, he was impatient to see a job completed. The story is told that on one occasion he received, as present from the Sultan, a magnificently bound and illuminated volume of Arabic verse. In answer to his question about how long it would take to translate it into Turkish, he was told at least three months. He tore the book into three parts and threw it down: 'Here, do it in one month.'*

But the largest, most spectacular project in Egypt he steadfastly refused to undertake. It must have held out a special attraction to him because it would, physically as well as symbolically, have separated Egypt from Asia. Nevertheless, because he sensed – only too accurately as it turned out – that the Powers would never permit his country to control so valuable a possession, he did not grant permission for the construction of a canal across the Isthmus of Suez.

The project had been on Bonaparte's agenda in 1798, and work on it had actually started, at least to the extent of completing the first surveys. Their finding had been that a difference of 32½ feet existed between the levels of the Red Sea and the Mediterranean, and that a canal would therefore require the construction of locks, a prohibitively complicated undertaking.

* Another story has it that one of his French counsellors urged him to read Machiavelli's *The Prince*. He gave it to a translator and ordered him to bring ten pages every day. After the first day, he said, 'There is nothing new here.' After the second, 'I already know this.' After the third, 'I have nothing to learn from this man. Stop your translation.'

As early as 1821, however, Linant made his own survey, discovered that no difference existed and, like the true engineer he was, began urging Mohammed Ali to let him start digging.

The British strenuously opposed the idea from the start. Over the years, this opposition ripened into an article of faith so strongly held that when the Canal was finally completed, in 1869, Britain was the only Power in Europe which pointedly boycotted its inaugural ceremonies. As to the reason for the objection, it was stated succinctly by one of Britain's consuls in Egypt, Sir Frederick Bruce:

> For both commercial and military purposes, we are nearer to India than any European nation except Spain and Portugal, which are nothing. When the canal is opened, all the coasts of the Mediterranean and Black Seas will be nearer to India than we are. ... At present, India is untouchable. It will no longer be so when Bombay is only 4,600 miles from Marseilles.

Therefore, if Britain could help it, there was to be no canal. And under no circumstances a French-dug canal.

Not that France had any notion of sponsoring or supporting any such enterprise. What interest there was came from Linant, and from a single private and highly eccentric individual, Claude Henri de Rouvroy, Comte de Saint-Simon. An amateur philosopher, mathematician, biologist and sociologist, Saint-Simon had advanced ideas about social organization, and the personal means to pursue them. Among his pet theories was the economic utility of constructing canals. The Isthmus of Suez had struck him as a logical place for such an enterprise – Panama was another – but unfortunately he died, in 1825, before he could generate interest in the project. Though his far-flung notions had cost him his fortune, they had also earned him a small corps of devoted disciples. One of them, Prosper Enfantin, took up the Suez scheme as his life's work. In addition to whatever practical utility such an artery might provide, Enfantin, who had mystic notions of his own, saw in it the opportunity to 'make the Mediterranean the nuptial bed for a marriage between the East and the West, and to consummate the marriage by the piercing of a canal.'

In 1832, Enfantin landed in Egypt with a group of followers. Their symbolism included costume as well as geography, for they arrived wearing flowing white trousers (the colour of love), red vests (the colour of work) and purple tunics (the colour of faith). They also let their hair grow long, and affected to wear flowers and beaded necklaces.* According to contemporary

---

* In other habits, too, they anticipated the times. Suzanne Violquin, a French nurse working in Egypt, described a visit she made to their permanent encampment on the banks of the Nile: 'The conversation turned to hashish, and everyone in turn and in the most casual manner described the hallucinations he had experienced, with no damage whatever to their well-being. Then they offered me their little boxes, and proceeded to partake of their contents themselves.'

accounts, they began singing as soon as they debarked, and only prompt action by the police prevented the workmen on the dock from tossing them back into the sea. It was just as well, for their safety, that they sang in French, for one of their songs declared:

> ... We will place one foot on the Nile,
> The other upon Jerusalem.
> Our right hand will reach out towards Mecca,
> Our left hand will cover Rome
> And will rest upon Paris.
> Suez is the centre of our life of Labour.
> There we shall perform the Act
> Which the world awaits
> In order to proclaim that we are
> Male.

Linant, whatever his own feelings about this kind of thing, recognized in Enfantin a potential ally and introduced him to Mohammed Ali, who with his usual politeness made arrangements for the Saint-Simonians to visit the Isthmus and begin their studies. He may have been sincere, but more likely he saw in Enfantin a way to put off the British, who had for some time been pestering him with an alternative project.

What they wanted was to build a railway which would connect Cairo with Alexandria and, ultimately, with Suez. Such a railway would serve their purposes admirably, for it would speed the delivery of mail to and from India, and make the journey immeasurably more comfortable for travellers who were obliged to go overland by horseback or in jarring and unreliable stagecoaches. Linant and the other Frenchmen were opposed to this scheme, partially for the sound reason that it would be costly and return no benefit whatever to Egypt, few of whose citizens travelled between London and Bombay, and partially because they sensed that the construction of a railway would set back indefinitely any prospect for a canal.

Not wishing to antagonize Linant and unwilling to accede to the British, whom he disliked and very sensibly mistrusted, Mohammed Ali temporized. Some day, perhaps, he would be ready to build a railway. For the present, there were other projects more in need of his immediate attention. To Enfantin, who had returned from the Isthmus with a choice of possible schemes for a canal, he was more cordial. He agreed to the appointment of an international commission which would study the alternatives and make a final recommendation. Enfantin hurried back to Paris and assembled a *Société d'Études* which included five Frenchmen, ten Germans, and two Englishmen. A three-man delegation, consisting of one engineer from each nation, was dispatched in November 1846 to make a field evaluation. Their finding, made public in May 1847, was that the canal scheme was, in its totality, impractical. Enfantin was crushed, and immediately suspected

duplicity on the part of the British delegate: 'I have every reason to believe
that he had been more interested in working on behalf of a railway than a
canal, which is to say exactly the contrary of what he gave us to believe when
he joined us.'

For a mystic, Enfantin showed shrewd worldliness: the Englishman's
name was George Stephenson, and his father had been the inventor of the
steam locomotive.

In the end, nobody won. The Peninsular and Oriental Shipping Company did not get its railway, and its passengers had to endure a desert
crossing for a few more years. Enfantin and his colleagues took their matri-
monial ambitions elsewhere, and Suez, for the moment, retained its
virginity.

The last years of Mohammed Ali's reign were sad. Portraits of him during
this period show a delicate, white-bearded patriarch dressed in high Turkish
style and seated cross-legged on a divan. One hand absently toys with a
ceremonial scimitar or water pipe; the face is serene, the smile composed,
the eyes look out with gentle understanding. In reality, the mind behind
those eyes had at last begun to cloud. In 1847, upon being told that work on
the Nile Barrage was falling behind for lack of materials, he commanded that
the Pyramids be dismantled and used as building stone; only Linant's hastily
contrived technical objection prevented the order from being carried out.

For years, Mohammed Ali had hoped to visit France, and early in 1848
arrangements were finally completed: he would go on a state visit as the
honoured personal guest of his good friend, King Louis-Philippe. He left in
February aboard the privately chartered French steamer, *Alexandre*, and
had just reached Malta when news arrived that revolution had broken out
in France and Louis-Philippe himself had fled Paris. Immediately, the old
man began devising fantastic plans to invade France, crush the insurrection
and restore the monarchy; he issued orders which were never forwarded to
mobilize the Egyptian army and navy. It was deemed unsafe to proceed to
Marseilles, but Mohammed Ali refused to return home, so as a compromise
the *Alexandre* headed for Naples. There, Ibrahim joined his father and,
together, the two quietly made their way back to Alexandria. There was by
then no longer any question of Mohammed Ali's capacity to rule. Ibrahim
had of necessity already begun to assume authority; in July, he was formally
invested as regent by the Sultan.

He was then himself 59 years old. Lord Cromer,* in his two-volume

---

* Sir Evelyn Baring, 1st Earl of Cromer, is conceded by the British, if not by the
French and certainly not by the Egyptians, to be the 'Father of Modern Egypt'. A member
of the great Baring banking family and the youngest of nine sons in his generation, he
arrived in Cairo in 1876 as Britain's watchdog over Egyptian finances, and remained to
rule the country as its pro-consul until 1907. More, much more, will be heard from and
about him in the course of this story.

Modern Egypt, ticks him off in 30 words: 'Ibrahim, the son and successor of Mohammed Ali, was a distinguished soldier, and a man of great personal courage. It must be added that he was a half-lunatic savage.'

Whatever the justice of this estimate – and it seems unduly harsh because his first official acts were to abolish the death penalty in Egypt, and secure for prisoners the due process of law – Ibrahim had little time left to live up to it: his reign lasted just 61 days. Worn out by a life of almost continuous war, unsuited to the role of administrator, preoccupied with his father's failing mind, he died on November 10th, 1848, while the old man still padded aimlessly around the halls of the palace.

According to the rule of succession established in 1841, the heir presumptive was the eldest male member of the family. Although Mohammed Ali still had a living son, Said, he also had a grandson, Abbas, who was ten years older, and therefore stood next in line.

There is a family legend to the effect that as preparations were being made for the transfer of power, Mohammed Ali happened to wander into the chamber where the Council of State was meeting. He greeted everyone, took his customary seat, and warned, 'You have come to prepare Abbas's accession, but he will crush every one of you and none will be spared.' Then he rose and left with great dignity.

It was an accurate prediction. Abbas was possibly the most unfit ruler any country has endured in modern times. One of the most scholarly and respected Egyptian historians, Mohammed Sabry, characterizes him as 'deceitful, reactionary, cruel, superstitious, rapacious, despotic, lazy, hypocritical, avid for pleasure and luxury'. Charles-Roux, in his semi-official *History of Egypt*, adds the comment that 'perhaps this estimate is excessively generous.'

Abbas was the son of Toussoun. Orphaned when only three, he was raised in the cloying, hothouse atmosphere of the harem, compounded equally of sensuality and ignorance. Here, he was master; as princeling, his favour was sought and bribed with every conceivable device. Of all Mohammed Ali's male descendants, he was the only one who disobeyed orders and refused to learn a foreign language. Hating all things Christian, he professed instead to be devoted to Allah. But the consuming passion of his life, to which he surrendered himself on the day he mounted the throne, was to destroy everything which Mohammed Ali had begun to build. Under the guise of ridding Egypt of alien influence, he abolished the public schools and closed the country's only hospital. Clot was banished, as were dozens of other Europeans who had served the old man. Factories were shut down, and their workers sent home to their villages or to beg in the streets of Cairo and Alexandria. All work on irrigation projects was halted. Abbas personally supervised the destruction of the Nile Barrage which he insisted represented a 'colossal crime against the laws of Nature'.

Whatever energy this orgy of destruction left him, Abbas lavished on the construction of fortified castles for himself. Because he preferred the company of horses and dogs to that of human beings, he located them on bleak, inhospitable sites, such as the barren desert between Cairo and Suez. The largest – of which nothing now remains but the stumps of fat, ugly towers – he had built, torn down and rebuilt four times, each time making it larger and more uncomfortable. He freely looted mosques, including the one dedicated to his father, of marble and alabaster. To speed up the work on his palaces, he disbanded Mohammed Ali's disciplined army of 120,000 men and turned them into crews of carpenters and masons. For his own personal protection, he hired 6,000 Albanian mercenaries whose loyalty he tried to purchase with free brothels and the promise of immunity in the discharge of their duties.

Abbas was 35 years old when he inherited Egypt, but for the first six months, while Mohammed Ali still lived, he had to be satisfied as merely a regent. When the great day finally came, it happened to coincide with the circumcision of his son, El Hami. To mark the double celebration, Abbas ordered a week of festivities, punctuated by a personal salute of 100,000 rounds of cannon – at a cost of approximately 2·5 million francs. Niggardly with the public purse, he was expansive on his own behalf: the furnishings used to fill his five palaces cost 7 million francs.

Stories of Abbas's cruelty abound – classic oriental horror tales of suspected courtiers whose lips were sewn together; of faithless high-born ladies who were served at ceremonial dinners with the severed heads of their lovers; of one particular mistress who incurred Abbas's displeasure and was punished by being turned over to the rude attention of a platoon of guards, while he watched contentedly from a balcony. Some of these stories were undoubtedly inventions, but it is hardly necessary to establish their authenticity in order to believe them possible. The most telling evidence is one portrait of Abbas which survives in the Bibliothèque Nationale in Paris: drawn in profile, it shows a beardless, weak-chinned man with watery eyes and the shadow of a moustache – the unknown artist could have visualized it from the pages of Krafft-Ebing.

However black the night Abbas caused to descend upon Egypt, he could not affect the interest others had in it. 'The politics of every State', Napoleon had observed, 'are determined by its geography.' Egypt still lay astride the route to India.

During the height of French influence and pressure to build a canal, Lord Palmerston, then Prime Minister, had written to Murray, his consul-general in Cairo: 'Lose no opportunity of impressing on the Pasha and his ministers the costliness and impractibility of such a project, and you should point out that those who press such a scheme do so solely for the purpose of diverting him from the railway.'

Now, with 'those who press such a scheme' out of the way, Palmerston began daily to badger Abbas about the railway. He had two advantages.

First, Murray knew Turkish, the only language which Abbas spoke. Second, Abbas needed European support from some quarter in his perennial struggle with the Sultan, who relentlessly pushed to recoup some of the concessions wrested from him by Mohammed Ali.

The negotiations involved furtive meetings, uncertain intermediaries, provisional agreements. Finally, Abbas weakened. In dead secrecy he signed in the middle of the night of July 18th, 1851, a contract with a British engineer. It provided that 'Whereas His Highness Abbas Pasha is about to undertake the Construction of a Railway between Cairo and Alexandria,' it was agreed that the said engineer 'shall by himself or [with] other competent persons ... superintend the planning, laying out and construction of the said Railway and of all works and buildings of whatsoever nature thereto belonging or necessary. ... '

The 'said engineer' was none other than the same George Stephenson who had, four years earlier, so effectively sabotaged Enfantin's canal project. According to the terms of the contract, Stephenson was to be paid £56,000 sterling,* for which he would provide all technical services. His Highness would pay for materials, and provide the necessary labour. After the years of indecision, British efficiency wasted no time taking over: the first order for materials – '24,000 tons of forged or molten iron' – was placed with English import houses in Alexandria on September 1st.

While the iron-makers of Birmingham rubbed their hands, the French wrung theirs. Shortly before the climax of negotiations, their consul had telegraphed home: 'British influence here is all-powerful at this moment, and threatens to assume the form of an outright protectorate.' Later, when the contract became public, he amplified on his fears: 'The railway ... will place into British hands what is at once the greatest commercial interest and the only political interest which Europe has in this country. ... It is tantamount to handing Egypt over to Great Britain.'

With the simple substitution of the word 'canal' for 'railway' and 'French' for 'British', this could have been the text of a dozen telegrams which British consuls had sent home five years earlier, at the height of French influence over Mohammed Ali.

Abbas had little time to savour the nicety of this turn of fortune. On the night of July 13th, 1854, while at his palace in Benha, he was assassinated by two of his servants. In a country where even natural death by old age is viewed with suspicion – sometimes judicious suspicion – this act provoked wide speculation which has never been resolved. One historian simply concludes, 'One does not know at whose instigation they acted,' leaving the implication that candidates were plentiful.

But though Abbas was dead, there still remained for him one final and appropriately grisly curtain call. By right, the throne now belonged to Said, but some members of Abbas's immediate family decided to stage a *coup*

* A pound was then worth 5 dollars, or 25 French francs.

d'état and install his young son, El Hami. Unfortunately, the boy was then away in Malta. A messenger was dispatched to fetch him; meanwhile, Abbas's body was dressed in street clothes, set in a carriage and driven through the streets of Cairo.

This story, more appropriate to the age of the Borgias than to the second half of the nineteenth century, is confirmed by Sir Frederick Bruce, the British diplomat who had previously expressed his country's views on the canal. Moreover, Bruce asserts that it was he who personally defeated the scheme. By his own account, he handled the whole unpleasantness as if he had caught a fellow club member cheating at cards:

> I was at the time shooting on the Nile. One of my people heard strange rumours and sent a boat to inform me. ... I went immediately to the Citadel, confronted Elfi Pasha (the chief conspirator) and asked why he had not sent word to Said, the successor. He answered that Said's right to the succession was not clear. ... I replied that Said's right was perfectly clear, and that I should take measures unless he did so, to inform him instantly of what had happened. ... He saw the plot had failed, so submitted and sent off a courier to Said in Alexandria.

In retrospect, virtue did not bring its own reward. Whatever might have been El Hami's foreign policy inclinations, Said's turned out to be exuberantly pro-French.

Said was Mohammed Ali's last son, born to him when he was 53 years old. All the struggle, most of the intrigue, and much of the bloodshed were behind the old man. He was absolute master of Egypt, a valued friend and confidant of European statesmen. Day by day, he was creating a country. It may be presumptuous and, on available evidence, psychologically speculative to suppose that the old man wished this young boy to be everything he himself could not have been, but Mohammed Ali did take particular interest in his proper rearing. From the age of seven, Said was put in the hands of a private French tutor, Koenig Bey, and force-fed the equivalent of a European education. His father, who had a great number of other matters to occupy his mind, summarily interrupted affairs of state once a week to listen to long, detailed reports of the boy's progress. They were good, but not glowing: Said was a pleasant lad who was willing enough, but showed no particular aptitude or initiative.

As part of his education, the boy was gradually introduced to the foreign advisers, distinguished visitors and resident diplomats who surrounded Mohammed Ali's court. Within that circle, no one made a deeper impression on Said than the dashing French vice-consul, Ferdinand de Lesseps. There is a story, repeated in almost every history of Egypt, that de Lesseps, with great prescience, bought Said's affection with heaping plates of macaroni, served to him surreptitiously from the consular kitchen to supplement the spartan diet imposed by Mohammed Ali. The story is probably untrue, but even without this gastronomic touch, it is easy to understand how the tall, handsome, worldly Frenchman, who was an expert horseman and a crack shot, would have gained the admiration of an awkward Turkish youth just entering his teens.

The friendship was interrupted in 1837 when de Lesseps was assigned to duty elsewhere. Said, then fifteen, was appointed a midshipman in the Egyptian navy, where, in a manner not unknown to other ruling houses, he quickly rose through the grades to become Admiral of the Fleet. A graphic word-picture of him was composed by the French writer, Edmond About: 'A Gargantua, a good-natured Colossus, a *bon-vivant*, a surprisingly heavy drinker, with a hand made to strike elephants, big-faced, high-coloured, overflowing with kindness, frankness, generosity and courage, but withal cynical, despising men and not always respecting himself.'

About was a novelist and writer of adventure stories, and his portrait was drawn entirely from hearsay, but the description conforms both to photographs of Said, and to first-hand recollections of his character. Schneider, the Austrian consul in Cairo, who was no novelist but who had more than a casual interest in what kind of viceroy Said would make, wrote home to Vienna: '[He] no doubt possesses a great heart and large gifts of the spirit. He has European training and speaks French and English to perfection, which facilitates discussion with him. But he appears possessed of a large dose of insouciance and instability in his decision.'

Had he been less circumspect, the Austrian consul could simply have reported that Said was a great big fun-loving boy who had never grown up and who was happiest in the company of his troops, with whom he enjoyed living under canvas in the field. While diplomats sat and waited for him in Cairo, he staged elaborate military exercises in the desert, moving regiments of infantry and batteries of artillery as if they were cast of lead. His own personal bravery occasionally spilled over into idiocy, as Cromer noted:

> ... In order to prove his courage, which had been called in question by the European press, it is said that he caused a kilometre of road to be strewn a foot deep with gunpowder. He then walked solemnly along the road smoking a pipe, and accompanied by a numerous suite, all of whom were ordered to smoke, – severe penalties being threatened against any one whose pipe was not found alight at the end of the promenade.

Meanwhile, in Cairo and especially in Alexandria, his accession was the signal for the foreigners banished by Abbas that it was time to resume business as usual. There had been some 3,000 of them – Greek, French, Italian, British, German – living in Egypt in 1838. More had come during

the closing years of Mohammed Ali's reign, as word spread that there was
money to be made in helping the old man propel Egypt into modern times.
With the help of his French advisers, Mohammed Ali had been able to keep
the more voracious of these volunteers in check. But now, they descended
like locusts. Whatever Said wanted to buy, they could supply at a price.
And even if he did not want to buy, there were means available to make him,
or the Egyptian treasury, pay for it. Because Egypt was legally only a
Turkish province and not an independent nation, resident foreigners had
always enjoyed a measure of extra-territorial rights which were jealously
guarded by their respective consuls. At the first hint of conflict, the consul
would huff and puff and threaten to blow the matter up into an issue that
could be settled only by the Sultan in Constantinople. Under Abbas, this
tactic was largely an irritant, bordering on small-scale blackmail. Under
Said, it became the most profitable profession in Egypt. A man claimed that
a shipment of cloth had been allowed to sit on the dock for several days and
been discoloured by the sun; he sued for twenty times its retail value.
Another man claimed his warehouse had been undermined by the Nile
flood and blamed the government for not preventing it; he demanded a
sum that would have paid for ten new warehouses. In each of these instances
the plaintiff's consul would appear at the Citadel and demand payment.
Said, preoccupied with yet another field exercise, would wave his hand and
order the matter settled. Because of the uncertainty of auditing practices
then in use, it is impossible to estimate how much money was extracted
from Egypt during this period, but one statistic offers some intimation:
during Said's reign, the number of foreigners in Egypt rose at the rate of
some 30,000 a year. Few were attracted by the climate, or the proximity to
the Valley of the Kings.

Far and away the happiest recipient of the news of Said's ascendancy to the
throne was Ferdinand de Lesseps, who through no fault of his own had
been retired from the service of his country and had passed the previous
five years as a country squire, managing La Chenaie, his mother-in-law's
estate in the Loire valley.

Some families are in banking, others in the military or the theatre. The
de Lesseps were in diplomacy. One or another had represented the interests
of France in foreign courts since the time of Louis XV. Ferdinand was born
at Versailles on November 19th, 1805, and grew up as a diplomatic brat,
learning good manners, how to sit a horse well, and what to say to a dowager
countess. At 19, he was appointed to his first post, as a lowly secretary in
Lisbon. Then followed Syria, Tunis, and finally Egypt. He was a vice-
consul in Alexandria when Enfantin made his appearance there and, in the
tradition of vice-consuls everywhere, was assigned the duty of shepherding
this rather peculiar visitor. He remained in Egypt until 1837, rising to the

rank of Consul-General. After that it was Rotterdam, Malaga and Barce-lona. Here, he dutifully made a point of being nice to a family of obscure, distant Spanish cousins among whom was an unusually pretty little ten-year-old girl named Eugénie de Montijo. His career, which until then had followed a smooth course, came to a sudden end in 1848 when, as Minister Plenipotentiary in Rome, he fell foul of the complex power struggle un-leashed by the Revolution. He was 49 years old, with nothing more impor-tant to do than repair the roof of an old manor house when, on September 15th, 1854, word about Said reached him. As he later wrote:

> I was busy among carpenters and masons ... when the postman appeared. Great was my surprise to learn of the advent to power of the friend of our youth, the intelligent and sympathetic Muhammed Said. ... I hastened to write a letter of congratulations. I told him that political conditions at home had given me the leisure to present my respects to him in person. ...

The letter immediately elicited an invitation. On November 7th, de Lesseps was in Alexandria; four days later he was in the middle of the Libyan desert, reliving old times with Said who, as usual, was putting his army through field exercises.

It was not a difficult sale to make; de Lesseps had had many years to review his arguments, and Said was not disposed to be critical. As de Lesseps recalls it:

> At five o'clock I rode to the Viceroy's tent. ... He grasped my hand and bade me sit beside him. We were alone. My studies and reflec-tions about the Canal passed rapidly through my mind. I felt I had such complete knowledge of my subject that it would be easy for me to inoculate the Prince with the same supreme confidence I felt. I therefore set forth my ideas without entering into details. Said followed with interest. I entreated him that if any lingering doubts beset him, he should do me the honour to let me hear them. He put to me with rare judgment several pertinent questions. My replies must have satisfied, for he turned to me and said: 'You have convinced me. I accept your plan. During the remainder of the trip we will discuss ways and means of bringing it about. The matter is settled. You may count on me.'

The two friends returned to Cairo on November 23rd, and exactly a week later their agreement was formally signed. It began:

> Our friend M. Ferdinand de Lesseps having called our attention to the advantage which would result to Egypt from the junction of the Mediterranean with the Red Sea by a passage navigable by large vessels ... we have accepted his suggestions and have given him and

do give him by these presents the exclusive power of constituting and directing a company. ...

The document then went on to define the terms of the contract, which any modern court of equity would probably reject as being tantamount to fraud perpetrated on an irresponsible idiot. Edward Dicey, a British journalist, wrote: 'Never has there been a concession so profitable to the grantee and so costly to the grantor, as that given by Said to the Suez Company.'*

If Said was the most incompetent man in the world to grant the Concession, de Lesseps was close to the least qualified to whom it should have been entrusted. He had no engineering training whatever, and no understanding of the technical problems involved; he had no business experience and had never tried to put together a large company, much less run it; he had no close connections with any of the great European banking houses which were the logical sources for his capital. He did have one high trump card which was to prove useful: on January 29th, 1852, his little Spanish cousin had married Napoleon III and become Empress of France.

He also had the Concession, and for four years he travelled tirelessly across Europe trying to raise money on it. The Rothschilds listened and intimated that they could handle the matter – de Lesseps was trying to raise 200 million francs – in consideration for 5 per cent. De Lesseps turned this down as outrageous. In the end, he sold a little more than half the shares and unloaded the rest, 177,642 out of 400,000, on his good friend Said.

The course selected for the canal ran from Suez in the south through two natural lakes and a long straight line to the sea. Here, the ceremonial turning of the first spadeful took place on April 25th, 1859. No more desolate setting for it could be imagined: a low, featureless sandbar with salt marshes on one side and empty desert on the other. But one day, the visionary de Lesseps knew, a great harbour city would grow here, and it would need a name. He had an appropriate one ready: Port Said.

Meanwhile, almost forgotten in the excitement over the canal, work on the railway had continued. Starting from Alexandria, it had reached kilometre 104, on the Nile, at the time Abbas met his untimely end. Two years later, in 1856, it was in Cairo, where a magnificent new five-track station had been built to receive it. The 144-kilometre spur to Suez was finished quickly, with funds made available by Britain. This kindness was prompted not by any desire to gain favour with Said but, again, by considerations totally irrelevant to Africa: the Sepoy mutiny had broken out in

---

* Among other conditions, it gave the Company rights to all land bordering the canal for a width of two miles; it specified that Egypt was to supply, at its cost, four-fifths of the labour; it absolved the Company from paying taxes, and it provided that Egypt should receive only 15 per cent of the profits, after all charges had been deducted.

India in 1857, and it was necessary to transport large numbers of troops as rapidly as possible to deal with it.

The locomotives were, naturally, British – type 2–4–0, made by Robert Stephenson and Co. – as was the rest of the rolling stock: 111 passenger and 514 freight cars. In fairness, they were well built; many were still in service at the time of World War I. Fares were reasonable, and the service generally good and reliable. The 120-mile trip from Cairo to Alexandria took approximately seven hours, including a six-minute crossing of the Nile by special ferry at Kafr-el-Zayat. On May 14th, 1858, this ferry – actually nothing more than a flat barge 80 feet long on which the carriages were transported one at a time across the 400-yard-wide river – was to play a decisive role in Egyptian history. The members of the viceregal family had spent the day with Said at his palace in Alexandria and were returning to Cairo by special train when a tragic accident occurred. It was normal practice to secure the wheels of the carriage with chains during the crossing, but just this once the precaution was overlooked and a carriage fell into the water, carrying with it Prince Ahmed, heir-apparent to the throne. Fat, clumsy, and unable to swim, Ahmed drowned, putting his brother Ismail – they were both sons of Ibrahim – next in line.

Having performed his unwitting disservice to his country – the harm, financial and political, which the Canal caused Egypt is yet to be calculated – Said remained on the throne for another four years. They were not happy: the foreign vultures became more daring in their demands and insolent in their manner; the military games began to pall. On January 18th, 1863, at the age of 41, Said died.

Edwin de Leon, the American consul, noted: 'He had mounted the throne a gay, hopeful, ardent man with vigorous health, boundless power and almost inexhaustible wealth. He left it but nine years later for a premature grave; his strength wasted by disease and trouble; hope, fortune, friends all lost.'

It was the last occasion any foreigner would have for some time to be condescending towards an Egyptian ruler. Ismail had been waiting in the wings; over the next sixteen years he proceeded to earn, to the last gaudy touch, his epithet of 'The Magnificent'.

There is a parochial tendency among westerners to think of Progress – the kind of progress which vaults continents, humbles nature, amasses fortune and leaves indelible traces – as a peculiarly western attribute, personified by men such as Vanderbilt, Krupp, Nobel, the elder Rockefeller, and of course Cecil Rhodes himself, the epitome of the Builder. Possibly, the historic reputation of Mohammed Ali has suffered from this bias. As regards his grandson, Ismail, there should be no doubt: non-western in his reasoning and instincts, he nevertheless saw himself as a Builder – an attitude which led him to post slogans from Smiles's *Self-Help* on the walls of his palaces, and order that clothes closets be installed in his harem. And on the record, and despite the concerted efforts of a generation of self-serving memorialists who tried to paint him as a profligate voluptuary, he was a Builder – right down to his highly-developed sense of acquisitiveness.

Educated in Europe and a graduate of St Cyr, he was at the time of his ascension to the throne 33 years old and the wealthiest man in Egypt. Mohammed Ali had taken Egypt's land merely to distribute it; Ismail acquired, outright and for his own profit, one-fifth of all the arable soil in the country. Mohammed Ali had been obliged to monopolize Egypt's trade and industry, but the fruits of his success largely returned to the national treasury. Under Ismail, the distinction between his personal revenues and those of the state grew hazy, and in time vanished altogether. In laying out Egypt's network of railways, he consulted the best engineers, then decided on routes which led past sugar refineries and cotton mills which he happened to own.

But all this was still in the future. On January 20th, 1863, it was an earnest, slightly portly man, a 'thrifty, saving landlord', who formally received the diplomatic corps at the Citadel, and addressed them in flawless French: 'I am firmly decided to devote to the prosperity of the country that I am called upon to govern all the perseverance and all the energy which I possess. The basis of all good administration is order and economy in finance; I shall seek this order and economy by every means possible.'

He then went on to say that he himself would set the example by abandoning the casual practices of his predecessors and establish a civil list which he would, under no circumstances, exceed. He promised to apply his energy to agriculture, and therefore to abolish the *corvée* – the system of mass enforced labour which Mohammed Ali had instituted in order to get his canals dug, and which had the consequence of reducing crops by taking away the hands available to till them.

In all, it was a measured, statesmanlike address. After the dizzying succession of Mohammed Ali, Ibrahim, Abbas and Said, all within 15 years, the foreign consuls, standing uncomfortably in full-dress uniforms, could only guess what this new viceroy would be like. Ismail's speech reassured them – all but one. Before the dean of the corps could deliver the traditional reply, de Beauval, the French Consul, interrupted with a question. Did His Highness's reference to the *corvée* signify his intention of interfering with work then proceeding on the Canal? Both he and Ismail, and every other man in the room, knew that, in accordance with the terms of the Concession, Egypt had been providing most of the labour for the project – an obligation which was requiring the use of one out of every three ablebodied men in the country.

'I have never supposed, Monsieur de Beauval,' Ismail replied, 'that France would countenance forced labour, on its own soil or any other.'

More formally, he wrote to the Frenchman:

I do not like this de Lesseps's concession. There is too much *'mon ami'* about it. My uncle signed it without reading it. ... He sacrificed Egypt to his chum, Ferdinand de Lesseps. I am prepared to deal liberally with that charming gentleman, but I must think of my country first. This concession is illegal ... I intend to fight it until it is adequately amended.

This decision took the matter out of local hands and into international courts, where it hung for eighteen months. Finally, it was agreed to put the matter to arbitration before – of all people – Napoleon III of France. On July 6th, 1864, he announced his decision. According to a contemporary comment, 'It astonished the jurists of all Europe and, had it not been of so serious a character, would have been regarded as a judicial curiosity.' It would have been less of a curiosity and source of astonishment had the jurists of Europe recalled that in addition to being Emperor of France, Napoleon III was also husband of Eugénie de Montijo.

Under the terms of the decision the contract was binding. Egypt was excused from some of its most blatantly unfair provisions, but, in exchange, was obliged to indemnify the Canal Company to the amount of 84 million francs – a colossal amount under any circumstance, but staggering to a country as poor as Egypt.

Ismail had exhausted his legal resources, and learnt a lesson: that it did not pay for non-Europeans – Ismail would never for an instant have thought of himself as an African, although that is what he was in the eyes of Paris and London – to attempt to deal on equal terms with European governments; the results would be insult, humiliation and, in the end, an expensive drubbing.

There were, however, individual Europeans who were more than willing to talk business with Ismail. The cotton which Mohammed Ali had introduced into Egypt had become one of its most steady, most dependable sources of income. With the advent of the American Civil War in 1861, moreover, its value had risen sharply. With five-sixths of their normal sources of supply cut off by the Northern blockade, the spinning mills of Manchester slowed down and in time stopped completely. Deprived of their miserable wages, people starved in the streets of the North, but meanwhile, on the docks of Liverpool, the price of Egyptian long-staple began to soar. It had been $6\frac{1}{2}$ pence a pound early in 1861; by late October it had risen to 12. In August 1862, it hit $26\frac{1}{2}$. Desperate attempts were made to grow cotton elsewhere – Spain, Australia, even the Fiji Islands. All of them failed, and each discouraging report fed the speculative fever. By the time Ismail came to power, Egypt's annual cotton crop had quintupled in value and *fellahin* all over the country were abandoning other crops to grow more of the wonderful white blossoms.

Ismail had been a successful businessman before he became a ruler. It took him little time to discover that any number of people would be delighted to lend him money. Unlike diplomatic officers, they were willing to remove their hats, bow, scrape, and only charge 7 or 8 per cent. The first loan, placed on September 24th, 1864, with Frueling and Geschen, of London, was for £5·7 million sterling, and Ismail, like many borrowers after him, discovered that 7 per cent, discounted, actually came closer to 13 per cent. Two years later, there was another loan, through Anglo-Egyptian this time, for £3·3 million sterling, at 9 per cent discounted. The Civil War had ended and the price of cotton subsided, but other arrangements could always be made: in 1868, Oppenheim, Alberti et Compagnie, of Paris, came through with £11·9 million, and accepted the Egyptian railway system and its revenues as collateral. In less than four years, the thrifty landlord had become the champion borrower of all time. Naturally, as his indebtedness grew, the terms became less favourable. Ismail's last loan, in 1873 and again with Oppenheim, was in the face amount of £32 million sterling, of which he realized only £17 million.

It is this borrowing spree which earned Ismail the opprobrium of a certain group of historians. Cromer, like the banker he was, merely sets out the numbers in his *Modern Egypt*, and assumes that any reasonable man will draw his own conclusion: 'In 1863, the public debt of Egypt amounted to £3,293,000. In 1876, the funded debt amounted to £68,110,000. In addition to this, there was a floating debt of £26,000,000.'

Milner goes further in his *England in Egypt*: 'Ismail ... is as fine a type of the spendthrift as can well be found, whether in history or in fiction. No equally reckless prodigal ever possessed equally unlimited control of equally vast resources.'

There is no question that Ismail spent a lot of money – exactly how much is still a topic for doctoral dissertations. But as in all shopping sprees, it is more interesting to inspect the purchases than to total the bills. Ismail's list included, in wholesale lots, public improvements of every kind: 5,200 miles of telegraph line; 910 miles of new railways, reaching southwards from Cairo 231 miles to Assiut and including the first line in the Sudan; 420 bridges (including one at Kafr-el-Zayat to replace the ferry which had brought him to the throne); pavement and sewers for most of the main streets of Alexandria, as well as running water throughout the city; 8,400 miles of new irrigation canals; 15 new lighthouses; 4,685 elementary schools, including the first girls' school in the Moslem world; institutes, libraries and faculties of every kind, as well as more than a dozen newspapers and periodicals.

This, however, was like buying underwear or kitchen utensils: sound, practical purchases, but not likely to impress visiting company; and impressing company – European company – was essential to the achievement of Ismail's plan. He had had five years – the period between the unfortunate railway accident and Said's death – to think about what he would do when he became viceroy. What he settled on was to complete the work started by Mohammed Ali: to amputate Egypt once and for all from the decaying Ottoman Empire and graft it on to the political body of Europe, while at the same time making it the dominant power of a slowly stirring Africa. How Rhodes, or other Builders, would have tackled the job makes for interesting conjecture. Ismail, remembering that Mohammed Ali had twice unsuccessfully tried to do it by force, resolved instead to do it with showmanship and some fancy gilt mirrors.

His first opportunity came in 1867. Paris was to play host that year to a world's fair, the newest fad in the international game of one-upmanship. Napoleon III cordially invited Egypt to participate in the *Exposition Universelle*, for which an area of 41 acres had been set aside along the Champ de Mars. Ismail accepted.

Other countries were satisfied with folkloric exhibits – Swiss chalets, a model Belgian village – or with displays of their technological virtuosity. Ismail ordered erected in the heart of Paris three magnificent pavillions, occupying an area of 60,000 square feet and, together, representing the golden ages of Egyptian history. The first was a Pharaonic temple, designed expressly by Mariette, the great Egyptologist, as a 'living lesson in archaeology'. A double alley of sphinxes led to a massive portico decorated with statuary and murals depicting scenes from the life of Ptolemy; inside was a peristyle done in the style of the pre-Christian era, ringed with columns whose capitals recorded the military conquests of antiquity; the inner chamber, a faithful copy of a tomb from the Fifth Dynasty, contained frescoes of hunting and fishing scenes, and reproductions of village life. Thus, according to the guidebook prepared by M. Mariette, 'the visitor, in a few paces, could pass through 40 centuries of history.' The second building was a Saracen *selamlik*, a gem-like palace of contrasting white and sky-blue stone carved to the delicacy of lace and surmounted by a golden cupola. Inside was a great hall, modelled like St Sophia in the shape of a Greek cross; light filtered in through tiny windows near the roof; every inch of floor, walls and ceiling was covered with inlaid stone, rare marquetry and silver filigreed stalactites set off against gold and alabaster backgrounds. The furnishings were equally sumptuous, for this room was to serve as Ismail's private hideaway during his visits to the Exposition. The third pavilion was a contemporary *okel*, a combination of covered bazaar, inn, atelier and storehouse. As a contrast to the other two buildings – for it was intended to represent the new, business-like Egypt – the *okel* was made of simple brick, graceful but utilitarian. Inside, around a central court, opened small shops in which artisans plied their crafts in leather, jewels, gold, straw, silk, wood and bronze. Souvenirs could be purchased; there was also a barber's shop, and an outdoor café. Upstairs was a museum which, among other attractions, offered a collection of 500 mummified skulls, a 150-foot-square relief map of Egypt on which were traced such landmarks as the route taken by Moses when he led the children of Israel, and a sample of virtually every object produced in Egypt, from fermented dates and rose water to cannons and gunpowder. The *okel* occupied the extreme corner of the fair-grounds; as the visitor stepped out, he was treated to one final wonder. Lying peaceably at anchor on the Seine, just off the Pont d'Iéna, was a *dahabiah*, one of the long, graceful boats used for travel up and down the Nile. It had been towed across the Mediterranean and was authentic in every detail, from its 14-man crew in their white uniforms and red tarbooshes, to the charcoal stove in the galley and the gilded crocodile carved as figurehead into its prow.

The newly-named Khedive Ismail – he had just purchased the title, which was the Persian word for 'sovereign', from the Sultan – sailed from Alexandria on June 10th aboard his private yacht, the *Mahroussa*, and landed in Toulon on the 15th, where he was accorded a salvo from the shore batteries and all the honours due a visiting Head of State. In Paris, which he reached the following evening, he was greeted at the Gare de Lyon by Baron Haussmann, prefect of the Seine, an honour guard of the 43rd Infantry regiment, and the full complement of 52 Egyptian students then doing their graduate work in France. An imperial carriage, escorted by mounted lancers, carried him to the Louvre palace, where apartments had been prepared for him and his retinue. His first call was on the Empress, who received him in full regalia; the Emperor, the newspapers noted, had reluctantly absented himself because of a sudden attack of rheumatism.

The next twenty days were a continuous round of receptions, balls and ceremonies carefully balancing culture (*Don Carlos* at the Opera), the martial arts (a full-dress review of the Paris garrison), business (repeated visits to the fair and formal calls from the principal bankers of France) and just plain fun (an evening-long banquet offered by the City of Paris, which for this occasion had caused the massive Hôtel de Ville to be transformed into a charming verdant grotto, complete with flowering shrubs and three working waterfalls). Napoleon III, recovered from his indisposition, called on the Khedive on the 19th, and the two became almost inseparable, lunching at Versailles or watching the steeplechases at Vincennes. Somewhere during this giddy whirl, Ismail managed to call at his tailor to order fourteen dozen pairs of trousers, eight dozen jackets and as many frock coats, and also to present the Empress with a small box containing earth from around the base of the tree under which the Virgin was reputed to have rested during her flight into Egypt.

The *Exposition Universelle* was a tremendous success, setting a new attendance record of 6,805,967, and the Egyptian exhibit easily eclipsed all the others in the eyes of both the crowds and the judges, who showered it with three gold medals, four silvers and more than a dozen bronzes. The Khedive took advantage of this new esteem to advance, in every way he could, the notion of Egyptian autonomy. For example, an international monetary conference was being held in Paris, to which Egypt had not been invited. Ismail insisted that, since his country minted its own currency independently of the Sultan, it should be permitted to send a representative. In reply, M. de Moustier, the French Foreign Minister, apologized for the unintended slight, accepted the credentials of an Egyptian delegate, and reminded the Khedive politely but firmly that France did not care what kind of money he used so long as he paid his debts on time.

London had, with careful impartiality, been placed next on Ismail's itinerary. After his reception in Paris, however, it proved to be something of a disappointment. To begin with, the Channel crossing was unseasonably rough. Then, the British protocol officials chose to be stuffy. Because Ismail was not, technically speaking, a Chief of State but merely a high-ranking subject of the Sultan, no more elaborate provision had been made for his stay than the reservation of a suite of rooms at a commercial hotel – Claridge's, to be sure, but nevertheless a come-down from the Louvre palace. Fortunately at the last minute a proper town residence, Dudley House, was emptied and put at his disposal. The official programme again included culture (Covent Garden this time, and *Fra Diavolo*), the military (the First Battalion of Scottish Guards, with pipers and banners), business (meetings with the directors of the Peninsular and Oriental, and the Manchester Cotton Supply Association), and assorted civic ceremonies. But a train ride from Paddington to Windsor and luncheon with its august occupant was no match for proper French *cuisine*, nor did the Royal Agricultural Society's display at Bury St Edmunds measure up to Versailles. The press, too, was far less friendly. The Paris papers had run long, flattering accounts of Ismail's comings and goings, and *Le Journal des Débats* had reminded its readers of the hospitality which Egypt had traditionally accorded French travellers since the time of Bonaparte. On Ismail's arrival in London, *The Times* merely noted that he was 'gracious', but observed that he 'remained impassive and scarcely interested in anything around him'.

Ismail left London on July 19th, stopped in Paris for some last-minute shopping – 81 embroidered ladies' silk gowns at a total cost of 47,000 francs – and proceeded to Vichy, where he spent three weeks resting and taking the waters. He returned home on September 16th, after stopping off in Constantinople to pay his respects to the Sultan. A surprise awaited him: all the public buildings in Alexandria and Cairo had been illuminated in his honour, and the festivities which had been prepared lasted for three days. Their cost was later estimated to have been in excess of one million francs.

The rest of that year and all of the next – 1868 – were occupied with financial crisis, internal troubles arising from Ismail's attempts to curtail the extra-territorial rights of foreign residents,* and expensive setbacks in the attempted colonization of the Sudan. It was probably with some relief therefore that, in May 1869, the Khedive packed his bags and again set off for Europe. This time, the itinerary was more elaborate because the main purpose of the trip was to drop off personal invitations to what Ismail confidently expected would be his greatest performance: the opening of the Suez Canal. He had not wanted the Canal, out of the same appreciation of *Weltpolitik* which had given pause to Mohammed Ali, and also for hard-headed economic reasons understandable to any businessman: to dig it under the terms of de Lesseps's concession, even as amended by Napoleon III, would bleed the entire Egyptian economy dry, and was in fact doing just that. The *Compagnie Universelle du Canal Maritime de Suez* had platoons of lawyers who, with the aid of French consular officials and constant pressure from Paris, fought to enforce every syllable of the contract. As a result it had been impossible to eliminate the *corvée*, and vast areas of arable land lay untended because tens of thousands of peasants were obliged mindlessly to move sand. Left no choice, Ismail decided to turn the project to his advantage.

In the biography commissioned by King Fuad I, Ismail's son and the first ruler of an independent Egypt, the Khedive's reasoning is given as follows:

> Ismail foresaw clearly that the achievement of the great work ... heralded the entrance of Egypt into the mainstream of international affairs. ... [and] determined to derive from this grandiose accomplishment the greatest possible credit. ... Thus he insisted that the inaugural ceremonies be carried on in a manner to impress the imagination of the participants, and that of generations to come.

If he failed, it was not for want of trying. There was first the matter of the guest list. Ismail's tour took him to Venice, Florence, Berlin, Paris, London and Brussels, and he also sent personal emissaries to The Hague and to the Livadia Palace in Yalta, where Tsar Alexander and his family were spending the summer. The results were gratifying: acceptances from Empress Eugénie, who was to be the principal attraction of the festivities; the Austro-Hungarian Emperor; the Royal Prince of Prussia, the brother of the King of Holland; the Duke of Aosta, son of Victor Emmanuel of Savoy. Many sovereigns – conspicuously Alexander – declined for fear of offending the Sultan, who had not been invited. Great Britain, not unexpectedly, stayed away, and President Ulysses S. Grant sent his regrets, explaining that he could not undertake to assume such an honour without the consent of Congress, which would not convene until December. Nevertheless, Ismail did not need to resort to his second-string list, which included personages less

---

* According to custom dating back to the sixteenth century and jealously guarded by their consul-generals, foreigners were exempt from taxation, and not subject to Egyptian law, civil or criminal.

in need of impressing, such as the Shah of Persia, the Sultan of Morocco and the Bey of Tunis. As he wrote happily to his principal minister, Nubar Pasha, it was necessary to limit himself. 'With the most earnest of good will,' he said, 'and making full use of my resources, I can only place eight palaces at the disposal of the sovereigns and princes who wish to honour me with their presence.'

The programme of ceremonies was, in a word, exhaustive. The official date for the opening of the Canal was November 17th, 1869, but the first guests arrived in Alexandria on October 15th. They included the press corps, all of whose expenses were graciously picked up by the Khedive, and a fair sampling of literary notables: Zola, Théophile Gautier, Ibsen.

Gautier in particular fell into the spirit of the occasion and paid his passage with some evocative descriptions. About the train ride from Alexandria to Cairo, now a mere four-hour trip, he noted:

> Many of the voyagers had equipped themselves as for a journey to the upper reaches of the Nile. Despite the fact that the temperature was no higher than in Marseilles, they wore white linen helmets with veils and neck-pieces to shield themselves against the sun. And, lest this not be adequate, a blue length of cloth was rolled turban-fashion around this peculiar headgear.

On October 22nd, after four days of partying in Cairo, a group of 100 select guests – scholars, scientists, artists, businessmen and members of Paris's elite Jockey Club and their ladies – left for a three-week trip up the Nile as far as Aswan and the great temple of Philae. Steamers to transport them had been provided by the Khedive.

Meanwhile, the important guests began arriving. First was the Empress Eugénie, whose Imperial yacht, *L'Aigle*, dropped anchor in Alexandria early on the morning of the 22nd. The Khedive immediately went aboard to greet her, but was told that she had not yet issued from her apartment; discreetly, he left and came back two hours later. Then, with the entire French colony of Alexandria lining the streets, the two sovereigns proceeded to the railway station, one wearing a simple grey dress with a tiny straw hat, the other in *tenue de ville*, without decorations. For Eugénie, the next year would bring Sedan, deposition, and the start of an exile that was to last fifty years and be marked by widowhood and the loss of her only son. But for the next month, she was to be Empress not only of France, but of the Arabian Nights as well. There were to be trips on the Nile such as Cleopatra might have enjoyed and sight-seeing in grand style – a chalet had been built expressly for her use at the foot of the Great Pyramid, which Ismail showed her in the glow of a magnificent fireworks display.

By November 15th, with the arrival of the Emperor of Austria and the Prince of Prussia – Vienna made sure to beat Berlin by several hours – the cast was complete. Off the sandbar where, ten years earlier, de Lesseps had turned a shovelful of dirt there now lay a fleet of eighty ships, flying every flag of Europe and completely filling the harbour. Ashore, the ceremonies began with a joint Moslem-Christian religious service, the first ever held, conceived by the Khedive as a symbol of the brotherhood of man before God. Afterwards, an Egyptian honour guard greeted the guests – royalty, M. de Lesseps and members of the administrative council of the *Compagnie*, the senior officers of the vessels in port, ambassadors, consuls, members of the clergies. According to the account in the *Journal Officiel*:

> An enormous crowd covered the beach, a multitude come from every corner of the world and presenting the most brilliant and varied spectacles. All races were represented. One saw men of the Orient, dressed in resplendent colours, chiefs of African tribes enveloped in their great mantles, Circassians in military dress, officers of the Anglo-Indian army in their sun helmets, Hungarian magnates in their national costumes.

After a night spent aboard their ships or in Port Said,* the guests were finally permitted to do what they had come for. At eight thirty in the morning, with the *Aigle* leading the way, the great procession of ships began its voyage to the Red Sea. There had been the inevitable last-minute accident: during the night, the Egyptian corvette *Latif*, which had been sent ahead, managed to run aground; Ismail himself rushed to the scene and personally oversaw its removal and the re-positioning of the navigational buoys. No other difficulties developed; one by one the flotilla entered the canal, at ten-minute intervals. There was a moment's anxiety aboard the *Aigle* when it was discovered that M. de Lesseps, who had been standing on the bridge next to the Empress, had disappeared. A search of the ship found him, fast asleep in one of the cabins.

The first day's trip terminated at four o'clock on the southern tip of Lake Timseh, roughly halfway to Suez. Here too, a new city was in process of being built. Although it had already been named – with irresistible logic – Ismailia, it still consisted of tents and unpaved streets. The only edifice of note was the palace which Ismail had commissioned in which to offer a banquet to his assembled guests who, including the self-invited, numbered between four and five thousand. The sovereigns worked their way through an eighteen-course meal in a special salon which had been reserved for them; the rest scrambled to get something to eat. Improvised kitchens had been set up in the desert surrounding the city, and 500 cooks and 1,000 waiters recruited from restaurants as far away as Leghorn and Genoa.

---

* The city had not lived up to de Lesseps's hopes. One visitor noted that 'In its impoverished character and in the habits of its population, which are entirely given to money-grubbing and crude amusements, it is like a San Francisco in miniature. One sees storehouses, factories and brothels side by side ... with a Casino at which people come to lose at night the money they may have made during the day.'

While in the palace the Empress, now dressed in a gown of cerise satin covered with silver stars, accepted the arm of the Austrian Emperor for the *grand défilé*, less fortunate guests consoled themselves with the knowledge that of drink there was no limit.

The rest of the trip became somewhat disorganized. Some of the guests, after their long night, chose to remain in bed; others headed back for Cairo and some, in disgust, for home. But the *Aigle* resolutely took her place at the head of the line and, having made another overnight stop, steamed out of the canal and into the Red Sea on the morning of the 20th. In her log, her captain entered: 'Dropped anchor in the Gulf of Suez at eleven thirty in the morning.' Empress Eugénie added her signature to this entry, and graciously requested de Lesseps to do the same.

There were more activities scheduled in Cairo, including horse races, and a little stag dinner to demonstrate the talents of a noted belly-dancer whose speciality was a number in which she pretended to escape from an enraged bee. For mixed company there was the opening of the new Opera House (not with *Aida*, which had been commissioned for the occasion but finished two years too late, but with the same composer's *Rigoletto*), the new Theatre and the new Circus. Also, since no full-dress occasion of the period would have been complete without it, there was a balloon ascent, under the direction of the noted Parisian aeronaut M. Poilay. (He took off from the centre of Cairo, heading for the Pyramids, but was blown twenty miles in the wrong direction.) After that, all that remained for Ismail was the chore of seeing the remaining dignitaries off to Alexandria, and on their way back to Europe.

He had every reason to feel pleased with himself. That the two months of festivities had 'impressed the imagination of the participants' was unquestionable; measured in sheer ostentation, nothing like it had been seen since the days of Louis XIV, or possibly Nero's Rome. The guests had been punctilious in treating the Khedive as a peer; no mention had been made of the absent Sultan. Cairo itself – or at least large sections of it – had become a full-fledged European city, a regular stopover for the jet set of the day. In addition to the new theatres and public buildings, wide avenues had been cut through the maze of ancient streets – in emulation of the same Baron Haussmann who had greeted Ismail in Paris. A marshy swamp had been filled in and turned into a splendid public garden, and new residential suburbs were growing rapidly. The final certification of the city's new status came when a French visitor complained that rents were exorbitant, but that nevertheless new houses were being snapped up faster than they could be built.

All this, and Ismail's other projects, had cost enormous amounts of money, and the pinch on his finances, at first nagging, became uncomfortable. The Suez Canal had turned out to be an immediate commercial success, but unfortunately the Concession had been amended in such a way that none of the revenues accrued to its major shareholder who, in 1875, was obliged to sell out.

The purchaser, as is well known, was Benjamin Disraeli, who, without taking the time to secure Parliamentary approval, negotiated a personal loan of £3,976,582 from his friend Nathan Rothschild to complete the transaction. It gave Britain an interest in Egyptian internal affairs and, providentially, control of the canal which she had so long and so myopically opposed. For Ismail, however, the relief was only temporary. The money went quickly, and after it was gone British voices joined the French chorus in hounding him to pay his debts.

The clothes on Ismail's back may have been Parisian, but the blood in his veins was unadulteratedly Turkish. Needing to remain solvent, he tried to play one creditor off against the other: a message went to London, requesting 'the services of gentlemen to superintend the receipts and revenues of the country'. Ismail could hardly imagine that Paris, confronted with this threat to its position, would not make some sort of counter-offer. Again, he miscalculated western mentality by failing to appreciate the ability of money to erase national differences. The Europeans disagreed on methods: the French would have confiscated the Pyramids, if only there were means to cart them away; the British were disposed to keep the goose alive while it could still lay eggs. They compromised by sending Ismail a joint commission of gentlemen: a Frenchman to supervise collections, and an Englishman – Sir Evelyn Baring, later Lord Cromer – to oversee disbursements.

Iron-fisted tax collectors were dispatched into the provinces. The due date for every coupon became the occasion for a new crisis. In 1878, it seemed as if nature itself was conspiring against Ismail: the Nile flood had been unusually low, with the result that 800,000 acres of land which could have been cultivated had to be left fallow; in addition, an epidemic broke out among the cattle. By midsummer, famine such as had not been known in Egypt for generations gripped the country. A British official, sent to make a survey, reported: 'It is almost incredible the distances travelled by women and children begging from village to village. ... The poor were in some instances reduced to such extremities of hunger that they were driven to satisfy their cravings with the refuse and garbage of the streets.'

City dwellers fared no better; civil servants, who made up a large part of the working force, had not been paid for months; shopkeepers closed and went out of business.

Nevertheless, another payment came due and the tax collectors again went out. The money was raised, but, as Cromer wrote: 'The great diversity of currency and the fact that many of the coins were strung together to be used as ornaments bore testimony to the pressure which had been used in their collection.'

Early in 1879, political unrest exploded in the streets of Cairo for the first time since Mohammed Ali had consolidated his power. On February 18th a group of 2,500 Army officers who had been cashiered without pay staged a demonstration during the course of which several public officials were mistreated. Order was restored only through the personal intervention of the Khedive, who, sceptics immediately claimed, had instigated the trouble in the first place. If they are right – and there is evidence to support it – Ismail can be credited with having invented a peculiarly Arab form of political expression which future rulers would perfect to a fine degree. For him, however, it was in the nature of a last hurrah; if he had hoped to prove that he, and only he, could rule his hot-blooded subjects, the demonstration failed to impress the Europeans.

Guarded conversations had already begun in Paris and London, exploring ways in which Ismail could be removed from the throne. On May 15th, 1879, a new voice made itself heard: the German Ambassador in London informed the Foreign Office that the German Consul-General in Cairo had been instructed to lodge a formal protest about certain acts which the German Government deemed prejudicial to its nationals. Until now Germany – which is to say Bismarck – had been satisfied to sit by and let the French and British wrestle with Ismail. The May 15th note was merely diplomatic jargon to say that if the French and British now wished to kick Ismail out, Germany would not only withhold objection, but would lend its considerable weight to the enterprise. With Europe united – Vienna had ceased to be a Power, and Russia was for the moment busy in the Far East – Ismail's days were numbered.

The Sultan, to whom the Powers addressed themselves, had no affection for the man who had repeatedly snubbed him and whose avowed goal it was to rob him of one of his most profitable provinces. On June 26th, Ismail received a telegram – sent over the line he himself had built – addressed 'To the Ex-Khedive, Ismail Pasha,' and reading in part: 'It has been demonstrated that your continued occupancy of the position of Khedive can have no other consequence than to aggravate the present difficulties. In consequence, His Imperial Majesty the Sultan ... has decided to name to the office of Khedive His Excellency Mohammed Tewfik Pasha. ... '

An eyewitness described the receipt of the telegram: Ismail read it, folded it carefully and ordered that Tewfik, his eldest son, be sent for. As soon as he appeared, Ismail crossed the great hall to greet him, knelt and kissed his hand, saying, 'I salute you, my sovereign.' Then he rose, kissed him on both cheeks, blessed him, wished him good luck and left. Cromer, not given to sentimentality, writes that 'The scene is said to have been affecting.'

The following day, Ismail presented himself at the palace and waited his turn to sign the list of those who had come to congratulate the new ruler. This done, he packed his things, collected a few friends, some favourite wives, and three million francs in cash, and left Cairo for the last time. He had hoped to spend his remaining years – he was only 49 years old, and in excellent health – in Constantinople, but the Sultan would not hear of it. Fortunately, his good friend Victor Emmanuel of Italy had a suitable villa – *La Favorita*, at the foot of Mount Vesuvius – which he was honoured to put at his permanent disposal.

The departure was, again according to Cromer, 'dignified':

> ... On arrival in Alexandria, Ismail Pasha embarked on board his yacht, the *Mahroussa* ... whose decks were crowded with officials and European residents who had come to take leave. His Highness met everyone with marked respect and consideration. Though his features bore traces of strong recent emotion, he bore up manfully, and was quite cheerful, addressing a pleasant word of thanks to everyone who took leave of him.

Ismail had another sixteen years to live. His last request, made shortly before he died on March 2nd, 1895, was that he be allowed to end his days in the land of his birth. It was denied.

In his summary of Ismail's career, Cromer makes much of hubris – 'Ismail had power, rank and a degree of wealth,' he writes, 'such as has been given to few individuals. With reasonable prudence he could have satisfied every legitimate ambition and left a name which posterity could have revered.' Then he adds: 'Any chance moralist who may have watched the *Mahroussa* steaming out of Alexandria harbour on that summer afternoon must perforce have heaved a sigh over one of the most striking instances that the world has ever known of golden opportunity lost.'

Cromer was not entirely right in stating that Ismail's ambitions had been unsatisfied. He had wanted to lead Egypt away from Asia and align it with Europe. He achieved the first goal and only narrowly missed the second; Egypt had become, if not a European nation, at least a European colony. He had wanted Egypt to become a predominant power in Africa and started it on that course; this too happened, but not in the manner nor under the flag Ismail had envisioned.

But the greatest gift which he gave his country – one which not even Mohammed Ali had had it in his power to make, and which was worth every penny of the 100 million pounds, give or take a few millions, he spent – was something it had never had before. Somewhere between the fancy dress balls and fancier displays, the fireworks and illuminations, the opening of schools, the introduction of newspapers, the establishment of Arabic as the official language – a step which Ismail ordered in 1870 – the arrogant incursions of foreigners with their blatant thievery and contempt for the country and its institutions – somewhere in those packed, jumbled sixteen years, Egypt found the beginnings of a sense of national consciousness.

It was at first a small and fragile thing, not always recognized even by those at whom it tugged. But it was to grow and, before long, to make its presence known, along the Nile and well beyond the confines of Africa.

PART FIVE

Wadi Halfa to Khartoum

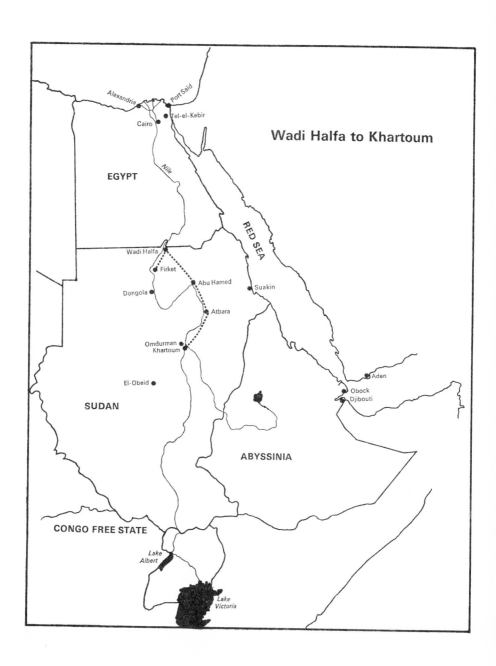

Wadi Halfa to Khartoum

CROMER writes: 'With the deposition of Ismail, the main obstacle which had stood in the way of Egyptian reform was removed.' He does, however, concede that some problems still remained: 'The Treasury was bankrupt. The discipline of the Army was shaken. Every class of Egyptian society was discontented: the poor by reason of the oppressive measures taken by their ruler; the rich because their privileges which they had enjoyed were threatened; the Europeans because the money owing them was not paid.'

Of this catalogue of woes, the last item called for the most urgent attention. Cromer and de Blignières, his French counterpart on the Debt Commission, had already drafted a suitable solution: the Law of Liquidation. It provided that henceforth one half of Egypt's total revenues, which stood at approximately nine million pounds a year, would go to pay off the debt. Of the rest, after deduction for tribute to the Sultan and other fixed charges, there remained a little more than two million pounds on which to run a country whose population now numbered between nine and ten million people. As one of his first official acts, Tewfik signed a decree enacting this arrangement. Furthermore, he agreed that he would not remove the Debt Commissioners without permission of the European Powers which had appointed them, thus placing Egypt under their absolute control and reducing his own duties to that of his country's chief tax collector. These acts earned him Cromer's praise as a demonstration of 'splendid constitutional temperament'.

Tewfik had probably been more stunned than Ismail by the Sultan's decree of dismissal; by one account, he slapped the face of the messenger who brought him the news. Weak by character and pliant by disposition, he had grown up in the shadow of a flamboyant father. Moreover, he was not even a legitimate son. It was common knowledge in Cairo that his mother had been a favourite concubine in Ismail's harem. Even without this stigma, however, he was not likely to initiate any experiments in independence; he had before his eyes the fresh example of what happens to Khedives of Egypt who fail to heed their foreign advisers.

For their part, France and Britain had reason to be pleased. Neither was yet prepared to assume sole control of Egypt, yet neither trusted the other not to do so if the opportunity presented itself. Dual Control, as the new system came to be called, was a happy compromise. As Salisbury wrote:

When you have got a ... faithful ally who is bent on meddling in a
country in which you are deeply interested, you have three courses
open to you. You may renounce, or monopolise, or share. Renouncing
would have been to place the French across our road to India.
Monopolising would have been very near the risk of war. So we
resolved to share.

However satisfactory the new arrangement was for the Europeans, it did
little to solve the rest of the problems which Cromer had enumerated. On
the contrary, foreigners continued to enjoy rights tantamount to immunity
under the law. Smuggling flourished on a grand scale because foreign ships
could not be searched without consent of their consular officers. Every
manner of fraud and breach of contract could pass unpunished because
aliens could only be arrested and prosecuted with this same consent. One
particularly vicious and resented trade, practised mainly by Greeks and
Levantines, was the lending of money at usurious rates of interest – 20 per
cent a month or more – and the subsequent seizure of the debtor's property
for non-payment. But these were minor matters; Cromer reported that 'On
the whole, I think the start has been favourable. A general feeling of
satisfaction prevails.' Visiting journalists interviewed each other in the bar
of Shepheard's Hotel and told their readers that Tewfik's administration
was, in the words of one of them, 'the best Egypt has enjoyed'. The final
accolade came from the *Contemporary Review*, which concluded that 'The
Liquidation Law [has] put the finances on a sound footing. ... Its effects
have been just and beneficial.'

There were many groups in Egypt who, for different reasons, did not
agree with this estimate. Among them were the constitutional reformers
who had rejoiced at the weakening of the Sultan's power, only to find it
replaced by a heavier hand; the Moslem conservatives alarmed by the
spread of Christian influence; the great landowners who sought to preserve
their own privilege under the guise of ridding the country of foreigners; the
small group of intellectual nationalists who had begun to advance the
radical notion that Egypt should be governed by Egyptians. And there was
the Army, which had a special reason for dissatisfaction. Traditionally,
senior ranks had been reserved for Circassians – Turks, Albanians, Kurds,
and other non-Egyptians. Under Said and Ismail, a number of *fellahin*
officers had been commissioned. Now, with the army being cut in half as an
economy measure, they were the first to be dismissed.

Similar combinations of elements, disparate and even mutually hostile,
have appeared at other times in history, and tried to attempt to achieve
their several objectives in common action – generally abrupt and violent
action. In Egypt, these elements had, by early 1881, accumulated to the
kindling point, and needed only a spark to set them off. It could have come
from anywhere. Unfortunately, it came from the Army.

The British Consul-General, reporting the incident, called it a 'schoolboy outbreak' and ascribed it to 'the general lax discipline of the Egyptian Army'. On February 1st, 1881, three *fellahin* colonels led by one Ahmed Arabi had presented Tewfik with a petition demanding the removal of the Minister of War, who, they claimed, was systematically weeding the army of non-Circassian officers. Tewfik had replied by ordering the petitioners arrested and tried for treason. The order could not be carried out, however, because the colonels' troops, all *fellahin* themselves, mutinied. They broke into the War Ministry, upset tables and chairs, forced the Minister to flee through a rear window, and triumphantly carried the three colonels off on their shoulders.

The Minister of War – an old-school Turkish pasha named Osman Rifki – was removed, but the British insisted that the colonels be transferred to posts far outside of Cairo. Instead of obeying, on September 9th they ordered their schoolboys, 2,500 strong and hauling 18 field pieces, to march on the Abdine palace. This time, there was no talk of arrest or treason. Tewfik tearfully embraced the colonels and told Ahmed Arabi, 'You three, you are soldiers. With me, you make four.'

Whatever it did for Tewfik's ego, the episode marked the start of the First Egyptian Revolution – so designated by the colonels who carried off the second one 71 years later. Its course and outcome were largely determined by the unlikely nature of its leader.

Ahmed Arabi was born in 1840 in Horiyeh, a village exactly like hundreds of others in the Delta – a cluster of mud huts, a small mosque and a water wheel. Wilfrid Scawen Blunt gives this portrait of him in his *Secret History of the English Occupation of Egypt*: 'A typical *fellah*, tall, heavy-limbed and somewhat slow in his movements, he seemed to symbolize ... the laborious peasant of the Lower Nile. ... His features in repose were dull ... and it was only when he smiled and spoke that one saw the kindly and large intelligence within. Then his face became illumined as a dull landscape by the sun.'

The illumination, in view of subsequent events, was largely in the eye of the beholder. Largely through Blunt's proselytizing, the Egyptian nationalist movement became the season's conversation piece in London. An Irish Member named Justin McCarthy rose in the House to ask rhetorically whether 'Arabi [was] the Cromwell of a great movement against an Egyptian Charles; the Garibaldi of a struggle for national liberty against a foreign rule.'

In Cairo, the immediate effect of Tewfik's espousal of the revolution had been the appointment of a new Government headed by Cherif Pasha, an elder statesman long associated with the struggle to free Egypt from Turkish intervention. But times had changed, and Cherif's platform had long since become irrelevant. Egypt's masters now no longer resided in Constantinople, but in London.

And in Paris. There, successive Governments regardless of their political orientation had become collection agents for the private creditors whose principal interest in Egypt was to assure prompt payment, with interest, of Ismail's obligations. Arabi – Cromwell, Garibaldi or whoever he might be – represented a threat to that orderly process, and therefore had to be squashed. The method chosen was to send a note expressing confidence in Tewfik, who, until his recent aberration, had shown himself so admirably docile. To preserve a united front, Britain was asked to co-sign it. (Why Gladstone, who had replaced Disraeli as Prime Minister, agreed to do it is uncertain. Cromer's explanation – sheer stupidity – is as reasonable as any.)

The effect of the Joint Note, which was delivered on January 8th, 1882, was that of 'thunder out of a clear sky'. At face value, it was innocuous enough, not even mentioning Arabi but merely reaffirming British and French resolve to 'guard by their united efforts against causes of complication, internal and external, which might menace the order of things established in Egypt.' But everyone in Cairo knew that there were no 'external' complications threatening Egypt save those which the signatories of the Note might themselves be contemplating, and the only 'internal' complication was the nascent nationalist movement itself. Cherif Pasha's comment on seeing the text – that 'They could not have found a better way to destroy us' – proved prophetic. Within six weeks, his Cabinet was out of office and replaced with a band of extremists including Ahmed Arabi, who was appointed Minister of War.

Now events acquired a counterpoint of their own. The *fellahin*, thinking the new Government would rid them of the moneylenders, became assertive to the point of occasional insolence. The Powers, determined to undo the mischief caused by the Note, took turns pressing Tewfik to act. On May 25th, he yielded and dismissed the Government, but could find no one willing to replace it. Three days later, Arabi was reinstated and, in the absence of a prime minister, became effective ruler of the country. Tewfik and his court moved out of Cairo to the safety of one of his country palaces; the frightened foreign consuls followed him. Meanwhile, insolence rose to insubordination and, eventually, insurrection. On June 11th, riots and looting broke out in Alexandria; six Europeans were killed and another 45 or so wounded, including Sir Charles Cookson, the British Consul-General who had shrugged off the first mutiny as a schoolboy prank. By June 17th, some 14,000 foreigners – for the mob made no distinction between Europeans, Levantines or Turks – had fled the country and another 6,000 were anxiously awaiting their turn to be evacuated.

Sitting at anchor off Alexandria, where they had been since May 15th, were two naval squadrons, one British and one French. To the British commander, Admiral Sir Beauchamp Seymour, inactivity was as galling as it can only be to a man who, in rapid succession, had taken part in the

Burmese campaign, fought the Russians on the Black Sea, commanded the Naval Brigade in New Zealand during the Maori wars, guarded Britain's coasts as commander of the Channel Fleet, and intimidated any number of insubordinate seaports by his presence off shore. On June 29th, he had signalled the Admiralty that 'Alexandria is apparently controlled by the military party,' but had not received the expected permission to show the flag. Five days later, he added the information that the harbour batteries were being fortified. Again, he was disappointed: his message was relayed to the Sultan, who promised to order the work stopped. On July 6th, he sighted renewed activity and sent a warning ashore announcing that unless it ceased he would open fire. Four days later, he followed with a last word: 'I shall carry out the intention expressed to you in my letter of the 6th inst., at sunrise tomorrow, the 11th inst., unless previous to that hour, you shall have surrendered to me.'

Before a reply could be formulated, dawn of the 11th inst. came, and with it Seymour gave the order to start firing.

British ships were the only ones to respond; late on the afternoon of the 10th, the French squadron had weighed anchor and filed away, its decks swarming with the last of the refugees. Paris had decided that intervention would be harmful to its interests elsewhere in the Moslem world, and instructed its commander to 'disassociate himself' from any action. For this caution, it was to pay a heavy price.

The bombardment of Alexandria lasted two days. On the evening of the 13th, a party of 150 marines went ashore and reported that the city was virtually deserted. To prevent looting by desert Bedouins who had already begun to move in, Seymour ordered 3,000 troops brought over from Cyprus. Tewfik, who had sat out the bombardment in safety, rushed back to Alexandria and placed himself under their protection.

Despite Seymour's zealousness, Gladstone still hoped to negotiate some kind of settlement. On July 24th, the House of Commons took matters out of his hands by appropriating immediate credits of £2,300,000 for an expedition empowered for 'operations in any part of Egypt'. The nature of the vote, 275 to 19, made it not so much an expression of confidence as demand for action.

Five days later it was the turn of the French Chamber of Deputies. Sensing it had committed a serious blunder by withdrawing its fleet, the Government argued in favour of joint action with Britain. In opposition, Clemenceau delivered one of his most impassioned speeches: 'All Europe is covered with soldiers; the world sits in waiting; all the Powers are reserving their freedom of action; do not, I entreat you, irrevocably now commit that of France.'

The words were guarded, but the meaning clear enough. Only one Power mattered to France – Germany. Clemenceau was warning his colleagues that an adventure in Egypt would weaken France and play into German hands. Still suffering from the shell-shock of 1870, they agreed and voted for 'total abstention' from any joint action.

'The history of the next two months', Cromer writes, 'may be summarized in a single sentence. England stepped in and with one rapid blow crushed the rebellion.'

The instrument to administer that blow was General Sir Garnet Wolseley. A land-locked version of Sir Beauchamp Seymour, his service record included the Burmese War, Balaklava and Sevastopol, the Indian Mutiny and the relief of Lucknow, the uprising led by Louis Riel in Manitoba, the Ashanti campaign in West Africa, the Zulu wars. Incredibly, he not only survived this global mayhem, but was a mere 48 years old when, on August 13th, 1882, Duty deposited him on the banks of the Nile. His parting words to envious colleagues in London were that he would have the whole mess cleaned up in one month.

Strategically, the situation was as follows: Arabi and his army, estimated to amount to some 70,000 troops, were in Cairo. The British, with half that number, were in Alexandria. Between them lay the Nile Delta, flat and latticed by a network of canals, dikes, ditches and railways, all of which could serve as natural fortifications for a defending force. There was, however, another way to reach Cairo: through Port Said, the Suez Canal and the unobstructed desert. Its sole disadvantage, from the point of view of the invader, was that it could be cut off behind him by the simple expedient of blowing up the Canal. Both Wolseley and Arabi knew this, as did Ferdinand de Lesseps who had arrived in Alexandria in July and was frantically trying to secure from both sides guarantees that they would observe the sanctity of his precious handiwork. Arabi wrote to him on August 4th: 'As I scrupulously respect the neutrality of the Canal, especially in consideration of its being so considerable a work and one in connection with which Your Excellency's name will live in history, I have the honour to inform you that the Egyptian Government will not violate that neutrality.'

Wolseley had no reply for de Lesseps, other than to order the movement of his entire force through the Canal to Ismailia. Arabi, even though he had ample opportunity to block its passage, respected the promise he had made. (Years later, Wolseley recollected happily: 'If Arabi had blocked the Canal, we should still be at the present moment on the high seas, blockading Egypt.')

The British took Ismailia, which was undefended, on August 21st, and proceeded to deploy their forces. Arabi's men had entrenched themselves as best they could at Tel-el-Kebir, roughly halfway between the Canal and Cairo. Surveying the position, Wolseley elected to attack by night, and assigned a naval officer skilled in celestial navigation to lead his forward elements. 'The enemy', he was able to write in his official report on the

battle, which took place on September 13th, 'were completely surprised. ...
Our troops advanced steadily without firing a shot, in obedience to the
orders they had received; and when close to the works, went straight for
them, charging with a ringing cheer.'

The Egyptians had fired their first shot at four fifty-five a.m.; by six
forty-five, the English had captured Arabi's headquarters, and the ground
was littered with the dead – 2,500 Egyptians and 57 British. Surprise had
hardly been necessary; most of Arabi's troops were untrained and hap-
hazardly-equipped *fellahin*. He himself, in 28 years of military service, had
never led so much as a company in combat. As Blunt observed, 'He would,
I imagine, have been quite unable to manœuvre a division even on parade.'
In any case, he did not linger long at Tel-el-Kebir to try his hand at command under fire. At the first exchange, he boarded a train and rushed back
to Cairo in order, as he later explained, to organize the city's defence.

There was no defence. While the rest of Wolseley's troops mopped up
the battlefield, two squadrons of the 4th Dragoon Guards, led by Major
Watson, R.E., made a dash to the city. They headed straight for the
Citadel, whose garrison, 8,000 strong, meekly surrendered. Watson calmly
entered alone and politely asked to see the commandant. Informed that he
was still asleep, he said, 'Then wake him up, and tell him to surrender.' The
order was carried out; still rubbing his eyes, the commandant appeared and
handed over the keys to the fortress. It was September 14th; Wolseley had
been one day out in his prediction. (Arabi surrendered himself voluntarily
and pleaded guilty to treason. By pre-arrangement, the mandatory death
sentence was commuted to perpetual exile.)

Officially, Britain still wanted no part of Egypt. On January 3rd, 1883,
identical notes went off to Berlin, Vienna, Rome, St Petersburg, Constantinople and Paris: 'Although for the present a British force remains in
Egypt for the preservation of public tranquillity, Her Majesty's Government
are desirous of withdrawing it as soon as the state of the country and
organization of proper means for the maintenance of the Khedive's authority
will admit of it.'

At the same time, Her Majesty herself, ever alert to the value of real
estate, was taking a different position with her Foreign Secretary: 'The
Queen feels very anxious that nothing should be said to fetter or hamper our
action in Egypt. We *must* have a firm hold on her *once and for all.*'

In any event, there was an immediate problem: having destroyed one
Egyptian army, Britain was obliged to replace it with another.

The task was assigned to Sir Evelyn Wood, V.C., another hero of
countless colonial wars and all-round utility Victorian General. Wood
arrived in Cairo on December 21st, 1882, and was handed a new uniform –
that of Sirdar (Commander-in-Chief) of the Egyptian Army – a budget

which just covered the recruiting of 25 British officers, and the job of preserving internal order and protecting Egypt against a threat which, unnoticed in the rush of events, had been gathering across its southern border, in the Sudan.

Egypt's property by right of Mohammed Ali's conquest, the Sudan was enormous (one million square miles, the size of all Europe eastward to the Elbe), unbearably hot and virtually empty. Mohammed Ali had done little about this part of his empire, save to appoint resident governors who used the pretext of their post's hardships and the immunity afforded by its great distance from Cairo to extract for themselves all they could of the country's meagre wealth. Said made a rapid tour of the Sudan in 1856, found it in deplorable state and never returned. Ismail never ventured into it at all but, pursuing his goal of making Egypt the dominant power of Africa, launched grandiose plans to develop its resources. There were to be vast irrigation works, and a regular steamer service on the Nile as far south as Wadi Halfa, where the Second Cataract barred navigation; beyond that, there was to be a railway, reaching to Khartoum, 440 miles away. There were to be schools, a public health service, regular postal delivery. The boundaries of the country were to be pushed out, by exploration first and military force if necessary.

To oversee all this activity, Ismail hired – charmed is probably a more accurate term – outstanding, eminently qualified Europeans. The first was Sir Samuel Baker, the great explorer who forced his way 1,000 miles up the Nile from Khartoum to Gondokoro in May 1870, and remained for three years. His successor was Colonel Charles George Gordon.

Securing Gordon's services was perhaps the greatest coup of Ismail's life, in its way more spectacular than the displays which surrounded the opening of the Canal. Gordon was a legendary figure, the incarnation of St George – a knight errant who travelled the world with a sword in one hand and the Bible in the other. He had fought brilliantly at Balaklava, had saved the life and the throne of the Emperor of China who, in gratitude, had offered him a roomful of gold which Gordon had rejected as being of no use to him.

Gordon was in Galatz, Rumania, serving as Her Majesty's representative to an international commission to regulate navigation on the Danube, when Ismail's offer reached him. He accepted on condition that his salary be reduced to one-fifth of what his predecessor had received, out of suspicion that the money would be extorted from the poor peasants he was coming to help.

Gordon had no trouble attracting extraordinary men to work under him: the Italian, Gessi, the American, Chaille-Long, who brought with him a small contingent of former Civil War officers, the German, Schnitzer, who turned Moslem and called himself Emin Pasha, and later the Austrian, Slatin, and the Englishman, Lupton – as varied a group of soldiers of fortune as ever gathered in a single cause. For five years they fought to create a country, and nearly succeeded. They overcame the fearsome climate and their own isolation, gained the respect if not always the affection of dozens of native tribes. Gordon made plans of his own, more realistic, for the beginnings of some sort of rational economy. In the end, they were defeated, not by the size of the task but by the Egyptian pashas and other functionaries who had burrowed deep into the flesh of the country and whose parasitic survival depended on undermining Gordon's efforts.

Ismail's grandiose schemes never materialized. Expansion was halted in the west by desert, and in the east by the Abyssinians, who fiercely defended their highlands. There was no irrigation, no crops, no steamer service. A letter posted in Cairo still took 28 days to reach Khartoum. The railway was begun in Wadi Halfa on February 15th, 1875, under the direction of a British engineer named John Fowler. *Bradshaw's Railway Manual* celebrated the occasion:

> The Viceroy of Egypt has actually commenced one of the most gigantic undertakings ever attempted in his territory. ... At the terminal point of all ancient and modern conquest, ... the Khedive ... is preparing to drive an iron road and a team of iron horses, not only to the confines of Nubia, but into the heart of Africa.

The cost of the railway had been estimated at £1,421,000, but funds ran out well before it could strike any vital organ. To be precise, the rails reached Sarras, 33 miles from where, with great pomp, they had started.

Gordon quit in disgust in August 1879. Before leaving, the man who had once led the Ever-Victorious Army said: 'The government of the Egyptians (in the Sudan) ... is nothing else but one of brigandage of the very worst description. It is so bad that all expectation of ameliorating it is hopeless.'

As if in confirmation, he was immediately replaced by a local pasha named Mohammed Raouf whom he had himself twice previously dismissed from lesser posts for excessive cruelty. Gessi and the others remained, but without central support their principal concern became their own survival. As for replacing that support, Cromer made clear his – and therefore both Egypt's and Britain's – position: 'If we are to become responsible for the government of the Sudan, we may at once, for all practical purposes, abandon all hope of getting away from Egypt at all.'

Instead, it was the Sudan which was abandoned – to its own devices, to the slave traders and to the Egyptian overlords and tax-collectors, 'swaggering bullies, robbing, plundering and ill-treating the people with impunity', as they were described by Colonel Stewart, a British officer sent down shortly after Gordon's departure to report on the state of the country.

Historically and politically, Europeans have found it convenient to treat the

Sudan as a single country. In reality it is two, divided into unequal parts by the miracle of the rainfall line which runs almost exactly along the 13° parallel. Below, it is wet, lush and black – part of pagan Africa. Above, it is dry, unchanging and unchanged from the way it looked to G. W. Steevens, the *Daily Mail* correspondent who visited it in 1898:

> Nothing grows green. Only yellow halfa grass to make you stumble, and sapless mimosa to tear your eyes; dompalms that mock with wooden fruit, and Sodom apples that lure with flatulent poison. For beasts, it has tarantulas and scorpions and serpents, devouring white ants and every kind of loathsome bug that flies or crawls. Its people are naked and dirty, ignorant and besotted. It is a quarter continent of sheer squalor. Overhead the pitiless furnace of the sun, under foot the never-ceasing treadmill of the sand, dust in the throat, tuneless singing in the ear, searing flame in the eye.

The Arabs had a briefer description. 'When Allah made the Sudan,' they said, 'he laughed.'

Above the rainfall line, the Sudan was Moslem. So, too, was Egypt, but there the comparatively soft life and worldly pleasures of Cairo and the Delta had attenuated the faith into an accommodation with God. Here, it was a force powerful enough to sustain a man through monstrous adversity, the kind of force which produces holy men and strange ascetics. The Sudan was full of them – pious wanderers who plodded from village to village, mumbling their prayers and shaking their begging bowls.

There were also the messiahs who rose almost as regularly as the Nile to proclaim that they had arrived to fulfil the prophecy of the Book. They were as harmless and ineffectual as the beggars, and little attention was paid to them. Because of this neglect, it is necessary to resort to biographical reconstruction in telling the story of one of them, who turned out to be not so harmless, and not so ineffectual.

Mohammed Ahmed was living the quiet life of a hermit in a cave on the Nile island of Abba, 160 miles south of Khartoum, when he proclaimed himself to be El Mahdi – the Messiah. He had been born on another island, Darar, between the Third and Fourth Cataracts, the son of a carpenter and boat-builder. His father moved south, to Omdurman, probably in search of a better supply of timber, and died while Mohammed Ahmed was still a boy. Because there were three older brothers, he was allowed to pursue his studies at a number of religious schools in and near Khartoum. He early showed great powers of application and impressed not only his teachers, who came to mistrust his calm self-assurance, but a growing body of personal disciples. He travelled, preached, meditated, and acquired a reputation for great sanctity and the ability to perform miracles. Finally he quarrelled with one of his religious superiors over a point of theological interpretation, and thereafter retired to his cave on Abba.

Life on the island was not altogether austere. He had two wives, both named Fatima and both his cousins, who lived ashore but daily ministered to his needs – a bit of porridge and dried fish, and the upkeep of his one coarse cotton shirt. The most reliable description – no photographs exist – paints him as 'Tall, rather slight, of youthful build, ... with large eyes and pleasing features, Mohammed Ahmed bore externally all the marks of a well-bred gentleman. He moved with quiet dignity of manner. ... '

Appearances, however, were deceiving:

> ... There was nothing unusual about him until he commenced to preach. Then indeed one understood the power within him, which men obeyed. With rapid earnest words he stirred the hearts and bowed their heads like corn beneath the storm. And what a theme was his! No orator in France in 1792 could speak of oppression that here in the Soudan was not doubled. What need of description when he could use denunciation; when he could stretch forth his long arm and point to the taxgatherer who twice, three times, and yet again, carried off the last goat, and last bundle of straw, from yon miserable man listening with intent eyes!

Sensing the mood of his audiences, Mohammed Ahmed began directing his eloquence against all foreigners, but particularly the Egyptians; Moslems though they might claim to be, they were defilers of the faith, and oppressors of the people.

Stolid Sudanese peasants and labourers who had been left unmoved by the Koranic disputations of previous messiahs responded to this one. Hundreds flocked to Abba Island. Because it was holy ground, and in any case too small to hold them all, they built a makeshift village on the bank facing it. Bonfires were lit; banners unfurled, proclaiming 'Mohammed Ahmed, Mahdi and successor to the Prophet of God'. The sermons continued daily, taking as their text increasingly political topics. 'Better', the Mahdi told his followers, 'thousands of graves than a single coin in taxes.'

This last message registered as far away as Khartoum. Mohammed Raouf, Gordon's successor, ordered two companies of troops to go down and bring back the dangerous heretic. What happened next is described by Winston Churchill in his *The River War*, with the author's comment that it was 'characteristically Egyptian':

> Each company was commanded by a captain. To encourage their efforts, whichever officer captured the Mahdi was promised promotion. At sunset on an August evening in 1881 the steamer arrived at Abba. The promise of the governor-general had provoked the strife, not the emulation of the officers. Both landed with their companies and proceeded by different routes under cover of darkness to the village. ... Arriving simultaneously from opposite directions, they

fired into each other, and in the midst of this mistaken combat, the
Mahdi rushed upon them with his scanty following and destroyed them
impartially. A few soldiers succeeded in reaching the bank of the river.
But the captain of the steamer would run no risks, and those who could
not swim out to the vessel were left to their fate.

That fate was to be torn to pieces by the Mahdi's 350 aroused disciples.
The date of the comic-opera engagement at Abba Island, August 12th,
1881, deserves to be noted; it marked the beginning of the Mahdist revolt.
Immediately, word went forth that a sign had been given, a miracle achieved
which proved beyond doubt the divine inspiration of the Mahdi's mission.
For had he not confounded his enemies and caused them to destroy one
another? Had not his faithful followers, armed only with sticks and spears,
triumphed over the rifles of the infidels? The Mahdi did nothing to discourage these speculations, but for himself decided that prudence militated
against expecting another such miracle. He announced that, like the
Prophet Mohammed before him, he must now undertake a *hegira*, a long
flight into the desert.

Mohammed had gone from Mecca to Medina; the Mahdi chose to lead
his small band of ragged followers, armed now with captured rifles which
few of them knew how to fire, southward along the Nile, then westward
until they reached the fastness of the Nuba mountains. Here, in a land as
inhospitable as it was inaccessible, he established his headquarters and
waited for either Government troops or the ripples of the holy war he had
declared to reach him.

The troops came first. In his report to Cairo, sent ten days after the
encounter at Abba, Raouf had minimized his own casualties and actually
claimed victory – had not the Mahdi and his survivors fled the scene? As
for the cry of holy war, it was a consequence of the hot weather and the
stupidity of the Sudanese, and would soon dissipate itself in tribal rivalries
and the enforced inactivity of the rainy season. This explanation satisfied
Tewfik, but it did not relieve the anxiety of the Governor of Fashoda,
through whose province the Mahdi had passed. He had seen how, like iron
filings swept up by a magnet, his own subjects had abandoned their hovels
to follow this newest messiah. Acting without orders, he collected a mixed
force of 400 soldiers and 1,000 black tribesmen, and set off to annihilate the
dangerous movement before it could spread. Instead, it was he who was
ambushed and wiped out. Again word spread: another miracle had taken
place.

By midsummer of 1882, the Mahdi stood at the head of a host of 30,000.
It could hardly be called an army, for it included women, children, the
lame and the old, and its weapons still numbered more spears and rusty

swords than firearms, but it was savagely loyal, sternly disciplined, and waiting for the next prophetic command.

It came in August 1882, and directed the faithful to capture El Obeid, the capital of Kordofan and, after Khartoum, the largest city in the Sudan. Flags flying and drums beating, they left their mountain camp and moved north, picking up recruits and followers in every village. On September 4th, the Mahdi sent messengers to the city's governor demanding that he surrender. His reply was to order the messengers executed, but their loss was more than compensated for by the streams of inhabitants who deserted to join the attackers. They had made a wise choice, for they were the last beings to leave the city alive for a long time.

The siege of El Obeid lasted for four months during which nobody, nothing moved in or out. Father Ohrwalder, an Austrian missionary who had taken refuge inside the city and suffered not only the siege but also a subsequent eight years as the Mahdi's prisoner, described some of its horrors:

> The poor began to starve quite at the beginning of the siege, and soon were dying in considerable numbers. ... All the camels and cattle being finished, donkeys, dogs, mice and even crickets were consumed, as well as cockroaches, which were considered quite tidbits; white ants too were eaten. ... The air was poisoned by the numbers of dead bodies lying unburied, while the ditch was half full of mortifying corpses.

With the fall of El Obeid and its inevitable sacking, the Mahdi gained some 6,000 rifles, 6 field guns, great quantities of ammunition and approximately £100,000 in cash. In addition, his personal prestige, which now reached into every remote corner of the Sudan, received supreme recognition: seventeen months after he had declared holy war, the British took notice of his existence.

Nothing precipitous was proposed. It was the position of Her Majesty's Government that the Sudan was Egypt's affair, at least in tiresome matters of this kind; moreover, any substantive help would be self-defeating because it would only add to the Egyptian debt. As a gesture, however, an offer was made to provide seasoned leadership for the Egyptian Army in the Sudan, the force which the Mahdi had humbled at every occasion, and which was so shadowy that the honour of commanding it went uncontested to the first applicant for the position – Colonel William Hicks, late of the Indian Army.

Hicks looked the part – red face, thick white moustache, fierce eyes and a ramrod stance – but he had been a desk officer, with thorough knowledge of regulations and no experience in leading troops, certainly not troops such as those he addressed on his arrival in Khartoum on May 4th, 1883:

I am desired by His Highness the Khedive to inform you that if you perform your duty faithfully and gallantly, so far from being left here in the Sudan – as it is reported you seem to expect – you will, at the expiration of the campaign, be allowed to return to your homes. ... I myself will take you back, and present you to the Khedive. I promise you this in His Highness's name.

This was a strange way for a commander to greet his army, but the army, too, was strange. Most of its men were deserters from Arabi's force who had been rounded up and brought to Khartoum in chains and unarmed. So uncertain had the Egyptians been of their loyalty that they did not dare issue them weapons and ammunition until they were safely in the Sudan, where there was nowhere to flee except into the dervishes' hands.

Hicks's first weeks must have been trying. Colonel J. Colborne of the King's Royal Rifles, one of the eight officers assigned to his staff, described one of the training exercises: 'When the guns were attempted to be brought into action, dire confusion reigned. Men ran against each other; the ground was strewn with cartridges. ... No one appeared to have the slightest knowledge of how to feed, aim or discharge the pieces.'

In addition to an infantry corps of 10,000, Hicks's force included 1,000 cavalrymen, and an artillery detachment of 10 brass mountain guns, 4 Krupp howitzers and 6 Nordernfels machine guns which could, in the hands of an experienced operator, fire 1,000 rounds per minute. There was also a body of 100 troops decked out in chain-mail and armour, and carrying maces and wide two-handed swords – relics of Richard-the-Lion-Heart's passage through Africa which any European museum would have been proud to display. Since no provision existed for the naming of such troops, they were identified on the rolls as *cuirassiers* – a term which had slipped out of the working military vocabulary after the introduction of gunpowder.

On September 27th, the army marched out, ranged in the shape of a huge hollow square with the 5,500 camels which carried its baggage, stores and ammunition in the centre, and 2,000 camp followers bringing up the rear. The unusual formation had been Hicks's notion, to guard against the danger of the sudden attacks for which the Mahdi was noted. It also assured that progress would be slow and unwieldy. Frank Power, who accompanied the expedition as correspondent of *The Times*, wrote: 'We march on a campaign that even the most sanguine look forward to with the greatest gloom.'

From Khartoum to El Obeid is a distance of 280 miles, an easy 12 days' journey by caravan. Hicks was on the road for 43 days, and never did reach his destination. An army on the march through the desert can, with care and preparation, carry every one of its requirements save one – water. As soon as Hicks left the banks of the Nile and headed westward, he dis-covered that the dervishes, who knew precisely where he was and where he was going, had preceded him and fouled every well on the road. His last dispatch back to Khartoum noted: 'We have depended on pools of rain-water for supply, which we have fortunately found.'

In mid-October, good fortune ran out and the army's route of march became a confused, desperate zigzag in search of water. The native guides proved less than helpful, leading the troops through high grass and thick bush which slowed them down still more and tore their uniforms to shreds. When Hicks suggested to the Egyptian commander, with whom his relations had been strained from the start, that there might have been something more than just bad luck involved, he was told, 'I have obtained these guides, and am quite satisfied as to their loyalty. I do not wish you to interfere with my people.'

Two other newsmen, Edmund O'Donovan of the London *Daily News* and Frank Vizetelly, an artist for the *Illustrated London News*, had also accompanied the army. At the end of October, O'Donovan filed his last story, from Er Rahad, 40 miles from El Obeid: 'We have halted for the last three days owing to the uncertainty of the water supply in front. ... The enemy is still retiring, and sweeping the country bare.'

For three weeks the dervishes had been sniping at the thirsty, helpless troops, picking off stragglers and adding to the confusion and sense of impending doom. On November 3rd, a letter arrived from the Mahdi, addressed to Hicks: 'Every intelligent person must know that Allah rules, and his authority cannot be shared. ... He who surrenders shall be saved. But if you refuse and persist in denying my divine calling, ... you are to be killed.'

Once again the prophecy turned out to be accurate. On November 5th, while they were wandering around a dry forest some thirty miles south of El Obeid, Colonel Hicks of the Indian Army and his men were attacked by an indeterminate force of dervishes. Nothing certain is known of the battle because it left only a hundred or so semi-coherent survivors. All others, including all the Europeans, were exterminated – either killed in the fighting or hacked to pieces after surrendering.

Cromer, in Cairo, found a scapegoat for the disaster: 'Thus the whole edifice of territorial aggrandisement in Africa, which Ismail Pasha and his predecessors, in an evil moment for their country, had planned, toppled to the ground. ... The bubble Government established in the Soudan collapsed directly it was pricked by the religious impostor who was now to rule the country.'

That was that, but there still remained some pieces to be picked up – roughly 40,000 Egyptians and several hundred Europeans stranded in Khartoum and some of the smaller cities in the Sudan, all of which were now the Mahdi's for the taking. On January 3rd and 4th, 1884, the Cabinet met in long session and concluded that the whole of the Sudan must be evacuated. Victoria reluctantly acquiesced; Cromer, informed of the

Government's decision, had no objection – indeed, he had himself proposed the notion. Given unanimous agreement – the Egyptians, of course,
had not been consulted – all that was needed was a man to oversee the
job.

In the four years after leaving the Sudan, Gordon had travelled a lot – to
India; to the lonely island of Mauritius, some 500 miles east of Madagascar,
where he spent a year as Commanding Engineering Officer; to South
Africa, where he tried unsuccessfully to negotiate peace with the insurgent
Basuto tribe. Nowhere could he find whatever he was looking for. He wrote
to a friend: 'The fiddle-faddle of my present life is a great burden. I do not
know how long I will be able to bear it.'

On January 7th, 1885, he returned to England from a year's stay in
Palestine where, characteristically, he had been simultaneously occupied in
locating sites mentioned in the Bible, and making plans for a canal to
connect Haifa, on the Mediterranean, with the Gulf of Aqaba. In his pocket
was a contract he had signed with Leopold II in Brussels the day before,
engaging himself to return to Africa and help establish what was to become
the Congo Free State. The visit home was brief – just long enough to post
his resignation with the War Office and to say goodbye to his older sister,
Augusta, who lived in Southampton. In less than two weeks, he was aboard
the S.S. *Tanjore* bound for Africa. His destination, however, was not the
Congo but Cairo.

What happened was that on the 8th he had agreed to grant an interview
to a newspaperman – the ubiquitous William T. Stead – during the course
of which he had talked freely of the plight of the Sudan, and what he would
do if he were in charge of it. The following morning, Stead's paper, the
Pall Mall Gazette, devoted a page and a half to the interview, under a headline which read CHINESE GORDON FOR THE SUDAN. The notion, which
had occurred to no one in authority, instantly took on the lustre of sheer
genius.

The press took up the cry *en masse*. Even the Liberal *Morning Advertiser*
told its readers: 'It is not too much to say that all England has been looking
for the employment of General Gordon in the present crisis in Egypt.'
Within days Gordon had withdrawn his resignation, informed Leopold,
who took it with ill grace, of his change of plans, and received a broad
mandate from the nation to do something about the Sudan.

Only Cromer had been untouched by the brilliance of the choice. His
own inclination was to leave things in the Sudan just as they were – any
action was bound to cost money. Furthermore, he had met Gordon before
and was unimpressed with his talents as an administrator. While Gordon
was still on his way to Cairo, on January 21st, Cromer had written to the
Foreign Secretary: 'It is as well that Gordon should be under my orders,

but a man who habitually consults the prophet Isaiah when he is in difficulty is not apt to obey the order of any man.'

Gordon arrived in Cairo on the night of the 24th, and in the morning paid a frosty duty call on the Khedive Tewfik, whom he despised. His conversations with Cromer clearly did not result in a meeting of minds. The point of disagreement seemed to be exactly what Gordon's orders were, and how much latitude he was to be granted in carrying them out. The objective was clear enough: to rescue the threatened Egyptians and Europeans stranded in the Sudan. But as to how it should be done, neither the Cabinet nor Cromer had concrete suggestions to offer – except, in the latter's case, that it be accomplished economically. Gordon, on the other hand, was bubbling with notions: he would meet the Mahdi and personally arrange for peace; he would cause the natives to defect from the Mahdist cause; he would fight his way out; he would simply sit still and wait for the sandstorm to blow itself out. He even had time to think of the longer-range future. On the way from Cairo to Khartoum, which he reached on February 18th, he stopped at Berber and sent off a telegram to Leopold, promising him that he would undertake the Congo assignment as soon as the present one was completed.

The events of the next eleven months have been related in scores of books, and well they might, for they contain all the elements of the perfect Victorian tragedy: a pure, God-serving hero; a villain, black and foreign; a harrowing race to an uncertain ending; the whole soaked in pools of gore and laced with intimations of sex – those poor white women, stripped naked and left at the mercy of grinning savages. Scene follows scene with reassuring predetermination: Gordon, far from leading the garrisons out, is himself surrounded and cut off by the dervishes; the Government, which has done nothing, finally bestirs itself to vote £300,000 for a relief expedition; not one but two forces are sent and equally mismanaged; Gordon himself spends day after day on the roof of his palace in Khartoum, scanning the Nile for a hoped-for plume of smoke; the Mahdi, choking with hate, sends his hordes to force their way across the river and take the defenceless city, butchering the men and consigning the women – at least the young and pretty ones – to their unspeakable fates; Gordon, struck down on the steps of his palace, is decapitated and his head presented to the Mahdi in a filthy handkerchief and propped into the crook of a tree, where it is stoned into bloody, unrecognizable pulp by the crazed dervishes; the rescuers arrive, gallantly but too late.

Too late. The two words flashed back down the Nile to Cairo, and to London. They appeared, on February 5th, as the headline of the *Pall Mall Gazette*, whose genial idea the whole scheme had been. Britain surrendered herself to an orgy of national grief, led by the Widow of Windsor herself. The news hit her hard. Sir Henry Ponsonby, her Private Secretary, recalled: 'She was just going out when she got the telegram, and sent for me. She then went out to my cottage, a quarter of a mile off, walked into the room, pale and trembling, and said to my wife who was terrified at her appearance: "Too late!" '

But grief alone seldom satisfies mourners. In London, it quickly turned into recrimination, and a search for the guilty. The most logical candidate was, of course, the Prime Minister. He had had the misfortune of going out to the theatre on the evening when the news reached the city; crowds hissed and booed him all the way back to Downing Street, and camped across the street for days to jeer at his every appearance. The initials of his nickname – Grand Old Man – were reversed, to spell out Murderer Of Gordon. A music hall song promised that when he died, he would 'sit in state, on a red-hot plate, between Pilate and Judas Iscariot'.

Other politicians and civil servants, less conspicuous, ran for cover. Cromer, little known outside governing circles, passed unscathed although he, as much as any single man except Gordon himself, was responsible for the disaster. Nevertheless, he was conscious of history's judgment; in explaining his part in the affair – in *Modern Egypt*, which was published in 1908 and is, if not always reliable, at least lucid in other matters – he resorts to 175 pages of pettifoggery. He speaks of a 'Gordon cultus' passing over Britain, and appealing 'powerfully to the imagination of a people who are supposed to be presumably cold-blooded and practical, but who in reality are perhaps more led by their emotion than any other nation in Europe.'

He tries to blame everyone – the public, the Egyptian Government (which had long since become his personal rubber stamp), Gordon himself – and finally settles on the lame, partisan conclusion that the whole sad affair 'must forever stand as a blot on Mr Gladstone's escutcheon'.

In the wake of great calamity, it often seems that no one – certainly no one with access to pen and ink – is ever directly to blame. So it was, and has remained, with the fall of Khartoum. But this much was certain: Gordon was dead, the Sudan was lost. And the means to avenge the first and regain the second were still far from ready.

Charged with creating the nucleus for a new Egyptian Army, Sir Evelyn Wood had no trouble filling the twenty-five vacant spaces which constituted his original staff. By late 1882, peace had broken out along the far-flung frontiers of empire, and good postings were hard to come by. Egypt, with its promise of action, rapid promotion, and the shower of knighthoods, D.S.O.s, C.M.G.s and other honours which seemed to accompany service on the Nile, was a plum. Several thousand officers – 'most of the British Army', according to one writer – applied. Strings were pulled, old school ties fingered. Under the circumstances, Wood chose extremely well; of his original recruits, twelve rose to wear general's stars.

The most successful among them was, on paper, the least promising. At

32, he was still only a lieutenant, and not even a line officer but an engineer, having passed through 'The Shops' – the Royal Military Academy at Woolwich – in 1871, average in every respect including his standing of 28th in a class of 56. For his first field assignment, he had drawn surveying duty in Palestine, a job he performed so conscientiously that after four years he was promoted to conduct a land survey of the island of Cyprus. He was stationed there in 1882 when the fleet which was to shell Alexandria was being assembled. He went absent without leave, wangled an invitation to watch the action from the bridge of the *Invincible*, Admiral Seymour's flagship, and even managed to go ashore in mufti and report on the state of the Egyptian defences. His letter of application to Sir Evelyn contained no hint of political connections, of which he had none, but did mention one important qualification which was rare among English officers: during his service in the Holy Land, he had learned passable Arabic. Probably on the strength of this, Wood accepted and, on December 28th, 1882, cabled to Lieutenant Horatio Herbert Kitchener, R.E., safely back on Cyprus, offering him a two years' engagement in the Egyptian Army. Kitchener accepted the appointment, which carried the acting rank of major and placed him as second-in-command of a cavalry regiment. Like the rest of the Army, it existed only on paper; Kitchener's first job was to recruit both men and mounts, and start training them. The correspondent of the London *Daily News*, John Macdonald, recalled meeting him at that time, January 8th, 1883:

> At the barracks, we found some 40 men waiting. I remember Kitchener's gaze at the awkward, slipshod group, as he took his position in the centre of a circular space round which the riders were to show their paces. ... Neither audible nor visible sign did he give of any feeling aroused in him by a performance mostly disappointing and sometimes ridiculous. In half an hour or so, the first native officers of the new *fellah* cavalry, the least unfit, were chosen. It was then that Kitchener made his longest speech. 'We'll have to drive it into those fellows,' he muttered, as if thinking aloud.

After this unpromising start, Kitchener's career picked up tempo. He received his baptism of fire during the ill-fated Gordon Relief Expedition of 1884, to which he was assigned as Intelligence Officer. In 1886, after a brief home leave during which he was presented to the Queen, he was made Commandant of the Suakin district, a precarious enclave on the Red Sea which the British held only under constant siege. It was there, in 1888, that he received his first and only battle wound, a 'serious, comminuted fracture of the right lower jaw', caused by a dervish bullet.

But it was less as a field commander than as a staff officer that he showed aptitude. Rising through a series of administrative posts, he served as assistant adjutant of the Army, then as chief of its police department. In every assignment, he was generally disliked by his men, whom he drove as hard as himself, and with the same uncommunicative determination he had displayed while selecting candidates for the Egyptian cavalry. A bachelor – by reason of a tragic love affair, it was said – he would not countenance marriage among his subordinates because he believed it distracted them from their work. He was cold, unconcealedly ambitious and, on occasion, surprisingly vain, as when he designed a special sky-blue uniform for the Egyptian cavalry. On April 13th, 1892, less than ten years after he had joined the Egyptian Army, Kitchener was suddenly and unexpectedly promoted to its command as Sirdar. It was an appointment which, in the words of Philip Magnus, one of his biographers, 'was received with surprise and disgust by the entire Egyptian army'.

For his part, Cromer found the appointment admirable: 'Sir Herbert Kitchener possessed a quality which is rare among soldiers. ... He did not think that extravagance was the necessary handmaiden of efficiency. On the contrary, he was a rigid economist, and ... suppressed with a firm hand any tendency towards waste.'

The new Sirdar faced an unenviable job. The Egyptian Army had proved that, with sufficient stiffening from its British officers, who now numbered almost 800, it could defend itself against the dervishes. The danger of their overrunning Egypt was over – an attack had been turned back with heavy losses at Toski, 60 miles north of the border, on August 3rd, 1889. But they still held the Sudan. Seven years after his death, Gordon was still unavenged; Khartoum still lay in ruins; and no British or Egyptian soldier dared wander far south of Wadi Halfa.

The British General Election of July 1892 had turned out the Conservatives and brought Gladstone back.* There would, for the time at least, be no encouragement for the retrieval of lost provinces, and certainly no money to equip the armies necessary for such enterprises. Kitchener was young – not yet 42 – and undeniably energetic, but the ardour which had commended him to Cromer was tempered with a heavy measure of caution – not the caution of the coward, for his personal bravery was unquestioned, but the caution of the commander who refuses all temptation to commit himself until he is certain, if not of victory then of overwhelming superior strength. Kitchener could not foresee when he would gain this strength by numbers; he therefore resolved to achieve it by superior cunning. Fortunately, he already had on his staff an officer uniquely equipped for the task.

Francis Reginald Wingate had not been one of Sir Evelyn Wood's original recruits, but in most respects he was better qualified than Kitchener himself to serve in Egypt. He too was a graduate of Woolwich, passing out in 1879 and taking up duty in Kandahar, where he settled down to the normal peacetime activities of a young bachelor officer on Indian service

---

* General Sir Garnet Wolseley, now Lord Wolseley, wrote to Kitchener: 'God must be angry with England when he sends back Mr. Gladstone to us as First Minister. ... '

– shooting, riding, dancing, polo. In addition, he applied himself to the study of languages, partly because of natural curiosity and partly because the Army granted additional allowance for this proficiency. As the seventh of eleven children of a Glasgow textile tradesman's widow, he had capital of £200, no private allowance, and a salary of £14 a month – not quite enough to run a string of ponies. He mastered Hindustani in eight months and tackled other barbaric languages such as Turkish, German and Arabic, which he learned during a tour at Aden. Eager to get on, he applied for every exotic assignment that came along: the Punjab Frontier Force, the Hyderabad Contingent, the Egyptian Army. This last application was turned down routinely because the requirements called for five years of active service, and he only had two. Three months later, however, came a telegram from Sir Evelyn Wood offering a post as his own aide-de-camp – again, it was the Arabic that had done it – at a stipend of £450 a year.

Wingate's duties brought him into direct contact with high-placed Egyptians – not only in the Khedival palace where ignorance reigned, but in the houses of intellectuals and nationalist leaders, where he received an appreciation of the Mahdi totally at variance with the then conventional British view of him as a sun-struck zealot.

By 1885 he was Assistant Military Secretary. In this post, much of his duties consisted of shuffling papers during the day, and attending dinner parties at night. In between, he pursued his own interest: the study of the nature and extent of the Mahdist movement. Eventually, he managed to excuse himself from the social circuit by wangling an appointment as Assistant Adjutant for Intelligence. Since few of his superiors could understand what he was talking about – a dervish was a dervish, and the only trustworthy ones were those with a soft-nosed bullet in their belly – he was left largely to his own dossiers.

He established, to his own satisfaction at least, that a dervish was distinctly not a dervish. The Mahdi had died in June 1885, surviving Gordon by only five months,* and had been replaced by his chief lieutenant, Abdullahi, who took the title of the Khalifa. A soldier rather than a mystic, he tried to sustain by force what the Mahdi had kindled by fervour. As a result, dozens of independent tribes had been forcibly impressed into service and the entire Sudan looted to provide sustenance for the army.

To someone who could understand not only Arabic, but the Arab mind as well, the situation presented an opportunity to turn discontent into a functioning intelligence network. This Wingate did, first alone and then with Kitchener's encouragement.

In *The River War*, Churchill writes:

Up the great river, within the great wall of Omdurman, into the

---

* He died, it is supposed, of poisoning at the hands of one of his wives. He had grown enormously fat, and on his infrequent outings from his harem was carried about on a platform like some grotesque living shrine.

arsenal, into the treasury, into the mosque, into the Khalifa's house itself, the spies and secret agents of the Government – disguised as traders, as warriors, or as women – worked their stealthy way. ... Information – whispered at Halfa, catalogued at Cairo – steadily accumulated ... until at last every important Emir was watched and located, every garrison estimated, and even the endless intrigues and brawls in Omdurman were carefully recorded.

Wingate also received important information from several Europeans, captives of the Khalifa, who managed to escape and make their way back to Egypt. The first of them was Father Ohrwalder, the Austrian missionary who had been at El Obeid. A far more valuable recruit was Rudolph Slatin, Gordon's former lieutenant, who had been taken prisoner shortly after the fall of Khartoum. His imprisonment had been ghastly. In order better to taunt and humiliate him, the Khalifa had him permanently chained at the ankles, and made to serve as his personal slave and door-keeper. No intelligence chief could have wished for a better-placed spy; after his own escape, Slatin became Wingate's deputy and right-hand man.

In addition to bringing information, the captives served another useful purpose. The accounts of their captivity, edited and translated by Wingate, became immediate best-sellers in England, aroused the indignation of the public, and served to remind the politicians that there was still unfinished work to be completed in the Sudan.

On March 1st, 1896, an Italian Army led by General Baratieri was wiped out by the Abyssinians at Adowa, prompting one of the first jokes of its kind on diplomatic record. 'I could have wished', Salisbury noted, 'that our friends the Italians had less capacity for being beaten.'

Adowa presented Britain with a double crisis: it jeopardized the entire eastern flank of the Sudan, which Baratieri was supposed to be guarding against possible French designs, and it raised the fear that the dervishes, emboldened by the success of the Abyssinians against white troops, might try another attack. The Cabinet met on March 12th and agreed to strike the first blow. Cromer and Kitchener, neither of whom had been consulted, received orders that they were to move in strength into the Sudan.

The campaign's jump-off point was to be Wadi Halfa. One of the oddest-looking towns on earth, it clung for more than three miles to the eastern bank of the Nile, yet nowhere was more than 400 yards wide, and in some places only 40. At the north end was a small group of substantial tree-shaded villas, mosques, minarets, a bazaar – all enclosed within a low mud wall. South of this stretched the barracks, low and long with small glassless windows, the arsenals, the military hospital, the workshops and the neat rows of officers' cottages. Where they ended began the Arab part of town, a

tumbled collection of mud huts and narrow alleys. Guarding the land side
and southern approaches were first the desert, then three large bastions and
five detached fortresses, mounting siege guns.

There were other signs of impending activity. G. W. Steevens of the
Daily Mail reported: 'Railways run along every dusty street, and trains and
trucks clank up and down till Halfa looks for all the world like Chicago in a
turban.'

Kitchener had ordered the construction of a railway. It was to travel in
the direction laid out by Ismail twenty years earlier, but this railway was
not intended to bring civilization into the Sudan, nor to provide transport for crops of cotton. Its only purpose was to feed and supply an army in
the field. It was an expensive solution – the budget was £500,000, antici-
pating the use of conscripted labour – but even Cromer, who had to approve
the expenditure, was forced to agree that none other was feasible. South of
Wadi Halfa, the Nile is broken by 100 miles of cataracts, and foot transport
across the desert is impossible.

Cromer naturally assumed that it would be the cheapest kind available –
a narrow-gauge military railway. For once, Kitchener overruled him and
insisted on a gauge of 3 feet 6 inches – the same measure as the tracks which
Cecil Rhodes was then pushing from Kimberley to Bulawayo. The two
men had been friends for several years; had talked over long-range plans
together; had met only a few weeks earlier when Rhodes, on his way back
to the Cape, had stopped in Cairo and obtained from Kitchener a shipment
of Sudanese donkeys for use in Rhodesia. There is little doubt about the
reason for Kitchener's insistence.

It did, however, mean that every piece of rolling stock had to be built to
order.* This, plus the total lack of suitable labour, tools and materials
turned the project into an engineering nightmare. But, as Steevens writes:
'It is part of the Sirdar's luck ... that he always gets the best subordinates.
Conceive a blend of French audacity of imagination, American ingenuity,
and British doggedness in execution, and you will have the ideal qualities
for such work.'

The possessor of these international attributes was a 29-year-old French-
Canadian named E. P. C. Girouard. Educated at Kingston College in
Ontario, he had worked on the gangs which built the Canadian Pacific
Railroad before joining the service as a lieutenant, in the Royal Engineers.
He was on his way from Halifax, Nova Scotia, to duty on Mauritius when
Kitchener, who had come across his name and record in the files, requested
that he be intercepted in London.

Girouard was, like many of his compatriots, almost compulsively casual
in his relations with superiors. During his first interview at the War Office,
he saluted with his left hand, hiding the other which held a half-smoked

---

* Rhodes lent a helping hand by diverting to Kitchener's use three locomotives which
he had ordered for his own railway.

cigar behind his back. Among the members of Kitchener's staff, who tended
to run to apprehensive attention and the briefest of replies, his broad accent
and truculence at protocol were particularly distinctive. But he did know
how to build a railway, and this, if nothing else, governed his relations with
Kitchener. As Steevens observed, 'He is credited with being the one man
in the Egyptian army who is unaffectedly unafraid of the Sirdar.'

When Girouard arrived in Wadi Halfa, at the end of March 1896, the
33 miles of line which Ismail had built as far as Sarras were still intact.
Beyond it, another 54 miles had been hastily laid in 1884 at the time of the
ill-fated Gordon Relief Expedition, but all of it had been torn up by the
dervishes. The last rail had been fixed upright into the sand, and a rope
passed through one of the bolt-holes; the rope had rotted, but a clue to its
use remained – a human skull and bones, polished white by sun and wind.

Girouard simplified the ballet-like operations of a good, experienced
railway line-laying gang to the abilities of his labour force, which consisted
of *fellahin* dragged down from Egypt, whatever Sudanese could be rounded
up, and a crew of 200 convicts who were paroled for the occasion. The
result was a fairly bumpy ride and frequent accidents – locomotives that
flew off tracks and down 15-foot embankments were hoisted back on the
rails and continued along as if nothing had happened. There was little
likelihood that passengers would complain.

Prudence dictated that the tracks be extended along the Nile, assuring
at once protection and a dependable supply of water. But the Nile traces a
long, graceful curve, almost doubling back on itself. There was neither time
nor money for long, graceful curves when a simple straight line would do –
a line which ended at Abu Hamed, at the precise point where the river
again headed south. Every expert pronounced the idea insane: engineers
pointed out, with truth, that nothing was known about the terrain, its
gradients or surface; soldiers asked how the devil Kitchener proposed to
defend a slender line of communication which would be burrowing deeper
and deeper into enemy territory towards a goal which was in their hands.
It could not be captured without a strong force, but a strong force could not
advance until the railway was finished, and the railway could not be finished
until its terminal was captured.

Kitchener had little appreciation for the elegance of circular arguments.
His question to Girouard was what would he need to build a railway on a
straight line to Abu Hamed. The reply came back, in satisfactorily short
time, and in the form of a requisition several inches thick – and so complete
that once it had been approved Girouard did not have to come back and
ask for so much as a single coil of wire.

The logistical problems were overwhelming. Winston Churchill wrote:

It is scarcely within the power of words to describe the savage desolation of the regions into which the line and its constructors plunged.

A smooth ocean of bright-coloured sand spread far and wide to the distant horizons. The tropical sun beat with senseless perseverance upon the level surface until it could scarcely be touched with the naked hand, and the filmy air glittered and shimmered as over a furnace. ... Alone in this vast expanse stood Railhead – a canvas town of 2,500 inhabitants, complete with station, stores, post-office, telegraph office, and canteen, and only connected with the living world of men and ideas by two parallel iron streaks, three feet six inches apart, growing dim and narrower in a long perspective until they were twisted and blurred by the mirage and vanished in the indefinite distance. ... Every morning in the remote nothingness there appeared a black speck growing larger and clearer, until with a whistle and a welcome clatter, amid the aching silence of ages, the 'material' train arrived, carrying its own water and 2,500 yards of rails and accessories. At noon came another speck, developing in a similar manner into a supply train, also carrying its own water, food and water for the half-battalion of the escort and the 2,000 artificers and platelayers, and the letters, newspapers, sausages, jam, whisky, soda-water, and cigarettes which enable the Briton to conquer the world without discomfort.

Day by day, the rails moved forward, preceded by a surveying party which stayed six miles ahead and pegged out the route. There were minor skirmishes on some occasions, but for reasons which have not been explained the dervishes never attacked the vulnerable railhead in force, nor tried to cut the unprotected tracks behind it. Girouard was also extremely fortunate in the matter of water; the desert was completely uninhabited and unexplored, but he managed, apparently by sheer intuition,* to sink two successful wells – at Mile 77 and Mile 126. For want of any distinguishing natural features, the stations at these points were called Number 4 and Number 6, the names they still bear today.

One of the qualities which endeared Girouard to Kitchener was his ability to carry out an order as given. Measured with a ruler on a map, the straight-line distance between Wadi Halfa and Abu Hamed is 212 miles. The tracks, when they reached their destination on October 31st, 1897 – 169 days after work had started – ran 230 miles.

The railway had won the war. Steevens wrote: 'Halfa was the decisive point of the campaign. For in Halfa was ... forged the deadliest weapon that Britain had ever used against Mahdiism – The Sudan Military Highway.'

Winston Churchill, as ever, was more quotable: 'Victory is the beautiful,

---

* Intuition because to this day not a drop of water has been found anywhere else along the route.

bright-coloured flower. Transport is the stem without which it could never have blossomed.'

The rest of the campaign was predictable. The British, once in range of the dervishes, caught them in camp near the confluence of the Nile and Atbara rivers. The central attack was led by Colonel Hector MacDonald, a tough Scot who had served for ten years in the ranks of the Gordon Highlanders before receiving his commission during the Afghan wars. Under cover of artillery, his troops stormed the thorn palisades of the camp and captured the bulk of the enemy force. Kitchener arrived on the battlefield in time to take the salute of the troops, and congratulate them on their bloodied bayonets.

Now he was poised for the finish. Under his command was the largest army Britain had assembled in nearly half a century – 8,200 British and 17,600 Egyptian and Sudanese troops. In front of him, with no place left to retreat, were the Khalifa and more than 30,000 dervishes. On the horizon, eight miles away but clearly visible, was the tallest man-made structure in the entire Sudan – the Mahdi's tomb. Its 91-foot dome presented so irresistible a target for artillerymen that by the time the battle was over and correspondents were swarming to take photographs, it resembled a badly-shattered eggshell.

There is little left to say about the battle of Omdurman. Churchill, who had the advantage of being a participant, describes it in *The River War*, and no more comprehensive, sustained account of men coming together in numbers for the purpose of mutual extermination exists in the English language. If the British felt any apprehension at all, it was on the night before the battle; the army had been marching all day and had to have a few hours' rest, on the open plain of Kerreri just north of the city. Every officer, from Kitchener down to Lieutenant Churchill, knew what a night attack could mean:

> At night, when 400 yards was the extreme range at which … fire could be opened, it was a matter of grave doubt whether the front could be kept and the attack repelled. The consequences of the line being penetrated in the darkness were appalling to think of. The sudden appearance of crowds of figures swarming to the attack through the gloom; … the fire getting uncontrolled and then a great bunching and crumpling of some part of the front, and mad confusion, in which a multitude of fierce swordsmen would surge through the gap, cutting and slashing at every living thing … and out of which only a few thousand, perhaps only a few hundred demoralized men would escape in barges and steamers to tell the tale of ruin and defeat.

None of this happened. The Khalifa did not attack by night – possibly because of the agents Wingate had sent into his lines to warn him that the British were themselves planning a night attack, or possibly because he did not trust his own troops' valour under cover of darkness. Before first light, the British fell out and started grouping, and the issue was no longer in doubt.

The dervishes attacked in a line five miles long shortly after dawn; their shouts were first heard in the forward lines at six fifteen. The artillery opened fire at a range of 2,800 yards, the riflemen at 1,200. It was six fifty, and Churchill reports that soon afterwards the Sirdar snapped his field glasses back in their case and announced that the enemy had been given 'a good dusting'.

But the battle was far from over. The 21st Lancers, Churchill's unit, had been assigned to the left flank of the British lines, between the infantry and the Nile. They were an extremely colourful regiment, and every move that they had made – the arrival in Cairo, the round of parties, the departure for the Sudan, the rides into the desert – had been exhaustively covered in newspaper stories. There had been pictures, interviews, predictions. The only thing the Lancers had not yet done was to fight. Nor, by mid-morning, did it look as if they would. Colonel R. H. Martin, their commander, had been given specific orders that his duties would be to reconnoitre and, if the occasion arose, to harass the enemy. Straining in his stirrups, Martin could see that whatever action remained was not coming in his direction. Through his glasses, however, he noticed that a small group of dervishes had become detached from the main attacking body and were falling back on the city. They were 600 yards away, he reckoned, across clear ground. Without hesitation, he ordered the bugler to sound a charge – 'their first in war', Churchill noted. The 320 horsemen, crouching low over their lances, had just reached full gallop when they discovered that the clear ground was in fact broken by a deep ravine, and that the ravine – a dry water-course – was filled with a mass of 2,000 dervishes. In the ensuing hand-to-hand scramble several medals were earned, but 80 men were killed or wounded, and 119 of the horses put out of action – neutralizing the Lancers as a fighting unit for the rest of the day. As Maréchal Bosquet observed after the great charge at Balaklava, '*C'est magnifique, mais ce n'est pas la guerre.*'

Meanwhile, on the main part of the battlefield, the dervishes had regrouped for a second attack. Steevens, in his account of the day's doings, summed it up as 'not a battle, but an execution'. The Khalifa's horde carried, for the most part, the same swords and spears which they had used so effectively on that day long ago on Abba Island. This time, however, they were not facing confused and cowardly Egyptian garrison troops, but icy-cool Grenadier Guards and Cameron Highlanders manning machine guns whose barrels were growing red-hot from incessant firing. Nevertheless, by a freak of timing, the second attack almost carried the day. It caught the body of Kitchener's army while it was wheeling around. Fortunately, MacDonald was able, on his own initiative, to swing his black Sudanese soldiers around by half-battalions – a complex enough manœuvre for the most seasoned troops – and cover the exposed flank long enough to blunt the attack.

After the battle, the sharp-eyed correspondent of the *Daily Mail* caught a vignette: ' ... by a solitary candle, the Sirdar, flat on his back, was dictating a dispatch to Colonel Wingate, flat on his belly.'

There was no need for adjectives. Save for the slightly embarrassing fact that the Khalifa himself had escaped,* the report almost wrote itself. For the British, 49 killed – including 22 Lancers and Herbert Howard, correspondent of *The Times*, who was struck by a British shell fragment in Omdurman after the battle – and 434 wounded; for the dervishes, 11,000 corpses left on the field, and 16,000 wounded for whom there was no means of caring, and who were therefore abandoned to join their comrades by slow and painful stages. There were also 30,000 prisoners, nearly all of them women who had remained in the city. Kitchener informed Cromer that to the best of his knowledge they were either cooks or concubines, and that he had no use for them in either capacity, nor the means to feed them.

Omdurman had been a great victory, and like all victories would grow greater with each re-telling. Perhaps it was that prospect which prompted Cromer to make this observation:

> I have no wish to disparage the strategical and tactical ability which was displayed in the conduct of the campaign. It is, however, a fact that no occasion arose for the display of any great skill in these branches of military science. ... The speedy and successful issue of the campaign depended, in fact, upon the methods adopted for overcoming the very exceptional difficulties connected with the supply and transport of the troops. The main quality to meet these difficulties was a good head for business. ... Lord Kitchener of Khartoum won his well-deserved peerage because he was an excellent man of business; he looked carefully after every important detail, and enforced economy.

Or perhaps it was the highest compliment he could pay.

Two days after the battle, on September 4th, Kitchener crossed the Nile to Khartoum, accompanied by representatives of every unit which had taken part in the campaign, and all the British officers who could be spared from duty. In front of Gordon's palace, its upper storey gone, its blind windows long since filled with rubble, the troops formed the other three sides of a rectangle. At the Sirdar's signal, two flags rose with perfect simultaneity on freshly erected staffs – the Union Jack and the Khedive's red banner. The national anthems were played and an unusually lusty 21-gun salute fired – no blanks had been provided, so real ammunition was used. Then the Sudanese band struck up *Abide With Me*, Gordon's

---

* He evaded capture for more than a year, and was finally cornered and killed some 160 miles south of Khartoum.

favourite hymn. When it was over, Kitchener mutely motioned an aide to dismiss the parade and, alone, walked away into what had been the palace garden. His shoulders shook, and those near him said they could see tears streaming down his cheeks.

Officially, Britain's only role in the campaign had been to lend the Khedive a helping hand in reclaiming title to a mutinous province. This was the reason for the dual flag ceremony, the protocol of which had been carefully drawn up and dictated to Kitchener. But such diplomatic niceties had been lost on the correspondents, who, in unison, were struck by the same genial idea. As Ernest Bennett of the *Westminster Gazette* wrote: 'The territories regained to civilization by Lord Kitchener's genius will be united to our vast possessions in the South, and Mr Rhodes's magnificent idea of a British Empire in Africa, stretching from Cairo to the Cape, will at length be realized in actual fact.'

Only the faintest shadow stood in the way.

The French, shut out of Egypt since 1882, had watched events there with mixed feelings. The easy British victory at Tel-el-Kebir and the collapse of the Arabi rebellion had caused them to regret their own cowardice; the fall of Khartoum and the death of Gordon had rekindled their hope. They had admired Gordon extravagantly, to the point of paying him their supreme compliment. '*Ah, ce Gordon*,' a French journalist had written, '*il aurait dû être Français.*'

But he was not, and so long as he lived France could only cast greedy glances at the Nile. Their own African adventures had not gone well. They owned vast areas of North Africa and steadily added to them, sending explorer-soldiers to plant the tricolour on the shores of Lake Chad, in remote desert oases, along the rivers of that part of the great equatorial forest which did not belong to Leopold. The acreage they amassed was enormous – the French empire in Africa was the largest of any colonial power's – but almost worthless. In the late 1860s, in anticipation of the opening of the Suez Canal, they had also established two precarious toeholds on the Red Sea, at Obock and at Djibouti, across from Aden. Neither was worth much alone, but connected with the vast holdings to the north and east, they provided the basis for an attractive dream – a French African empire which would stretch laterally across Africa and destroy once and for all Britain's aspirations to achieve a similar, vertical goal.

With Gordon's death, and the rise of the Mahdi, the French reached into international law and produced the doctrine of *res nullius* – literally 'nobody's thing'. If nobody owned something, then whoever came to claim it was entitled to keep it. As far as the French were concerned, the Sudan – which is to say the upper Nile – was *res nullius*. They truculently maintained this position in the face of two serious discouragements: Salisbury's refusal to acknowledge their claim, and their own inability to support it militarily. All the while, they listened anxiously for the sounds of Kitchener starting south – a move they knew he would eventually make, and which would forever shut them out of the Sudan.

Finally, they made their own move – a dashing, Gallic gesture. It had not the slightest right to succeed, but it did, and as direct consequence brought the world to within an angry word of war – a war which would have made the name of Fashoda as familiar as it later did that of Sarajevo.

PART SIX

Crossroads at Fashoda

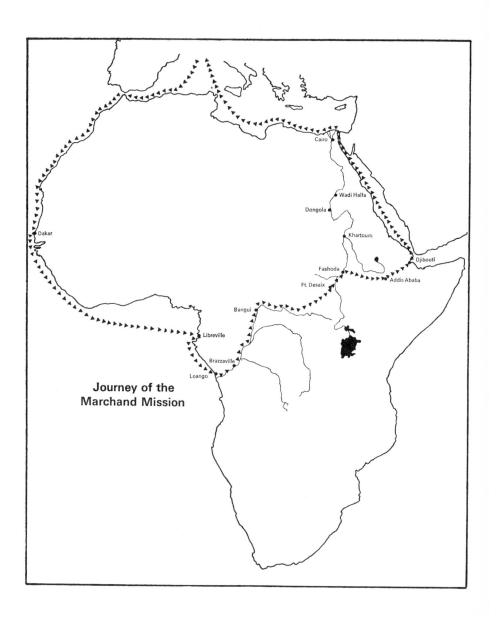

Dakar

Cairo

Wadi Halfa

Dongola

Khartoum

Fashoda

Ft. Desaix

Djibouti

Addis Ababa

Bangui

Libreville

Brazzaville

Loango

**Journey of the
Marchand Mission**

To anyone who valued national pride, and most French Army career officers did value it to some degree at least, 1895 was not a good year to be a French Army career officer.

There had been first of all the defeat at the hands of the Germans in 1870, a defeat which had left the Army not only humbled and dishonoured but also largely discredited. Marshal Bazaine, its Commander-in-Chief, had surrendered the fortress at Metz before the Germans could lob more than a few shells into it; afterwards, it had taken the better part of a day for his 184,000 able-bodied troops to march out and be taken prisoner. At his trial for treason, Bazaine said he had decided to preserve his army 'in order to defend the country against the more dangerous enemy at home' – the newly-proclaimed Third Republic.

In 1882, the politicians had given away Egypt. In 1889, with General Boulanger as its man on horseback, the Army almost regained its rightful place, but at the last possible moment the General panicked egregiously. It became common knowledge in France that instead of rushing to the Presidential Palace where supreme power lay waiting to be embraced, he headed for an *hôtel particulier* on the Left Bank to join his mistress, Mme de Bonnemains, who was in much the same posture. Two years later he committed suicide on her grave, and Clemenceau, once his staunchest supporter, composed his epitaph: 'Here lies General Boulanger, who died as he had lived, like a subaltern.'

Late in 1894, the nation was shocked by a scandal which implicated a member of the Army General Staff in espionage on behalf of the Germans. A military court promptly charged, tried and sentenced the culprit, an insignificant Jewish captain named Alfred Dreyfus, but to many people in and out of the Army his guilt had not at all been satisfactorily established and voices were already being raised in doubt. They would grow much louder.

The Army's greatest failure and frustration, however, derived from France's attempts to create a new colonial empire. The old empire, neglected through a century of uncertain experiment in government, had vanished – lost in battle, frittered away or sold outright. The drive for new colonies began even before the trauma of 1870 had worn off, and partly as a result of it. With nowhere to go in Europe, and a nagging need to find new markets for its goods, France cast eyes on the other continents.

Closest at hand was Algeria, which France had occupied in 1830, but which had remained little more than an uneasily-held armed camp. In 1870, it was divided into three *départements* and incorporated into metropolitan France, with full representation in the Chamber and Senate. If the hope was that this administrative act would exert a civilizing influence, it did not materialize. Immigration was encouraged and subsidized until Europeans accounted for more than one-fifth of the population, but neither they nor the Army could make Algeria economically justifiable or politically secure.

On the other side of the world, prospects appeared brighter. The small French establishment in Cochin, astride the delta of the Mekong River, was one of the few scraps which Britain, in culling over the Bourbon empire, had rejected as beneath notice. The Republic dispatched soldier-explorers who penetrated easily into the Indo-Chinese sub-continent, only to suffocate in its soft, yielding flesh. Here were no Moslem rebels who struck and vanished, no desert outposts where loneliness was the enemy's ally. The natives – Annamites, Cambodians, Laotians – were friendly. Their rulers, for all the peculiarities of their courts, were disposed to accept the amenities of French civilization. Yet warfare, supported by the Chinese to the north, continued unabated. The French commanded the sea and the rivers, but short of declaring war on China, there was no way to pacify the countryside. Fearful of outright rejection, the ambitious Prime Minister, Jules Ferry, called on the Chamber for repeated war credits, each time pointing out that a satisfactory conclusion to the enterprise was imminent. Victory after victory was announced; then the shocking news of the defeat of General De Négrier and the loss of the vital position at Lang-Son. Ferry was hooted out of the Chamber. As he walked across the Seine to tender his resignation to the President, mobs surrounded him, shouting, 'Into the water!' Peace for Indo-China was, in 1895, still around the corner.

Probably because it lies so close to Africa, Madagascar looks deceptively small on the map. Actually it is the third largest island in the world, bigger than France and only slightly smaller than Texas. Louis XIV was the first French monarch to have designs on it, and missionaries kept the option alive, but it was not until 1885 that the Republic decided to do things properly. By the usual route of minor quarrel, intervention, naval bombardment, landing parties, and treaty of friendship, France secured possession of the island's chief port, Diego Suarez. The interior was another problem: over a period of ten years and at a cost of 5,000 lives lost – twenty in combat, the rest to disease – the French managed to attain the position of close advisers to Her Majesty Queen Ranavalona III. But little progress was made towards effective control of the island, or its conversion into a ready consumer of Lyons textiles or Normandy butter.

It was Africa proper which held out the greatest promise for the fulfilment of imperial aspiration. Senegal, on the west coast, had been in French hands since the seventeenth century; a major port had been created at Dakar, and trading posts dotted the coast as far south as the mouth of the Congo.

Inland, north of the great river, France held hundreds of thousands of square miles of virgin land, the gift of a grateful foster-son, Savorgnan de Brazza. And past the forests lay more uncounted miles. 'Light soil,' Salisbury had once observed, but it stretched to the sea on the north and the west. And to the east – well, that was an open question, at least in the minds of French Army career officers.

The French had never succeeded in colonization by private charter. There was no Gallic equivalent of the British South Africa Company, or the Royal Niger Company. It was not that individual Frenchmen were incapable of carrying off a plan of grand design; the Suez Canal was evidence that they could. Nor was private capital lacking; it had been available to the extent of $300 million to finance the disastrous Panama project of 1888. If anything, private means were discouraged from taking on the challenge of colonization because a public instrument, ready and idle, lay at hand – the French Army.

The defeat which destroyed the honour of the Army had left its body intact, but purposeless. As hope for immediate revenge across the Rhine faded, brilliant young officers such as Lyautey applied for transfers to unfashionable colonial regiments. The Republic obliged them, sent them in inadequate number to pestilential corners of the world, and rewarded them with promotions, the assurance of action, and an occasional, addicting taste of glory. One officer who received a share of all three was Captain of Marine Infantry Jean-Baptiste Marchand.

Neither by family tradition nor by early training was Marchand the typical French career military officer. His father was a carpenter in the village of Thoissey, in the placid region between Dijon and the Swiss border, and Jean-Baptiste was the eldest of five children. Because money was short, he left school in 1876, at the age of thirteen, to become an apprentice to *Maître* Blondel, the local notary. His careful calligraphy was Marchand's only qualification for the work; before turning twenty he left home and enlisted in the Army. That he specifically chose marine infantry as his branch of service, and that Thoissey is almost as far from the sea as it is possible to be in France, probably say something about his childhood and youth.

Working his way through the ranks, Marchand earned his commission as *sous-lieutenant* in the 4th Marine regiment in February 1887, graduating thirtieth in a class of 460. The regiment had been training for service in Indo-China, but the French defeat at Lang-Son caused a change of plans, and it was sent to West Africa instead. Marchand had just turned 25; he would spend his next seven years there.

West Africa from the Senegal River to the Niger was a patchwork of concessions, trading stations and circlets of influence superimposed by force on the existing system of well-established native kingdoms. Profitable commercial products – once slaves, now palm oil – had attracted the interest of a half-dozen European countries; some of them – the Danes, Swedes, and Dutch – had been driven off, but the rest struggled to maintain their toe-holds. This political climate called for an odd military posture: soldiers fought elusive native chiefs while keeping an eye over their shoulder for other white troops. 'We soldiers', wrote General Galliéni, whose exploits made him a national hero, 'knew only that there were territories which ought to belong to us and that the English and Germans were in process of appropriating them. We wanted to beat them to it.'

Because of the near-total ignorance of civil authorities at home of local conditions or even terrain, the colonial officer became at once explorer, conqueror, administrator, dispenser of justice and court of last resort. During his years of West African service, Marchand filled all these roles.

The military aspects of his work were of a nature to delight and thrill schoolboys – forays into unknown steaming jungles, ambushes and fire-fights against fanatical blacks with names such as Sikou-Ba and Samori who stealthily attacked and sometimes overran emplaced machine-gun positions in unpronounceable places: Ouessebougou, Doseguela and Kodiokofi. The political aspect consisted of repeated attempts to unite the fragmented French holdings in Senegal, Guinea and on the Ivory Coast into a single strategically defensible unit. These attempts came to nothing, frustrated equally by British counter-measures and the parsimony of successive French Governments. Early on, Marchand learned to hate the first and despise the second.

The few photographs of Marchand that have survived from this period show him to be short and slight – by his own account, his normal weight was 69 kilograms, 152 pounds. To be sure, there were few fat colonial officers, but fewer still had his taut features and deep-set, unsmiling eyes. In West Africa, Marchand was twice wounded, nearly losing his right arm, mentioned in dispatches, and promoted to the rank of captain. He also nurtured a conviction which slowly matured into a plan. While on home leave in 1895, only his second in seven years, he proposed it to the responsible authorities.

The origins of the Marchand Mission – who gave what orders and authorized what action – are lost to historians. Many of the key documents, whose existence can be inferred from other sources, have been stripped out of the files of the Foreign and Colonial Ministries, and scholars still occasionally produce monographs which attempt to fix the blame for this face-saving vandalism. Certain facts, however, are clear: some time in late summer of 1895, Captain Marchand went to see Marcel Chautemps, the new Minister of Colonies, and outlined his plan to him. Marchand later claimed that he had originally gone to see Gabriel Hanotaux, the Foreign Minister, who in turn directed him to Chautemps. Hanotaux later denied this, and there is no evidence other than Marchand's word that such a meeting occurred. On September 21st, however, in a confidential inter-office memorandum addressed to Hanotaux, Chautemps described his own meeting with Marchand and suggested that the Captain's plan raised 'a question which touches more on general foreign policy than it does on purely colonial interests'.

That it did. What Marchand had in mind was to 'extend French influence to the Nile'.

Marchand's argument, and no French official would quarrel with it, at least in private, was that France's imperial aspirations in Africa were doomed to failure unless they were anchored with an outlet on the great highway of the Nile. There was no hope of ever securing lasting control over the west coast, and the Sahara presented an impenetrable barrier to the north. Unless the French could use the Nile – not own it outright, just use it – there was no sense wasting lives and money in subjugating and developing West Africa.

Unfortunately, the French had lost Egypt when their fleet sailed away from Alexandria in 1882. Egypt, though nominally a dependent state of the Sultan, was British. And the Nile, from the Delta to Wadi Halfa, was British; it could not have been more British if its masters had decreed that the slow-moving *dhows* and steamers had to travel on the left-hand side.

South of Wadi Halfa, however, was another matter. There was no traffic whatever. The river, its banks and the entire Sudan from the Red Sea to the watershed of the Congo, belonged to the Khalifa Abdullah and his dervishes, and had been in their hands since the killing of Gordon and destruction of Khartoum ten years earlier. An exhausting amount of diplomacy on the part of the British had been expended in keeping European hands off the Sudan, against the day when Anglo-Egyptian forces slowly being amassed could be sent down to reclaim it. A score of treaties and conventions had been signed – by England and Germany, England and Portugal, England and Leopold II, even England and France. Most of them, for all their seals and ribbons, were substantially meaningless. Salisbury himself, in a moment of candour, had written: 'We have been engaged in drawing lines upon maps where no white man's foot has ever trod; we have been giving away mountains and rivers and lakes to each other, only hindered by the small impediment that we never knew exactly where the mountains and rivers and lakes were.'

But in all the welter of agreements and accommodations, one simple and unmistakable phrase stood out. It had been pronounced by Edward Grey, Permanent Under-Secretary of State, in the House on March 28th, 1895. Surveying the gathering of imperialist vultures who were hovering over the Sudan, he had stated flatly that Her Majesty's Government would consider any intrusion into the valley of the Upper Nile as an 'unfriendly act'. As he said it, his voice, if not his finger, was aimed directly towards Paris. Hanotaux had replied with an elegant statement to the effect that his country

regarded Mr Grey's views as totally unilateral and therefore not necessarily binding on French policy, either now or in the future. Grey had not
pursued the debate, leaving the Fleet and the army which Kitchener was
training in Egypt to make the point for him.

Marchand's plan was to circumvent the Grey Declaration by stealth. He
would lead a small expedition – a dozen whites and perhaps a hundred
Senegalese riflemen – from the west coast, across the equatorial forest, up
the Ubangi river, which was in French hands, and around the Bahr-el-
Gazal, a trackless waste of swamps and marshland that stretched eastward
to the Nile. Once there, he would plant the French flag. He had no illusion
that he could keep it there by force, but he did not think that this would be
necessary. His sole object was to secure for France a negotiable stake on the
Nile. Once it was established, he naturally assumed that an international
conference would be convened to discuss, at great length, the relative
claims of the pretenders. That, after all, had been the classic pattern of the
political partition of Africa: explorers endured heat, privation and danger to
plant a flag; later, they or members of their expedition returned home with
crudely drawn maps, and diplomats gathered to officiate at the carving.
When it came time to carve up the Nile, France would get its share.

Marchand had selected the exact place – Fashoda – where he proposed
planting the flag. He had never been there – no white man had since 1880.
The German, Schweinfurth, who passed through in 1869, had pronounced
it 'pestiferous'. Fashoda sat on the left bank of the Nile, 480 miles south of
Khartoum. It had been chosen as the site for a fortress by the Egyptian
forces which first penetrated into the Sudan in 1830. By 1855 it had become
a government post whose sole function was to serve as collecting-point for
whatever tribute could be extracted from the Shilluk and Dinka tribes that
roamed the region. The troops ordered to perform this civilizing task
considered assignment to Fashoda as hardship duty. To bolster their
morale, special licence was permitted them in making what use they wished
of the natives' few possessions and the persons of their women. During the
Mahdi's rebellion Fashoda was therefore one of the first Egyptian positions
set to the torch. The fortifications and low-lying buildings described by
Schweinfurth had lain in ruins for ten years. Marchand did not know this
about Fashoda, any more than he knew exactly how to get there.

Nevertheless, his plan was accepted. A map-reading session prompted
the inter-office memorandum of September 21st, 1895, from the Minister
of Colonies to the Foreign Minister, which in turn set in motion the
bureaucratic machinery of the Republic. On November 10th, Marchand
complied with a request to submit an additional report; on November 21st,
Berthelot, who had in the interval become the new Foreign Minister, took
up the matter at a Cabinet Meeting; Guieysse, who had taken over as
Minister of Colonies, endorsed it; on November 30th, Berthelot signed the
letter formally authorizing the Mission. Then nothing happened until

February 24th, 1896, when Guieysse handed Marchand his instructions, which had been cleared with the new acting Foreign Minister, Bourgeois. Throughout all these developments a deep cloak of secrecy was maintained.

Marchand occupied the time between November 1895 and February 1896 in assembling the members of his expedition. In this respect he was given a free hand and he did an extraordinary job. As his closest aides, he chose two young officers whom he had known in Africa. Captain Albert Baratier, who had received his commission at St Cyr, was given the crucial task of supervising the transport of men and supplies. Lieutenant Charles Mangin, who like Marchand had come up through the ranks, was assigned the recruiting and training of the 150 Senegalese riflemen who would accompany the Mission and, should trouble arise with the dervishes, protect it. Both men not only discharged their duties to the letter but went on, as did Marchand himself, to become generals.

The rest of the Mission consisted of three other army officers, Captain Germain (Marchand's adjutant) and Lieutenants Largeau and Simon; a naval officer, Ensign Dye, because there would be navigation to contend with once the Nile was reached; four non-commissioned officers, all experienced Africa hands; a military surgeon, Dr Joseph Emily, who was also to keep a diary and write the best account of the trip; and an interpreter, Landeroin, who would show talent of an unexpected nature. At the outset they were joined by an artist-illustrator named Castellani who represented the magazine *L'Illustration*. He found neither the climate nor the discipline to his liking and left the expedition at mid-point.

In order to escape the attention of British spies, it was decided that the Mission would leave in four separate groups. Before they left, however, Gabriel Hanotaux, who was back in office as Minister of Foreign Affairs, told them: 'You are going to fire a pistol shot on the Nile; we will all accept its consequences.' Unlike other statements which he later denied having made, or tried to explain away, M. Hanotaux was fairly stuck with this one.

The first echelon of the Marchand Mission left France on March 25th, 1896. Twelve days earlier, shortly after midnight, General Kitchener had received urgent and most secret orders in Cairo. He was to move south immediately in the long-awaited campaign to clear the Sudan.

Though neither side knew it yet, the race was on.

Marchand left with the last group, sailing from Marseilles aboard the *Taygete* on May 25th, 1896, touching at Libreville, capital of the French Congo, on July 19th, and arriving at Loango, sixty miles north of the river's mouth, on July 24th. Even by local standards, Loango was not much of a place: eight long, flat, wooden buildings, facing the sea and set at unfriendly distance apart from each other. These were the *comptoirs*, the privately owned posts which served as commercial bases for trade with the interior; two were English, three Portuguese, one Dutch and two French. At one end of the row was a Catholic mission; at the other end a smaller but taller structure, *la maison d'Ubangi*, served as shelter for travellers waiting to join caravans heading inland. Farther back were the ruins of some abandoned warehouses and a cluster of 'permanent' mud houses which served as headquarters for the French administrative authorities. The whole urban sprawl lay under a piercing sun which baked it to a uniform dun colour, relieved in spots by patches of scorched, scrawny grass. Baratier, who had arrived on June 10th to start making arrangements, noted that it had not changed in the least since he had last seen it two years earlier.

It was not Loango's natural charm which had caused Marchand to select it as the starting point for the Mission. It had served that purpose for other expeditions dozens of times before, for one good reason: the Loangans, if they could be rounded up, were the finest porters on the west coast of Africa. Walking with their characteristic loping gait, they could make the 300-mile trip to Brazzaville, at the point where the Congo became navigable, in twenty days, carrying the standard 30-kilogram load on their head. Baratier writes: 'To look at them, with their scrawny bodies, their ribs sticking out, their palsied legs and their feet torn to shreds by chiggers, you would think them incapable of the slightest effort. Yet the Lord must have brought them into the world with a load on their head, for without them, the Congo colony could not have survived.'

Marchand's plan was to march from Loango to Brazzaville, then to steam up the Congo and Ubangi rivers to Bangui, the outer limit of French colonial control. From there, it was still 900 miles to the Nile, most of it across a gigantic uncharted plain. The few explorers who had nibbled at its edges reported that it was impassable: in the summer, it baked and cracked into iron-hard clay totally devoid of water; during the rainy season it became a swamp, too shallow and muddy to sustain either a man on foot or a boat. Marchand had envisaged leading his men around this plain, heading first north and then east to reach the river. The full distance from Loango to Fashoda he reckoned as approximately 1,450 miles, roughly the same as that from Paris to Moscow.

But it was not simply a matter of reaching Fashoda. In order to be able to lodge a defensible claim on behalf of France, Marchand had to establish 'effective occupation', as specified by the Berlin Conference of 1885 which had marked off the partition of Africa. To do this, he would have to create a chain of permanent posts along his route, and keep them provisioned at least long enough for the wheels of diplomacy to grind out a favourable judgment. Translated into the most practical of terms, this meant that he would have to make his secret dash to Fashoda carrying 15,000 30-kilogram loads – the irreducible amount of supplies the expedition would require.

The job of providing transport for this mountain of material was assigned to Baratier, who had an unsentimental idea of what it involved:

Speed was essential to the success of the Mission, and therefore any possibility of drawing on a fixed base of operations was ruled out. We would have to take with us everything we would need – provisions and ammunition – for a period of two to three years.

It was clearly impossible for us to carry all the food we would require. For just 100 men, a daily ration of 300 grams of rice would add up to more than 10 tons per year. We therefore had to count on living off the land.

Now, African natives seldom grow more food than they need for themselves and their families. To take it away from them condemns them to almost certain starvation and therefore usually provokes uprisings. Measures of repression are time-consuming and to some degree self-defeating because neighbouring tribes are likely to hide their supplies and scatter.

This was a messy way to travel, suitable for a Stanley who passed through the jungle like a scourge, leaving a trail of burnt villages and perforated corpses. The Mission would do it the other way, paying as it went.

But even this is complicated because the goods which attract one tribe may leave the next one cold. Some like red beads; others only white ones. Here, blue denim is much prized; there, white calico. It was moreover impossible to know exactly what we should bring because some of the regions we would cross had never been visited by white men.

The Mission brought along all these items, and also yellow leather, yard goods of every variety, Korans for the Moslems and gunpowder for the heathens, ceremonial sabres, brocades and gold stripes for chieftains, and 'because it is always useful to please the women,' mirrors, pearl necklaces, real and fake amber, coral, ribbons, and '*de la parfumerie*'.

Baratier's immediate problem was how to move this bazaar inland. Normally, he would have arranged for groups of 80 to 100 porters to leave each day – it was clearly impossible to assemble a phalanx of 15,000 of them – and start towards Brazzaville; as they arrived and returned empty-headed, they would start off again. Thus there would soon be a human chain stretched out in both directions along the 300 miles. Finally the end would catch up with the beginning and that would be that. Under usual circumstances, the whole operation would take perhaps eight or nine weeks.

But circumstances were far from normal. Several of the lesser chieftains whose territories lay astride the trail had become land-borne pirates, at first stealing a few loads here and there, and when their theft had gone unpunished, halting and stripping entire caravans. Since it was customary for the Loangan bearers to receive a small down-payment at the start and the bulk of their pay on delivery, they quickly stopped showing up for work at the *comptoirs*. When Marchand arrived in Loango, the Mission's supplies lay in untidy heaps, and Baratier was obliged to report that he could not recruit a single bearer. Worse yet, the first few he had sent did not reach their destination.

This would not do. Marchand, although he never wrote a full account of the Mission, nevertheless peppered his friends with letters. One describes his reaction on receiving this news: 'I confess that at that moment I thought the Mission was over, even before it had started. My stupefaction was immediate and total. All evening, I remained in this state ... I cannot recall in all my years in Africa – and soon they will be ten, and what years! – such total dejection.'

By morning, stupefaction had yielded to reason. Marchand knew what the problem was, and what had to be done to solve it. The problem, in a word, was Brazza – Savorgnan de Brazza who, in 1896, was commissioner-general of the French Congo. Though only 45 years old, the great soldier-explorer was a man broken in health and, largely, in spirit. No one in Paris wished – or indeed dared, for France owed the Congo to his single-handed effort – to criticize Brazza, but it was evident that his long service in the unhealthy climate of central Africa had affected him. His dispatches rambled on about bringing peace and security to the natives. The reason why caravans could not safely travel the trail between Loango and Brazza-ville was that Brazza had not sufficiently impressed the local chiefs with the inescapable consequence of their piracy.

To Marchand's complaints, Brazza explained that times were difficult and perhaps if the Mission waited a little, some accommodation could be made. Lieutenant Mangin, who had recruited the 150 Senegalese riflemen to escort the Mission, was disposed to be kind in his evaluation: 'M. de Brazza gives me the impression of a tired old lion who roars at the sight of our taking off on a hunt which he wishes he could only join.'

Marchand could not afford such largeness of spirit. After weeks of un-successful discussions, he finally put the matter squarely: either Brazza would issue the orders necessary to clear the way, or Marchand would take the first ship back to France and throw the whole matter in the lap of the Cabinet. Wearily, the commissioner-general of the French Congo told the captain of marine infantry: 'Write your own orders, and I will sign them.' According to Mangin: 'After Marchand secured command, it became my task to assure transport through the troubled zone. This was accomplished through certain rapid operations which had the virtue of rudely surprising the natives.'

A French account speaks of *'incendier quelques cabanes'* – burn down a few shacks. In fact, Mangin's riflemen set more than thirty villages to the torch, scattering the inhabitants and denying them a base of operation for further pillage.

On September 18th, exactly a month after his last stormy meeting with Brazza, Marchand left Loango. On November 8th, the Mission was in Brazzaville, its 15,000 charges trailing safely behind it. (On September 23rd, Kitchener had taken Dongala without any fighting; the dervish army, intact, still lay between him and Khartoum.)

For the last 300 miles of its course, the Congo is not navigable. Beyond the last of the cataracts, however, the river blossoms into a vast lake sixty miles long and fifteen miles at its widest – Stanley Pool. At the southern tip of this lake two scruffy villages – they are cities now, and capitals of their respective countries – stood and stared suspiciously at each other across the placid water. Brazzaville in 1896 was, in Baratier's phrase, 'a sensible place to build a town'. Leopoldville, on the Congo Free State side, was more substantial, in anticipation of the railway that would soon connect it with the coast.

Marchand's arrival was cause for celebration; the revolt of the porters had virtually cut Brazzaville off from the outside world, and some of the supplies he carried were addressed to the local officers' mess. As far as helping the Mission along, there was little that could be done. What they needed was river transportation to Bangui, 600 miles away. Baratier walked down to see what was available: 'It is hardly necessary to point out that the port of Brazzaville bore the same relation to a real port as the town itself did to a real town. It consisted of a small natural creek in which two half-dismantled boats sat and rotted. Our "fleet" included another boat, but it was somewhere upriver, chartered for private, commercial use.'

By contrast, the waterfront across the river was hustling with activity. Five ships were being loaded or unloaded. A sixth was under construction. Leopold's careful cultivation of commerce was obviously more successful, whatever its hidden costs, than Brazza's paternal benevolence.

Marchand may have reflected on this, and the fact that his own country, while making a grab for a foreign province, could not even vouchsafe him passages through territory which it already owned. But that was not his affair; he had a job to do, and pride could not be permitted to interfere with it. He took a ferry across the river, paid a formal call on the Belgian governor-general, and asked to borrow or rent a suitable boat.

The Belgian, Colonel Wahys, was delighted to oblige him. Mangin, who knew Wahys by reputation, recalled that he had served with the French expeditionary force in Mexico at the time of the ill-fated Maximilian affair, and ascribed his helpfulness to this prior association. A more reasonable explanation is that Leopold had ordered him to help Marchand in any way possible. The Belgian King's own designs on the Nile had been successfully checked by Salisbury, and the prospect of a dispute which would lead to a new international conference could only have delighted him. Leopold had proved on several occasions that he could hold his own at meetings of this kind.

The *Ville-de-Bruges*, a comfortable, substantial steamer commanded by a Swedish captain named Lindholm, was put at Marchand's disposal. It required two trips to carry all the cargo, and the last few miles above Zinda, where the Ubangi River became too shallow for the *Ville-de-Bruges*, had to be negotiated by a swarm of 65 native dugouts, but for once the local French administrator, M. Bobichon, was on the job, and by April 11th, 1897, the Mission and all its gear were safely in Bangui. (On April 11th, Kitchener was still in Dongala, and Lieutenant Girouard had only begun assembling the material he would need to build the Desert railway.)

If there was ever a time that the Mission enjoyed a few frivolous moments, it was now. Writing to his sister, Mangin reported: 'So far, a picturesque voyage ... every evening the porters relax by dancing to the music we play on our phonograph – a touch of Parisian boulevards in the heart of Africa.' He also took time to send her a recipe:

> It's quite good, elephant trunk *a l'étuvée*: you just dig a hole in the ground – 2 metres 50 should do it – and heat it well for twelve hours. Then insert the trunk, covered if possible with banana leaves, and cover lightly with dirt. Leave it in for another twelve hours. This gives a fairly firm flesh, lightly larded and very reminiscent of zebu hump.

Baratier found himself caught in the middle of a crowd on market day in a river village:

> Great pyramids of manioc, carefully wrapped in individual leaves, are the staple; but there are baskets of pineapples, gleaming dull gold, and next to them the brilliant yellow of bananas ... and some greens suitable to garnish a sauce. ... A fight breaks out and I am asked to pass judgment on the freshness of an egg. ... Another fight, this time between two competitors: their voices rise, they make threatening gestures and insult each other's ancestries. I understand not a word, but I comprehend everything as clearly as if I were standing in *Les Halles*.

Even with the Belgians' help, the Mission was four months behind schedule, and Marchand did not want to waste any time in Bangui. He sent Mangin and Germain ahead to scout, and was himself ready to follow when, on April 17th, he received word that the entire countryside along the route he had selected had been laid waste by the dervishes; not a living thing remained to eat or to act as porters. It would take several years 'to repopulate this immense desert'; until then, anyone foolish enough to wander into it would either starve or be massacred by freebooting bands of the Khalifa's followers.

This was, Marchand wrote, 'the total defeat of my three years of planning'. The choice was to go back or to try forcing his way directly to the Nile, across the swamps of the Bahr-el-Gazal. With 'death in my soul', Marchand decided to continue.

His immediate problem was to find a boat. On the northern route, he could have stayed on dry land; going this way, he would have to use every available piece of water he could find. It was said that the Soueh was navigable during certain parts of the year, also the Mbomou. Bangui lay near the edge of the Congo basin; Fashoda was on the Nile. No one had ever undertaken even a preliminary hydrographic survey of the region where these two great basins met; it was not even certain in which direction some of the smaller tributaries ran.

The only boat of any kind available to Marchand within 1,000 miles was the *Faidherbe*. Old and decrepit, it was sixty feet long, eighteen feet wide, and drew, fully loaded, a little less than five feet of water. It had a single deck, with no enclosed space, and one six-foot smokestack. Its power plant was an ancient boiler that consumed 900 cubic feet of wood per day, roughly as much as twenty men could cut if they worked all night. Its normal function, which it was barely able to perform, was to carry mail between the five or six stations on the Ubangi river. From Marchand's point of view, however, the *Faidherbe*'s most serious drawback was that it was riveted together and therefore was not, as many boats built for African service and its frequent portages, dismountable. This created a problem because the first likely navigable waterway along the new course was 120 overland miles away.

The job of turning the *Faidherbe* into a *bateau-démontable* fell to Captain Germain. With the aid of a Senegalese sergeant who had had some experience with machinery, he broke it into pieces by cutting through the rivets. There was, however, nothing which he could do about the boiler except separate it into two parts, each of which weighed a little more than a ton. How they were carried, on human backs, over gorges and ravines, through virgin jungle and across torrents, challenges not only description but imagination as well. Where possible, a road was cut, using axes to chop down trees and melinite – a rough-and-ready explosive made of picric acid, gun-cotton and gum arabic – to blast out stumps and rocks. The fallen tree-trunks were used as rollers to move the heavy pieces along, much as the great obelisk of Luxor had been transported to the sea on its way to Paris. Where no road could be cut, the pieces were simply manhandled by brute force and willpower, sometimes advancing 100 yards in a long, back-breaking day.

Meanwhile, Marchand pushed on ahead, creating forts and depots as he went. The phonograph and the Parisian records were forgotten now. It was hard going, and the journals describing this portion of the trip tend to be brief, as if written by men too tired at the end of the day to ponder over a paragraph.

At Fort Hossinger, which he reached on July 24th, Marchand paused to let Baratier search out a route. He came back seventeen days later, exhausted and half-starved but jubilant: the water was flowing northward. 'We are', he told Marchand, 'in the basin of the Mediterranean.'

Mangin, meanwhile, had forged ahead to found still another base on the ruins of an old Egyptian emplacement. He named it Fort Desaix in honour of the Napoleonic general who had remained behind to explore the northern Nile valley during the campaign of 1798-9. It is now the site of Wau, a provincial capital and major railway terminus. One hundred miles behind, Marchand waited impatiently while the pieces of the *Faidherbe* were being reassembled. Even here, at the extreme edge of empire, bureaucracy caught up with him. He had asked that three *baleinières* – open whaling boats – be sent to him, and they finally arrived. As he wrote: 'One must have admiration for our Administration. I asked for three boats, a total of about 1,300 metal parts. All but 27 arrived safely, but these 27 happen to be the main ribs. Without them I cannot put together a single craft.'

Germain managed to make do without them, as he managed to manufacture the rivets required to weld the *Faidherbe* back together – using bits and pieces of wire, utensils and ornaments, which he collected from the natives, melted down and reshaped. On November 22nd, the boat was lowered into the Soueh River and, to the surprise of everyone, stayed afloat. (On November 22nd, Kitchener was in Metemmah, 112 miles north of Khartoum, still carefully avoiding battle with the dervishes until his railway was completed and could bring him the mountains of supplies he had requisitioned. The race, if such it was, matched not a tortoise and a hare, but a herd of elephants and a thin, weary column of ants.)

Marchand was jubilant, and spoke of reaching not Fashoda but Khartoum itself in fifteen days. But not even he could change the seasons; the Soueh, which had sounded to a depth of thirty feet, began dropping rapidly after the rains stopped. By the end of December, it was falling before their eyes, revealing rocky outcroppings and the shadows of long, sinuous sandbars. They barely made it as far as Fort Desaix. The largest of the whaling boats, named the *Étienne* after a notoriously vociferous pro-colonial delegate, had to be emptied and pushed by hand through the rapidly vanishing rivulets of water. Had the Mission not lost time between Loango and Brazzaville, time which they understandably had not counted on losing; had there been better transport available at Bangui; had they made their overland crossing faster, which is almost physically impossible; had any of these things happened, Marchand would have been in Fashoda late in December 1897, nine months before the decisive battle at Omdurman. What might then have been the course of events is open to speculation. French commentators, and particularly those like Hanotaux who in their official capacities as Ministers had to answer for the outcome of the Mission, have written about possible alliances with the dervishes or with the Abyssinians that could have blunted the British thrust. Probably not, because Kitchener, once launched towards an objective, was a very stubborn man. All of this, however, belongs to the 'what-if' school of history. The fact was that the dry season intervened and Marchand was stuck in Fort Desaix until the rain came.

It came in May, pelting down daily until the sandbars they had been staring at for five months were at last submerged. The river was still too low to float the *Faidherbe*, but Marchand decided he could wait no longer. On June 4th, half the Mission piled into the flotilla of barges and dugouts and moved out; the rest would follow as soon as they could. (On June 4th, Kitchener and his entire Expeditionary Force had settled down into summer quarters around Berber, waiting for the hot weather to break.)

After the months of inactivity, sheer movement was exhilarating. To the delight of the native paddlers, the sails which Dye rigged up worked to perfection. Dr Emily's journal reads:

> Sunday, June 5th. Good day. Despite a violent storm which forced us to shore, we covered 45 kilometres.
> Monday, June 6th. 50 Kilometres today. A hippopotamus attacked the lead boat but Marchand killed it. ...
> Friday, June 10th. Lazy morning; didn't raise anchor until eight. ...

Gradually, however, the river's current slowed down until, on the 12th, it stopped completely. They were on the edge of the great swamp which Baratier had scouted. Emily writes:

> Before our eyes stretched an immense prairie, a sea of grass; to the horizon we could see only that endless greenness and the washed blue of the sky. Our blacks looked at us as if to ask 'Where is the way?' There wasn't any way. ... Every few feet, the water vanished under a matted tangle of roots, floating plants and oozing mud. The men would have to go over the side and push, arching themselves against the long supple poles they had carefully prepared. ...

On that first day in the swamp, the Mission covered two kilometres, and spent the night huddled together on their boats; there was no spot of dry land on which to pitch a tent or build a fire to discourage the swarms of insects. In the morning, under the blazing sun, they moved forward again – or what they thought was forward. By mid-day, it was impossible to move. Baratier decided the safest course was to return and try again. A day of back-breaking work. Progress: zero.

Forty years earlier, at the height of the great competition to find the sources of the Nile, not even the most stubborn or foolhardy of explorers had considered attacking the river from this direction. It was simply put down on the maps as impassable. Eighteen years earlier, Gessi, one of Gordon's lieutenants, had wandered into the great swamp by mistake, and had barely struggled out alive. Yet Marchand pushed on, and Dr Emily recorded his progress:

> Tuesday, June 21st. Made 500 metres by lunch-time, when the channel suddenly closed. The men worked the rest of the day and all night building a mud dam to trap some water and float the boats. ... Wednesday, June 22nd. The water rose to 15 centimetres. It is so foul that I cannot bring myself to wash my face in it. Yet we have been drinking it for ten days, after pretending to boil it. ... Today was a 500-metre day. ...

On the afternoon of the 24th, though the weeds were no less thick or tangled, they could sense a faint current underfoot. Shortly after five o'clock, as if a solid green curtain had suddenly been yanked away, they found themselves staring at an immense sheet of gleaming water, gently rippled by a faint breeze. The Bahr-el-Gazal, the sea of gazelles, is in reality a river, the most important western tributary of the White Nile, but it received its name because since time immemorial it had backed up every year to the edge of the swamp to form the great lake on which Marchand and his men now found themselves.

The physical hardships were over – the rest of the trip would be a leisurely sail downstream – but political problems now replaced them. Marchand's orders were to avoid conflict with the dervishes at all costs. Not only were there delicate diplomatic considerations involved – considerations which had great meaning to the functionaries at the Ministry of Foreign Affairs – but there was also the practical matter that the Khalifa had an army of some 60,000 troops and Marchand had 150 riflemen. During their crossing of the swamp, the Mission had barely seen any human beings – an occasional Dinka or two out hunting on the long, thin boats they manœuvred effortlessly through the weeds – but here, small villages began dotting both banks of the river. The inhabitants were Shilluks, black-skinned, tall and graceful men, and slender women who wore close-cropped hair and a bit of cloth which draped over their shoulder to cover one breast. They were not Moslems, and had taken little interest in the holy revolt which had been started by the Mahdi and kept alive by the Khalifa. To the urgent questions of Landeroin, the interpreter, they professed to have no knowledge about other white men, or about warfare to the north. Pearls and cloth and copper necklaces were exchanged for eggs and scrawny chickens. As for Fashoda, yes, it was not far away, four or five days by the river, but it was empty and deserted.

There was no way Marchand could test the honesty of the Shilluks' protestations about the dervishes, but regarding Fashoda they had been truthful enough. Late on the afternoon of July 10th, 1898, the Mission reached its destination, and he could see for himself. The town lay on the west bank of the river, partially screened by a stand of tall, sparse palms. Dr Emily wrote:

> It was nothing but a mass of bricks and mud. Ancient buildings, with not a beam, not a roof. Puddles had formed where courtyards had once been, and all around them walls had crumbled. ... Here, the frame of a door still stood, topped by the vault of an arch profiled against the sky. ... Farther, a large structure divided into three chambers, their thick walls still blackened by the explosion which had shattered them ... this was the ancient powder house. ... Other ruins which, by their more ambitious proportions and by the vestiges of lime which still clung to them, must have once been a government house. ... Everywhere, a thick carpet of weeds and, surrounding it all, a moat more than three kilometres in perimeter and full of stagnant water.

Nevertheless, it was Fashoda. At the end of their dinner that night, the officers and white non-commissioned officers of the Mission Marchand drank champagne – Montebello, no less – and toasted 'la plus grande France'.

In the morning, work resumed. Mangin and his riflemen began building fortifications; Dr Emily set up a small dispensary; Landeroin cleared a strip of land and planted the seeds which had been brought along – lettuce, cabbage, carrots. In this climate, they sprouted to ripeness in five weeks. A flagstaff was erected and, on the morning of the 12th, the flag was raised with full honours. Since the expedition had brought no cannon, four home-made firecrackers were set off as the Senegalese riflemen, at stiff attention, presented arms. The local Shilluk chieftain, Abd-el-Fadil, was invited as guest of honour and observed the ceremonies, and the soldiers, with impassive solemnity.

His official duties completed, Marchand settled down to wait. His original plan had envisaged that while he made his end run to the Nile, a far stronger force would come out of the Abyssinian highlands to meet him. How much stronger would depend on the ability of French diplomacy to secure the support of the Abyssinian emperor, Menelik. Since there had been no one to greet him at Fashoda, Marchand sent a small group south and east to meet the advancing column.

No such column existed. The effort had been made: for two years, the French had courted Menelik, promising him all manner of spoils. They had even enlisted the aid of their Russian allies, who sent a mission all the way from St Petersburg to Addis Ababa for the ostensible purpose of studying common elements of the Greek Orthodox and Coptic religions. The French had, at Menelik's request, equipped his soldiers with modern rifles, a gesture which the Italians noisily took pains to resent after their own débâcle at Adowa. Three separate missions had been charged with mounting the expedition which was to meet Marchand, but because of personal rivalries their efforts were not co-ordinated. One never left Abyssinia; the second penetrated to within ninety miles of Fashoda, but was forced to turn back because of lack of supplies. The third did succeed, but only by the thinnest of technicalities. Leaving in strength but failing rapidly, it managed to send two scouts as far as the Nile, which they reached on June 22nd, while Marchand was still struggling towards the Bahr-el-Gazal. Exhausted, starved and racked with fever, they did not even attempt to stay the night; one of them died on the way back. The orders they carried, composed in Paris and marked 'Very Confidential', read: 'Upon reaching the Nile, you will establish a permanent base. ... '

In Fashoda, time moved slowly; six weeks passed with no word from any direction. After three years of preparation, of struggle, of daily steeling himself against every sort of adversity, the wait must for Marchand have become the most unendurable form of torture. He had, on arrival, sent dispatches back to France; they would arrive in eight or nine months. Under the leaden skies of the gathering rainy season, one day followed another. A market-place of sorts had been set up and Shilluk women and a few curious men came to barter. The soldiers worked on the fortifications. Dr Emily, his medical practice in hand, spent his evenings trying to teach his house-boy how to read and write French. At daybreak on August 25th, Fashoda awoke to the sound of a general alarm. The smoke of two steamers, moving up the Nile, had been sighted. Neither could be the *Faidherbe*, for it would have come from the other direction.

They were, it turned out, the *Safia* and the *Tewfikia*, relics of Gordon's tiny Nile fleet which had been captured thirteen years earlier by the Mahdi. Their mission on this morning was peaceable: to collect the grain which the Khalifa, emulating his Egyptian predecessors, extracted from the Shilluks as tribute. It was probably with some surprise that their crews noticed a strange flag and signs of renewed activity in the ruins of Fashoda. Without warning, they fired off a volley and headed towards the town. This, as Mangin recalled, turned out to be a mistake: 'Had the poor devils just kept their distance and shelled us, we would have been powerless. As it was ... we adjusted our range of fire, first by the splashes in the water, then by the ringing sound our bullets made when they struck the thin metal of the boats.'

Instead of running the gauntlet, the dervishes decided to retreat against the opposite bank. Since the river was only 600 metres wide, this still left them well within range of the Senegalese riflemen. Finally, by eleven o'clock, they called it quits and turned back. Mangin and his men chased after them on foot, firing away into the distance.

They had beaten off the dervishes. In the round of mutual congratulations, Lieutenant Largeau remembered that the patron saint of this day, August 25th, was Saint Louis, who as Louis IX had been the first French king ever to bring the national colours to African soil – during the Crusades. On the spot, Fashoda was renamed Fort Saint Louis.

Euphoria had just begun giving way to concern, for the running fight with the dervishes had cost the defenders more than a third of their supply of ammunition, when another steamer was sighted. This time, it was coming from the south, and it was the *Faidherbe*. Stowed safely on its deck were 100,000 rounds of ammunition and enough food and supplies to last for at least four months.

The following day still more food arrived: a well-fatted live ox, curried to a high sheen. It was a present to Marchand from the Shilluk chieftain, Abd-el-Fadil, who also sent word that he would be pleased to have the opportunity for a chat with the white commander. The conversation, carried on through Landeroin, followed a predictable course. His people, Fadil said, were weary of paying tribute to the dervishes, yet he was afraid of retaliation should he dare defy them. Marchand made it clear that he was in a position to suggest a solution. If the Shilluks would place themselves under the protection of the French .... He went on to describe the might of the French armies, the extent of the territories under their sheltering wing, the advantages of such an alliance to the well-being of the Shilluks. Fadil, who had seen the soldiers first on parade and then in action, and who had watched reinforcements arrive, needed no geography lessons. He readily agreed to affix his seal to a treaty, which was quickly drawn up in French and Arabic. Even as the signatories sat down to a celebratory banquet, copies were sent on their long way to Paris.

As he drank to the health of his guest, Marchand had every right in the world to be satisfied. He had won the race. His impossible mission had been carried out. In twenty-six months he had marched across one of the most inhospitable parts of Africa. It would have been feat enough for a man trudging alone, but Marchand carried with him nearly a million pounds of supplies and, for a good part of the journey, a sixty-foot steel boat. He had been obliged, by his own reckoning, to impress into service 46,000 native porters. He had overcome extremes of weather and terrain, the hostility of native populations, and the fumbling of colonial bureaucracy. Perhaps most amazing of all, he managed to accomplish it without losing a single member of his Mission, whether to battle, disease or accident.

The Shilluk, now that he had concluded his alliance, was willing to share some information with his new protectors. There *had* been stories trickling down from Khartoum in the past few weeks that unusually large masses of dervishes were concentrating near the city. Some villages had been pillaged to provide food for his host, and some men had been impressed at sword's point to join the armies of the Khalifa.

What Fadil did not say, for he obviously did not know it, was that those armies had been utterly destroyed by Kitchener at Omdurman on September 2nd, the day before he signed his own treaty with Marchand.

Historic meetings have a way of generating conflicting, or at least differing, recollections. Regarding what happened in Fashoda on September 19th, 1898, there is almost total agreement, not only among the participants but among historians as well.

Kitchener received the news of Fashoda's occupation first-hand, from the survivors of the fight with the dervish steamers. If there was any doubt about the identity of the tenants, it was dispelled by examination of the bullets prised out of the *Tewfikia*'s decks; they were of European make. As the senior British representative in the Sudan, Kitchener undertook to handle the matter himself. On September 10th he left Khartoum with an appropriate entourage: the indispensable Wingate, three aides-de-camp, including Lord Edward Cecil, Salisbury's son, two Sudanese battalions, a company of Cameron Highlanders, and a detachment of artillery. The entire lot, some 2,000 men, travelled aboard five steamers and constituted, according to Lieutenant-Colonel H. L. Smith-Dorrien, late of the Sherwood Foresters and now in command of the XIIIth Sudanese, a 'very happy party'.

Smith-Dorrien's account of the trip makes perhaps the most interesting, and certainly the most grotesque reading – it could be the rousing clubroom recollections of an upcountry pig-sticking. He describes, for instance, how the 'happy party' came across the disabled *Safia*, tied up near an encampment of white tents: 'Our Maxims and quick-firers were all in action. We soon steamed in close, and I landed with troops. Some twenty-five bodies were found ... and the *Safia* was riddled.' Kitchener evidently became irritated at this useless target practice, because Smith-Dorrien quotes him as complaining, 'You d–d sailors can never see anything afloat without wishing to destroy it.'

On the afternoon of the 17th, they stopped at a village called Kaka where the Sirdar ordered a native runner to carry a message to Fashoda, some fifty miles away. It was addressed to 'Monsieur le Commandant de L'Expédition Européenne de Fashoda.' Then the flotilla dawdled along to allow time for the message to be received and digested.

It arrived in Fashoda at six in the morning, escorted by two Sudanese soldiers wearing red-plumed fezzes. Marchand opened it and read it aloud – it was written in French – to his officers:

Sir,
   I have the honour to inform you that on September 2nd I attacked the Khalifa at Omdurman and, having destroyed his army, have reoccupied the country. ... Considering as probable the reports of the presence of Europeans in Fashoda, I deemed it my duty to write you

this letter in order to acquaint you with the events which have recently taken place, and to inform you of my imminent arrival in Fashoda.

I have the honour to convey the expression of my most distinguished sentiments.

HERBERT KITCHENER
SIRDAR

While his own black troops examined with curiosity the two Sudanese, Marchand composed his reply. With an eye to the annals, it was entitled: 'Letter addressed to General Sir Herbert Kitchener, commander in chief of the Egyptian and British forces in the Sudan, from Captain Jean Marchand, commissioner of the French Government on the Upper Nile and Bahr-el-Ghazal.' Marchand warmly congratulated Kitchener on his victory over the 'fanatic savagery of the partisans of the Mahdi', then went on to inform him that he had, as of July 10th, occupied the Bahr-el-Gazal and the Shilluk country on the left bank of the Nile upon orders of his Government; and that he had brought this territory under the French protection by the instrument of a treaty which he had signed on September 3rd with the Sultan Abd-el-Fadil. He closed by expressing his best wishes and anticipated pleasure at greeting the Sirdar 'in the name of France'.

The reaction to Marchand's reply was brisk. Kitchener was, in Wingate's recollection, 'rather staggered' and ready to lose his temper. The intelligence officer 'begged him to be firm and to stick absolutely to what we had arranged'. Kitchener 'pulled himself together' and ordered two of his officers to go ashore, while the entire British flotilla drew up directly in front of the fortifications, guns pointing and curious soldiers lining the decks.

The two Englishmen, Commander Colin Keppel, the senior naval officer, and Captain Cecil, who spoke French, were greeted by Marchand, dressed like the rest of his officers in spotless whites. After an exchange of civilities, Marchand readily agreed to come aboard the *Dal*, Kitchener's flagship, taking Germain with him.

Smith-Dorrien anxiously observed the scene through field glasses from the roof of his own boat, some 200 yards away:

After much bowing and scraping and saluting, what I supposed to be a map was spread on the table, then followed much gesticulation. ... Distinct signs of hostility on both sides. I was beginning to think ... that I should see negotiations broken off, when up the ladder moved a native, bearing a tray of bottles and glasses, and these, full of golden liquid, were soon being clinked together by the two central figures, who until that moment I had believed engaged in a deadly dispute.*

* Twenty-three years later, Marchand recalled that 'it tasted atrocious.... Never did I serve my country more courageously than when I swallowed that vile smoked alcohol without betraying a grimace.'

Although he understood gentlemanly rules of behaviour, Smith-Dorrien did not number lip-reading among his skills. The conversation between Kitchener and Marchand had been polite, but entirely unsatisfactory. Kitchener had made a formal protest against Marchand's 'infringement of the rights of Egypt and Great Britain'. Marchand replied that he had acted under orders of his Government and therefore had no alternative but to remain where he was, pending further instructions. Kitchener said that he had orders of his own, and asked whether Marchand was prepared to resist their execution. The answer was that Marchand and his companions could only 'die at their posts'.

Kitchener then asked whether Marchand 'considered himself authorized by the French Government to resist Egypt in putting up its flag' in Fashoda.

Marchand found himself in a dilemma. He could not very well refuse the request. France had no quarrel with Egypt. On the contrary, good relations with the Sultan had been the basis of French diplomacy for decades. He agreed to the hoisting of the Egyptian flag, and Wingate and Germain were immediately ordered ashore to find a suitable site. After a thorough inspection, they agreed on a spot some 500 yards from the old fortress. Wingate would have preferred it to be closer to where the French flag fluttered on its staff, but Baratier protested: 'Indeed, why not over our beds?'

The two commanders remained aboard the *Dal* for the two hours which the inspection consumed. In Marchand's recollection, the Sirdar was expansive in his praise for the magnificence of the Mission's exploit – praise which Marchand accepted on behalf of his troops. 'I only regret', Marchand quotes Kitchener as saying, 'that you are not British.' Over luncheon, using knives, forks and glasses as props, Kitchener gave a professional account of the battle of Omdurman.

Meanwhile, from his post ashore, Mangin was looking out at the miniature fleet and daydreaming:

How well-kept those boats are! Those turret guns, they are 100s. ...
But our earthworks are three metres thick. It would take a lot of rounds from those 100s to breach them. And the armour on the gunboats is thin; good enough against the Winchesters and Martinis of the dervishes, but not our model 1886 bullets. ... The men are ranged six deep, on two decks. ... That makes a target about four metres high, and the range is 150 metres. ... What frightful ravage! Better not think about it.

Luncheon over, Kitchener excused himself to attend the flag-raising which had been laid on by Smith-Dorrien. It included Highland pipers, a twenty-one-gun salute and three cheers for the Khedive – given in Egyptian as 'Effendines Choke Yassa!'.

Afterwards Kitchener and his officers repaid Marchand's visit by dining in his mess, a straw-roofed former storehouse. The doorway was low and, in stooping to enter, Kitchener tore the seat of his trousers on his spur, a fact which Baratier duly recorded. Table talk was at first of a strictly neutral, professional nature. The British reported to the French, who had been without news for more than half a year, on the progress of the Spanish-American War. Gradually, however, the subject turned to European developments and the British commiserated with the French over the sad news from France.

Sad news? But didn't they know that the Dreyfus affair had exploded, that the Government had fallen? It was all over the Paris press. But of course, how could they know? The Sirdar promised to send over some newspapers.

Champagne was brought from the ample supply Marchand had carried with him, and toasts were drunk all around. On his way back to the *Dal*, Kitchener paused to admire some of the colourful zinnias which Landeroin had planted in his garden. The interpreter quickly picked a few and presented them to him. 'Flowers', said the Sirdar, 'flowers in Fashoda. Oh, these French!'

That was the end of the meeting between Kitchener and Marchand. They never saw each other again. The Englishman proceeded up the Nile for some miles, then turned back and headed for Khartoum without stopping. He did drop off a note, delivered by a junior officer, stating that he was placing the entire region under military law, and that as a result all movement of munitions of war along the Nile was prohibited. Since it was now well into the rainy season and any other kind of movement was out of the question, the order had the effect of pinning Marchand to the spot.

The military men had gone as far as they could, short of resorting to their professional skills. The next move was up to the diplomats.

In London, the offices of Prime Minister and Foreign Secretary were occupied by Robert Arthur Talbot Gascoyne-Cecil, Third Marquess of Salisbury. Born in 1830 at Hatfield, the family seat, he followed the prescribed course through Eton and Oxford, took a leisurely two-year trip around the world and, at the age of 23, stood for Parliament. He was returned unopposed and remained in the House for fifteen years when, on the death of his father, he succeeded to the title and moved to the Lords. In 1874, he joined Disraeli's Cabinet as Secretary of State for India and became Foreign Secretary in 1878. On Disraeli's death three years later, he became Leader of the Tories in the House of Lords, and in 1885, Prime Minister and Foreign Secretary, posts which he held with two intermissions until his retirement seventeen years later. He early showed a flair for the grand style of diplomacy and, on Bismarck's retirement in 1890, became the single dominant personality in European affairs. Nor was public service a novelty in his family; the third Marquess was by direct descent the great-

great-great-great-great-great-grandson of Robert Cecil, counsellor and confidant of Elizabeth. In the great park at Hatfield, visible from the study of its present occupant, still stood the oak tree under which that Queen had received the news of her accession to the throne.

In Paris, the new Foreign Minister of the French Republic was Théophile Delcassé. The only child of the town bailiff, he was born in 1852 in Pamiers, a market centre in the foothills of the Pyrenees, and educated in the local schools. On his third try, he received a degree from the University of Toulouse and, like most ambitious young men in the provinces, gravitated to the capital. There, he found work as tutor to the children of a minor Foreign Ministry functionary, a post he kept for six years. To supplement his income, he also held down a part-time job as an editor on the foreign news desk of *La République Française*, a small but noisy daily paper owned by Léon Gambetta, the champion of liberal egalitarianism. When his daytime employer, an ardent royalist, discovered the nature of Delcassé's moonlighting activities, he fired him, thrusting him into full-time journalism. In the intense, café-terrace atmosphere of Paris, the line between polemics and politics was thin, and Delcassé crossed it in 1889 by winning election to the Chamber of Deputies, again after two unsuccessful tries at public office. Within the rainbow of French politics, he joined the imperialist group and was rewarded in 1893 with the post of Under-Secretary for the Colonies. Despite its overseas exertions, France had not yet accorded them the recognition of a full-fledged ministerial portfolio. Nor was the Under-Secretary allowed to participate in Cabinet deliberations; Delcassé made it a condition of his acceptance that this be changed. In 1895, the Government fell and Delcassé moved to the back benches, where he continued to make speeches on behalf of colonial expansion.

Delcassé was swarthy, myopic and so conscious of his short stature that he wore lifts in his shoes. During his long political career he made few friends, was on the familiar 'tu' basis with only three colleagues and, except for rare receptions, never entertained at his home, a modest apartment at 11, Boulevard de Clichy, on the edge of Montmartre. In an age when deception was the basis of statecraft, he was the most secretive man who held high diplomatic office. He kept treaties which he had signed on behalf of France in his personal safe, sometimes not bothering to inform his colleagues of their specific content. Anatole France, in *Penguin Island*, caricatured him thus:

> The dwarf came into cabinet meetings with a briefcase bigger than himself and crammed with documents. He remained silent and answered no questions, even those put to him by the venerable President of the Republic. Soon afterwards he fell asleep, tired by his incessant work, until all that was visible above the green baize table was a small tuft of black hair.

He married, at 35, the wealthy widow of a former political associate, thereby assuring himself of financial independence. Work was his life, and his consuming concern was for his country, which he loved with a passion men usually reserve for a woman. He once wrote: 'A frivolous or mocking reference to France in a foreign newspaper stabs me in the heart. I cannot allow my country to be spoken of except in a tone of admiration. ... And I bleed inwardly when I am forced to admit that mockery is justified, that we are not what we ought to be.'

This was the man who, by still another government crisis, was suddenly propelled into the Quai d'Orsay. Delcassé's nomination as Foreign Minister was approved by the Assembly on June 30th, 1898, exactly ten days before Marchand was to reach Fashoda.

In the closing years of the nineteenth century, the new Foreign Minister of a European Power was very much in the position of a chess player asked to take over a seat at a match already in progress. Surveying the board and the disposition of his material, Delcassé could have wished that his predecessors had played a stronger or wiser game. Britain was at last moving in force to clear the Sudan. The French Army was in disarray: on January 13th, *L'Aurore* had published Émile Zola's *J'Accuse*, which tore open the entire Dreyfus affair; on August 31st, Colonel Henry, on whose unsupported testimony the Jewish Captain had been convicted, committed suicide under circumstances which implicated the Army General Staff in foul perjury and caused the resignation of three Ministers of War within seven weeks; radical labour unions, led by the building trades, called for a general strike; more than 60,000 troops were hastily concentrated near Paris, some bivouacked in suburban public squares. On the seas, Britannia ruled unchallenged; the French Navy existed largely on blueprints, because the credits to build it had never been voted. Even in the chancelleries, France was outmanned. The British Ambassador in Paris, Sir Edmund Monson, was an astute, experienced diplomat. The French had no ambassador in London; Baron de Courcel, who had held the post for many years, had retired and not yet been replaced. Nevertheless, Delcassé decided to make the first move.

Having dispatched Marchand to the Nile in 1896, the French Government paid scant attention to his progress for the next two years – a neglect to which Marchand's own letters attest. The battle of Omdurman on September 2nd, 1898, was a nasty reminder. On the 7th, shortly after news of the British victory was confirmed, Delcassé sent a casual note to Trouillot, the new Colonial Minister, pointing out that the fall of Khartoum had 'profoundly modified the situation which existed at the time of the Marchand Mission's departure'. He went on to express the hope that Marchand would stop somewhere short of Fashoda and that, in any case, he would 'apply himself less to accentuating his march', and more to the 'exercise of prudence'. Trouillot dutifully sent off a telegram to the French commissioner in Libreville which began 'Transmit Marchand by surest and fastest means following instructions. ... ' Of course, the message never reached its destination.

That same evening of the 7th, Delcassé approached Sir Edmund Monson at a diplomatic reception and took him aside for a private chat. After congratulating him on his country's great military success, he hazarded the assumption that Kitchener would not stop there, but would continue his march up the Nile. Should this be the case, it was highly likely that the Sirdar would soon make contact with Captain Marchand.

To Monson's question, Delcassé replied that, no, he had not actually heard from Marchand for several months, but that in any case the Captain was travelling through Africa as an 'emissary of civilization', and had no authority whatever to discuss political questions. This would be done exclusively by the two governments concerned.

Monson hurriedly left the reception to compose a telegram reporting this conversation to Salisbury, who received it that night. In the same diplomatic pouch there was also a communication from Renell Rudd, Salisbury's diplomatic agent in Cairo, stating: 'From information gathered by the Sirdar, one may conclude that there is at this moment in Fashoda, where the French flag has been planted, a force of eight European officers and 80 Senegalese soldiers.'

Thus Salisbury knew – and had every reason to assume that Delcassé also knew – exactly where the Marchand Mission was. Nor did Rudd's news come as a total surprise. Back in October 1897, eleven months earlier, Salisbury had tried to speed up Kitchener's cautious preparations by writing to him that 'if we wait another year, we may find that the French have anticipated us by setting up a French principality at Fashoda.' Should this happen, he added prophetically, 'the diplomatic crisis will be something to remember.'

Despite French attempts at secrecy, almost every white man in Central Africa knew about Marchand's presence and his destination; for some unaccountable reason, the Mission's baggage had been stencilled with a large black C-N, for 'Congo-Nil'. Moreover, months earlier, a Belgian newspaper had carried a report describing how the entire Mission had been annihilated by the dervishes, and several of the men had written home to reassure anguished relatives.

Now, on September 7th, *The Times* hinted that something was up. A long account from its Khartoum correspondent included this paragraph: 'It will be time enough to discuss the likelihood of French interference if we find that Marchand has actually established a post on the river between Fashoda and Khartoum. At present, this is a "nebulous hypothesis".'

On the 10th, the nebulous hypothesis dissolved. 'Important news arrived this morning,' *The Times* wrote. 'A force of white men have occupied Fashoda. Information tends to confirm that this force is French.'

On the 12th, there was still no official word: 'The [French] Colonial Office continues to disclaim receipt of any news of the Marchand Mission.'

Other British newspapers did not wait for confirmation. On the 13th, the London *Evening News* put the matter clearly to its readers:

> There is no need to argue the point. If a householder finds a man in his back garden, he does not go to arbitration about the matter or enter into elaborate arguments to show that he, the householder, is the owner of that garden. He simply orders the trespasser out, and, if he will not go out of his own accord, he has to go out in another fashion.

Across the Channel, *Le Temps* on September 17th made clear its position:

> Captain Marchand is at Fashoda charged with carrying out a mission to which we in France attach very real importance, and every act menacing his person – that is to say the Flag of which he is the guardian – will be considered on our part as carrying with it all the consequences usual in these incidents.

While the press was girding for war, activity continued on the diplomatic front. Monson delivered Salisbury's reply, with perhaps more forcefulness than necessary. He personally disliked and distrusted Delcassé, finding him 'unsatisfactory' and 'carrying the practice of subterfuge to an extent which I have hardly ever met before in a Minister of Foreign Affairs.' At this meeting, Monson reminded Delcassé of the Grey Declaration of 1895, which had warned that Britain would consider any intrusion into the Upper Nile valley as 'unfriendly'.

Whatever his preference, Delcassé had little else other than subterfuge to fall back on. He had inherited a nasty mess, and the closer he looked into it, the nastier it became. On September 10th, his Consul-General in Cairo reported that a bloody engagement had taken place between two of the Khalifa's gunboats and the white force occupying Fashoda – that would be Marchand's skirmish with the *Tewfikia* and *Safia*. On the 17th, an urgent telegram announced that the Sirdar himself, accompanied by a strong force, had left Khartoum for Fashoda.

Time was running out. On the 18th, Delcassé summoned Monson to the Quai d'Orsay and outlined France's position. To begin with, he repeated that he still had no official knowledge of Marchand's exact whereabouts – this was important to stall for time, and also happened to be the truth – but that this did not deprive the Captain of the same rights of conquest which the British invoked in Kitchener's name. As for the Grey Declaration – and Delcassé looked Monson squarely in the eye as he said this – it was France's view that there was no such thing as the Marchand Mission and therefore no unfriendly act. To be sure, there was a Captain Marchand, but he was merely a junior military officer who had been labouring selflessly to bring the benefits of civilization into the reaches of the Upper Ubangi river basin since 1893, two years before Sir Edward Grey had made known his unilateral position.

In his report to Salisbury, Monson repeated Delcassé's argument, adding only that 'I avoided using expressions which could be construed as menaces, but took pains to make as clear as words could convey the impossibility of our permitting French presence in Fashoda.' Before parting, the two men exchanged the hope that their differences would not develop into a quarrel.

The press had no such compunction. On September 20th, *Le Matin*, which was generally considered a semi-official organ, stated flatly: 'It is an insult to the French Government to think them capable of disavowing M. Marchand.' The London *Morning Post* replied that if there was no disavowal of Marchand's expedition, there would be 'no other course open but an ultimatum coupled with the mobilization of the military and naval forces of the Empire.' Thus the battle lines were drawn even before there was any public notice of confrontation.

That notice finally came on the 26th, in an exclusive story carried by *Al Moayad*, in Cairo. Kitchener, who had no use for press correspondents – he once called them 'drunken swabs' – had refused to allow any of them to accompany him to Fashoda. He did, however, send his own first-hand report back to Salisbury. It was concise, as complete as a newspaper foreign editor might wish from his star correspondent and, with one serious exception, truthful:

> I have just returned from Fashoda where I found Captain Marchand, accompanied by eight officers and 120 men, located in the old Government buildings. ... I at once stated that the presence of a French Force at Fashoda and in the Valley of the Nile was regarded as a direct infringement of the rights of the Egyptian Government and that of Great Britain, and I protested in the strongest terms against their occupation. ... In reply, Captain Marchand stated that he had precise orders to occupy the country and ... that it was impossible for him to retire without receiving orders to that effect from his Government. ...
>
> I appointed Major Jackson to be Commandant of the Fashoda district, where I left a garrison. ... We neither saw nor heard anything of the Abyssinians on the Sobat River, but we were told that their nearest post was situated some 350 miles further up. ...
>
> The Shilluk chief, with a large following, has come into Major Jackson's camp; the whole tribe are delighted to return to their allegiance to us, and the Chief absolutely denies having made any treaty with the French. ... *

* Not only did Fadil, once he had counted the number of British soldiers, deny it, but he also claimed that the French had forced him to drink an 'abominable philtre' which may have temporarily deprived him of his reason.

The position in which Captain Marchand finds himself is as impossible as it is absurd. He is cut off from the interior, and his water transport is quite inadequate; he is moreover short of ammunition and supplies, which must take months to reach him; he has no following in the country and nothing could have saved him and his expedition from being annihilated by the dervishes had we been a fortnight later in crushing the Khalifa.

The last paragraph was an unvarnished lie. Having visited their camp and drunk their champagne, Kitchener no doubt knew that the French had flour and bully-beef as well, and ample supplies of ammunition. Possibly he only intended to present himself as the Mission's saviour; the effect of his lie, however, proved more mischievous.

As for Marchand's equipment, it was in fact superior to that carried by the British. Major Jackson noted this with a professional eye:

The French were in better case to withstand the discomforts of a tropical rainy season. Each soldier was provided with an excellent type of water-proof ground-sheet which could also be used as a sleeping bag. He carried in addition a small but serviceable mosquito-net which added considerably to his comfort. ... Stores and supplies were carried in sealed tin cans of a size and weight suitable for a porter's head.

If nothing else, Marchand's years in the jungle had taught him something about how to cope with Africa.

As he read Kitchener's dispatch in London, one sentence leaped to Salisbury's eyes: 'We neither saw nor heard anything of the Abyssinians ... ' The Prime Minister had been aware of France's frantic efforts to enlist the aid of Menelik. Kitchener's report removed any lingering fear that this aid might be forthcoming. Salisbury now knew that he held all the cards.

Delcassé knew it too. On September 26th, he wrote a letter to a close friend in which he stated his position as he saw it: 'We have nothing but arguments, and they have got troops.' None the less, the diplomatic game had to be played out.

On his return to Khartoum, Kitchener had a bright thought. 'If the French Government', he telegraphed to Salisbury, 'will at once give intsructions for the explorer M. Marchand and his expedition to leave Fashoda and come down Nile, I can now send a special steamer with such orders to fetch them. I am quite sure that no one would be more pleased than M. Marchand and his officers to secure release from their unpleasant position.'

Salisbury took up the suggestion immediately, instructing Monson to offer, on behalf of Her Majesty's Government, 'assistance to a French explorer who finds himself in a difficult position on the Upper Nile.'

This was to be the face-saving device for a graceful French exit – a triumphant ride down the Nile for Marchand and his companions, followed by a splendid reception and the award of an engraved plaque from some geographical society. Delcassé only wished that he could accept it. His entire political philosophy rested on the creation of a firm Anglo-French alliance to balance the consolidated continental power of Germany and Austria. In time he was able to do it, by means of the Triple Entente which formed the nucleus of the Allied side in World War I, but in September 1898, any weakness in the face of British pressure would have been calamitous. The press, now in full cry, would see to that.

In an emotional interview with Monson, Delcassé begged him not to drive him into a corner. He showed the Englishman press stories hinting at possible French weakness and holding up to execration any public official who would risk being the 'author of national disgrace'. He readily admitted that public sentiment in England was also running high, but still asked for magnanimity: 'Do not ask me for the impossible.'

Monson refused to budge an inch. Reading the lengthy account of the meeting which he sent to Salisbury, it is easy to discern the fact that he, for one, was enjoying the conversation hugely. To Delcassé's apprehensive question of 'You surely would not break with us over Fashoda?', he replied that this was exactly what he feared. At one point near the end of the conversation, the Frenchman observed that in the event of war, 'We shall not stand alone; but I repeat I would rather have England for an ally than that other.'

'That other' was a reference to Russia, with whom France had signed a military treaty in 1895. To invoke it was, on Delcassé's part, pure bluff; both men knew that even if Russia were inclined to interfere in Africa, where it had no interests whatever, there was nothing that the Russian armies, landlocked several thousands of miles away, could do. As for a navy, Russia's was weak and far away.

Part of France's case – the claim to the Upper Nile by right of conquest – rested on the effectiveness of Marchand's occupation of Fashoda. To support this claim, the French had pointed to the string of forts – in fact, little more than hastily improvised supply depots – which the expedition had built along its route, as well as the beginnings of a road, and the repudiated treaty signed with the Shilluks. Since time was obviously on its side, Britain now decided to test that effectiveness.

The idea originated with Sir Thomas Sanderson, the Permanent Under-Secretary for Foreign Affairs. 'I do not think', he suggested to his superior, 'it will be a great calamity if Marchand is left a fortnight or so on short commons in order to demonstrate how helpless and derisory the supposed occupation is.' Salisbury thought the notion good and sent instructions to Kitchener: 'M. Marchand's position should be made as untenable as possible. If he is in want of food supplies, it will be very necessary to use circumspection in helping him to obtain them. Until he expresses his intention of going down the river, no such supplies should be furnished to him except in case of extreme necessity.'

Meanwhile, since he did not expect a man who had crossed Africa on foot to give in at the first hunger pang, Salisbury continued to establish a basis for possible negotiation. On October 8th he received from Kitchener the description of an acceptable new frontier line which granted large territorial concessions to the French, without injuring Britain's position on the Nile.

In Paris, Delcassé had given up on Sir Edmund Monson and begun working on his fellow cabinet ministers. Whatever they might have to say publicly, each of them knew the hopelessness of Marchand's position. On October 10th, *Le Matin*, speaking as the voice of the government, sent up a fragile trial balloon. The essential point to remember, the article suggested, was that France's policy all along had been actuated by the necessity of obtaining a commercial outlet for Central Africa, and in no way by a desire to thwart English policy on the Nile. Monson picked up the story and relayed it to London with the accurate comment, 'It is more than possible that this article ... may have been inserted in *Le Matin* by the Government here with a view to paving the way to a settlement of the question by negotiation.'

Public opinion on both sides of the Channel, however, shot down the balloon instantly. In Paris, angry crowds gathered at the gates of the British Embassy. In London, *The Times* took a stance: 'We cannot conceal from ourselves that Lord Salisbury and his colleagues have taken a position from which retreat is impossible. One side or the other will have to give way. That side ... cannot be Great Britain.' The *Morning Post* added: 'The British nation is indeed united in a way that it perhaps never was before.' A radical organization, the Yeovil Workingmen's Liberal Association, went on record to say that, while it continued to condemn in general the foreign policy of the Government, it approved its attitude in the present instance. Marchand and his men were characterized as 'scum of the desert', and 'irregular marauders'. *Punch* contributed a cartoon which was to poison Anglo-French relations for years to come: it showed a group of monkeys dressed in French Army tunics dancing around the erect figure of Lord Kitchener. 'What will you give us if we go away?' asked the caption, and answered, 'Nothing, but beware of what I will give you if you stay.' Reporting home, the German Ambassador in London came to the conclusion that, with this kind of public support, Salisbury would find it difficult to retrace his steps, even if he wanted to.

In the middle of this verbal barrage, an unexpected visitor arrived in Paris – Captain Albert Baratier. He had left Fashoda on October 10th, reached Cairo ten days later and, at eight o'clock on the morning of the 27th, sat in the anteroom of Delcassé's office, waiting to be ushered in.

The meeting, as Baratier described it, was unusual.

> The door opened and the minister appeared. With eyes and arms raised to the sky, he advanced towards me in rapid steps.
>
> 'Why did you go to Fashoda?'
>
> I replied that we went to Fashoda because we had been ordered there.
>
> 'What order?'
>
> 'The one which your predecessor gave us after he approved a proposal made by Captain Marchand, and a copy of which you have somewhere here in your office.'
>
> The minister asked me to sit down, pulled up a chair for himself and asked me in a plaintive voice, 'Can you see in what situation you have placed us?'
>
> I interrupted him. 'We have executed your orders, Monsieur le Ministre.'
>
> 'If Great Britain declares war on us,' he said, 'you are all lost down there.'
>
> I replied that this was not necessarily true, but that in any case, the lives of 13 Europeans and 150 riflemen should not influence the decisions of the government when the interests of France and her honour are at stake.
>
> Brusquely, M. Delcassé answered, 'You do not understand well the honour of France.'
>
> With this I started to leap up, but halted myself. I turned my head, for I could feel tears of pain and rage welling in my eyes.
>
> 'Captain ... Captain ... You don't understand.'
>
> 'Yes, Monsieur le Ministre, I understand.'

Baratier had two other interviews with Delcassé. At the first, the Minister said, 'Look at my hair. It's turned white in the last month. You cannot wish that we go to war against a nation as powerful as Great Britain.' At the second, he absently agreed to Baratier's demand that, should the Mission be forced to leave Fashoda, they be allowed to walk through Abyssinia and to the coast rather than accept the humiliation of a British escort down the Nile to Khartoum and Cairo. To Baratier's question about instructions to take back to Marchand, he replied that they would be sent directly. In Delcassé's mind, they were already framed, and Baratier, as he left Paris to go back to Fashoda, had no doubt what they would be. 'Once more I said goodbye to France,' he wrote, 'but with what sadness, what pain.'

On the Mediterranean leg of his trip to Paris, Baratier had had a distinguished companion – Lord Kitchener himself, heading from Khartoum to London. He too arrived on October 27th, but to a somewhat different reception. In Dover, a band played 'See the conquering hero comes!' and the Sirdar, dressed now in a grey lounge suit, made a brief speech expressing the hope that the Battle of Omdurman had at last opened the whole of the Nile valley 'to the civilizing influences of commercial enterprise'.

The climax of his return was a banquet on November 4th at the Guildhall. There, before 3,000 spectators, he was presented with the Freedom of the City of London, and a sword of honour whose hilt, made of 18-carat gold, bore the figures of Justice and Britannia as well as the initials K.K. – for Kitchener of Khartoum – picked out in diamonds and rubies. Lord Salisbury's welcoming speech was interrupted many times by applause, the loudest – a standing ovation – greeting his surprise announcement that the Fashoda crisis was over. On the previous evening, the French Government had agreed to recall Marchand.

Delcassé insisted on a final face-saving gesture. The Marchand Mission was being withdrawn, it was announced, because of concern for its health and well-being. The French press, which had done so much to precipitate tension, barely took notice. They had already thrown in the towel. *Le Lyon Républicain* spoke for the majority when it wrote on October 19th that 'The notion of two great civilized powers entering into conflict over possession of some fetid swamps is absurd.'

And it would have been, had only fetid swamps been at stake. On November 4th, in reporting to the Chamber on the successful conclusion of the Fashoda affair, Delcassé accepted full responsibility for the negotiations and intimated that certain accommodations had been reached. When they were finally made public in the Anglo-French Agreement of 1899, these accommodations proved to follow almost precisely the boundary lines proposed as acceptable by Kitchener to Salisbury back in October. They gave France possession of thousands of square miles of wasteland lightly populated by unruly natives, and in exchange extracted her promise to stay away from the Nile forever.

At the height of the crisis, Queen Victoria had written to Salisbury, asking whether it was true that Europe faced 'a war for so miserable and small an object'. On March 26th, five days after the formal signing of the Agreement, she granted Salisbury a lengthy audience. In her journal, she noted: 'We talked of many things and rejoiced at the success of the arrangement with the French, which gave us entire possession of the Valley of the Nile.'

On March 26th, Captain Marchand and his companions were in Addis Ababa. Fashoda and the Nile, which they had left on December 11th, was 480 miles behind them; ahead lay the French colony of Djibouti, where the cruiser *D'Arras* was waiting to bring them home.

After the Sirdar's departure from Fashoda on September 19th, a period of tense expectancy had begun. The French remained installed in the ruins of the old fortress, which occupied a small knoll, the only rising ground in sight. Major Jackson, whom Kitchener had appointed Commandant of the Fashoda District, and his XIth Sudanese regiment did the best they could. 'Our camp', Jackson recalled, 'lay some 300 yards south of the French. The low-lying ground on which it was placed was covered with tall rank grass and became a veritable quagmire after the torrential rains which fell every afternoon and generally during the greater portion of each night.'

Kitchener's orders had restricted the movements of the French forces, so they sat and waited and, according to the entries in their journals, took turns reassuring each other that it would all come out satisfactorily – that the Government in Paris would not capitulate. They were much cheered by the news, passed to them by the British, that Delcassé had become Foreign Minister. 'We all knew M. Delcassé', Baratier wrote, 'as one of those rare men who had a clear view on colonial matters and who, at the time of our departure, was most ready to advance the cause for which we marched.'

Marchand had further reason for optimism. On October 9th the steamer *Kaibar* which served as courier between Khartoum and Fashoda brought him a letter – the first official communication he had received since leaving France. It read:

> I am pleased to transmit to you the congratulations of the French Government which appreciates and will not forget the service rendered by you and your collaborators. You are hereby named *chef de bataillon*.
>
> The British Government has communicated to us the information it has received from General Kitchener regarding your meeting with him. It is imperative that I receive as soon as possible whatever account you yourself are able to furnish me regarding both this meeting and your subsequent situation at Fashoda.
>
> You will therefore assign one of your officers to convey your report to your diplomatic agency in Cairo, which will telegraph its contents to me.
>
> DELCASSÉ

It was this message which had prompted Baratier's departure – a happy occasion because whatever might now happen, they would have their day in court; Delcassé was not going to turn his back on them. But as the days passed, Marchand was seized with apprehension. Acting on his own, without orders or permission, he decided to go to Cairo. It was, after all, his Mission whose fate was being decided.

Mangin, the stoical professional soldier, was left in charge with little to do but write letters. One of them was addressed to a former commanding officer: 'For the past six weeks, we have been sitting here and staring at each other like two china dogs on a mantelpiece. We send them vegetables from our garden; in exchange, they send us newspapers which describe the

Dreyfus Affair and show our country to be transformed into an insane asylum.'

The letter went on to describe conditions in Fashoda, which Mangin translated into military terms. First he assessed the strengths of the British, then their weaknesses which he described in some detail: their boats, for instance, were manœuvrable but inadequately armoured against the French rifles or mortars. The black troops were for the most part unwilling Sudanese recruits who detested the English and Egyptians equally and who would, at the first opportunity, desert to the French side. As for the British officers, they tolerated the climate much worse than the French, and had only one desire: to return to Cairo. In sum, Mangin's professional assessment concluded:

> Whatever may be the result of the negotiations, we have high hopes. M. Hanotaux once told Marchand: 'Go to Fashoda and fire off a pistol.' This we have done. Now, if what they want is a cannon burst, we can accommodate them. Our men will make short work of the poor wretches who are huddled in front of them, and for whom they have the most profound contempt.

Fortunately, no cannon burst was called for. Mangin's letter was dated November 6th. He did not know that it had all been over for three days.

Neither did Marchand, until he arrived in Cairo and received the news from the French Consul-General, who met him at the railway station. According to one authoritative account, his first reaction was to observe the irony of history. Jacques Delebecque writes in his *Vie du Général Marchand*:

> Marchand was quiet for a moment, then fixed his companion with a penetrating look. 'But in this case,' he said suddenly, 'it is a great misfortune that we succeeded. We, who in the midst of our efforts, our thoughts, our sufferings, were supported by the idea that we were performing a useful service for our country, we find now that it was misfortune which we were bringing down on France. Better by a thousand-fold that we had failed. ... '

Biographers, even semi-official biographers – Delebecque had Marchand's help in writing his book – sometimes create quotations to suit occasions. What is certain is that Marchand felt frustrated, betrayed, and above all angry, with an anger that was to last for the rest of his life. For the moment, this anger fastened on Delcassé's comment about the health and well-being of the Mission. Marchand fired off an ice-cold telegram to the Minister:

> I have no choice but to bow before the decision of the Government ... but I formally refuse to accept the manner in which you wish to present it publicly, and further refuse, as chief of the French Mission, to evacuate Fashoda until you give the true reason. I believe I am a

soldier and know my duty ... but I am prepared to resign my commission rather than execute an order given under false pretences. ...

There is no record of Delcassé's reply, but it must have mollified Marchand
because he withdrew his threat of resignation. Or perhaps it was Baratier,
back from Paris, who talked him out of it. Together, the two comrades
remained in Cairo for a few days, where they were subjected to a round of
parties and ceremonial dinners by leaders of the large French colony who,
from their comfortable mansions, could not see that anything of value had
been ventured or lost 1,700 miles up the Nile.

This was the irony of the Marchand Mission. It entered French history
as a glorious episode. There were to be dozens of books written about it, all
stressing Duty, Honour and Country. Marchand was to become a hero, an
example for the young. Even as he sat in Cairo, accepting congratulations
that must have rung with great hollowness, the first *feuilleton* describing his
adventures was on the press. Before the author exhausted his imagination,
it was to go through 140 weekly installments – 2,200 pages in all. A diorama
was put up in Paris on Avenue de Suffren, in the shadow of the huge steel
tower that had recently been erected; it depicted the high moments of the
expedition – the crossing of the Bahr-el-Ghazal, the fight with the dervishes,
the meeting with Kitchener. In every account, whatever the medium, the
operation had been a boldly executed, brilliant success. As for the patient,
'*Eh bien, ça, c'est la politique.*'

Finally, Marchand and Baratier disengaged themselves from their hosts
in Cairo and slowly made their way back to Fashoda. There was no need to
hurry now.

Nor, since the civilians had had their say, was there any reason for
soldiers to quarrel. On December 10th, the day before the Mission's
departure, Major Jackson and the British officers gave a formal luncheon to
the French officers.

Major Jackson, whose home regiment was the Gordon Highlanders, was
of the old school. After coffee and brandy, he presented Major Marchand,
on behalf of the entire Anglo-Egyptian force, with a tattered rag. It was the
flag of the dervish steamer *Safia* which the French had driven off on
August 25th. According to Major Jackson, 'The flag was enthusiastically
accepted. An official record of the presentation and acceptance was
expressed by Major Marchand in a written address signed by all the
Officers of the French Mission.'

The next morning, the French and the Senegalese piled aboard the
Faidherbe. In his account, Baratier notes that 'We took with us all the
provisions we could, leaving behind for the British 20 tons which we had
carried across Africa.' So much for 'explorers in trouble', and health and
well-being.

As a delicate touch, Major Jackson ordered that the French flag remain aloft during the departure. Only when the tired little steamer turned a bend in the river and vanished from sight was it struck, and the Union Jack hoisted in its place.

In Djibouti, more congratulatory ceremonies awaited Marchand. To mark this most eventful day in the tiny colony's history, M. Martineau, the governor, ordered a special train to go to the end of the line and greet the visitors. Thus, the last thirty-four kilometres of Marchand's trip across Africa were accomplished by rail – along the only section of the great French Trans-African railway that had ever been built.

At that evening's banquet, M. Martineau made the principal speech. He began by likening Marchand to Xenophon, then moved easily to Brennus the Gaul, Godfrey de Bouillon and Napoleon, all of whom had led men on long expeditions with varying degrees of success. He invoked history, which alone was just and impartial, and which would inscribe this exploit among the deeds that honour humanity. As for himself, he felt proud that fate had granted him the privilege of being the first to salute such a hero. 'All of France', he promised, 'is preparing to do you honour.'

This was not exactly true. Most of France may indeed have been waiting, but their impatience was not shared by the Government and its responsible ministers. History-conscious as any Frenchmen, they remembered too well that another military man's return from Africa exactly 100 years earlier had led to the downfall of the First Republic. Already, some of the newspapers were suggesting that Marchand should go directly from the dock in Marseilles to the Élysée Palace in Paris and clean up the whole snivelling mess.

Even the non-political Mangin could understand what was going on. He wrote to his family: 'We have not been told where we are to land, much less when we will arrive in Paris. The "darkness of Africa" is nothing compared to that with which they have surrounded us.'

At seven o'clock on the evening of May 18th, 1899, the *D'Arras* weighed anchor and headed for the Red Sea. It was two months and one day short of three years since Marchand had landed in Libreville. On the long voyage home, he too wrote a letter, to Bobichon, the colonial administrator who had been so helpful to him in Bangui:

I have no desire whatever to play the role of idol of defeat, and I do not propose to let my countrymen atone for their defection in my name. This is not a time for congratulations, but for self-examination. ... We are behaving like a pack of mongrels, yapping as we back away. It is sad and makes me want to cry. I received a nasty blow in Fashoda. It will not be healed over by a ceremony in Paris.

Marchand stuck to his word. He listened impassively to the welcoming committee of businessmen and war veterans in Marseilles ('Marchand, yesterday unknown, today like a giant beacon you illumine the world and show all eyes that France, despite its grief and suffering, remains for ever the divine source of light. ... '). In Paris, he attended the minimal ceremonies which had been arranged. To the vast number of receptions, testimonials and celebrations arranged in every corner of France, including the launching of a frigate which had been hastily re-named after him, the Government conveyed the Captain's reluctant regrets; he had important work to do.

As soon as they decently could, the Government saw to it that this work took Marchand to China,* where he remained for three years as a military observer. For ever a marked man – Tsar Nicholas II insisted he spend a few days in St Petersburg on his way home – Marchand tried unsuccessfully to avoid controversy, but in the revolving-door politics of France he was too handy a symbol for anti-Republican orators. During one government crisis in March 1904, Marchand's name was invoked as living proof of Republican indecision and cowardice. Emile Combes, then Prime Minister, lost his temper and replied with the wish that Marchand 'could be sent to a colony where nothing would ever again be heard of him'. The remark was made during debate in the Chamber, and reported widely. Marchand responded by again submitting his resignation. This time it was accepted.

Nothing more was heard from him until 1905, when Théophile Delcassé suddenly resigned after seven years as Foreign Minister. In a long wrap-up story on his career, a feature writer for *Le Matin* happened to mention that, among his other achievements, Delcassé had been the 'father of the Marchand Mission'.

This was too much. Marchand sent off a letter to the editor which, because it was the first public comment he had ever made on the affair, appeared in a prominent place on the next day's front page. Marchand reviewed the history of his proposal, then added: 'I myself killed off *le commandant* Marchand because I wanted to spare others the remorse they may have felt over having stifled a soldier whose existence proved embarrassing to them.'

As for Delcassé, Marchand said, 'the only role he played in the entire enterprise was that of grave-digger.'

Marchand lived on to fight in the World War. He served well, was wounded twice and promoted to general, but did not have the good fortune to be in the right place at the right time – like Mangin, whose troops had the honour of driving the last Germans off French soil, or even his good friend Baratier, who died heroically in Champagne, leading his division into action.

The years after the war stretched long and empty for Marchand – until

---

* The other members of the Mission were scattered as far apart as French colonial holdings permitted – to the West Indies, Tonkin, back to Africa.

1934. After his death the Municipal Council of Paris voted to bestow the highest compliment at its command: a small street, two blocks long, in the 16th Arrondissement was named after him. More accurately, it was named after *La Mission Marchand*, which, had he been consulted, is what he would have undoubtedly preferred.

Right-wing critics to this day blame the Dreyfus affair for the failure of the Marchand Mission, and the consequent defeat of France's trans-African aspirations. On September 4th, 1970, among the crowd gathered in front of the Hôtel de Ville in Paris to celebrate the centennial of the Third Republic, there circulated hawkers selling a special issue of the monarchist newspaper, *Action Française*. One of its lead stories, on this day almost precisely 72 years after the meeting at Fashoda, charged the Government with having betrayed Marchand.

Perhaps Marchand was betrayed, but if so it was by his patriotism, abetted by his superiors' unwillingness to recognize the stubbornness of facts. Weak on land, impotent on sea, frustrated by the consequence of irreparable blunders committed years before, they deluded themselves into believing that all could be retrieved with one bold move. Marchand was a pawn sent out to put the queen in jeopardy. That is not a daring but an idiotic manœuvre, and it was not to hide guilt but to avoid the charge of inanity that someone purged the files of the Foreign and Colonial Ministries.

Shortly before leaving Khartoum for London, Lord Kitchener, by acclamation the greatest Englishman since Wellington, sent a telegram to his friend Cecil Rhodes in Cape Town: 'When are you coming up?'

From the sea to the lakes, the way for the railway was now wide open.

PART SEVEN

Closing the Gap

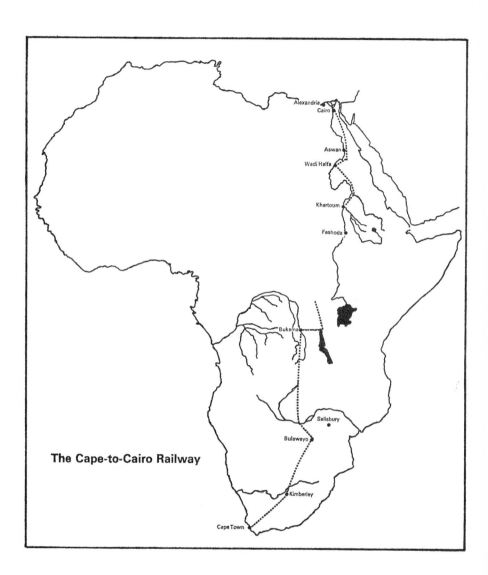

The Cape-to-Cairo Railway

As Winston Churchill had observed, the Boers interfered with most people's arrangements. Instead of Rhodes coming up, it was Kitchener who was obliged to come down – to Cape Town and eventually to Pretoria.

Before Kitchener's presence in South Africa had become urgently required, Sir Alfred Milner, the brilliant, self-assured High Commissioner, wrote: 'As for the Boer himself, provided I am once sure of having broken his political predominance, I should be for leaving him the greatest amount of individual freedom. First beaten, then fairly treated and not too much worried in his conservative habits, I think he will be peaceful enough.'

That was the view on November 28th, 1899, before Black Week and the emergence of Botha, Smuts, de Wet and de la Rey. A year later, in another of his closely reasoned *aide-mémoires*, Milner, who had so skilfully made the war inevitable, changed his mind: 'On the political side, I attach the greatest importance of all to the increase of the British population. ... If, ten years hence, there are three men of British race to two of Dutch, the country will be safe and prosperous. If there are three of Dutch and two of British, we shall have perpetual difficulty.'

Nor did Milner wholly trust to numbers alone: 'Next to the composition of the population, the thing which matters most is its education. ... Dutch should only be used to teach English, and English to teach everything else.'

The key to Milner's planning was the Rand. Its gold mines were going to be the lure which would attract the British immigrants needed to achieve his racial formula, while at the same time yielding the wealth which would turn South Africa into another India.

But when the mines reopened after the war, less than one-third of the 180,000 blacks who had laboured in them could be rounded up again. It had taken force, backed by the threat of starvation, to bring them into the deep, stifling shafts and galleries; now, there was ample work available above ground, rebuilding ruined homesteads and replanting untended fields.

Milner tried to import labourers from neighbouring Portuguese Mozambique, but they had acquired the lazy habits of their masters. He toyed with the explosive notion of permitting white men to work alongside blacks, but even with a tenfold difference in rates of pay, South Africa was not ready for such social experiments. Finally, he fastened on the idea of importing indentured Chinese coolies. It was hardly an original thought – Jan van Riebeeck had proposed it 250 years earlier – but it solved the immediate problem. Within three years, 54,000 Chinese were brought to the Rand and put to work at wages lower even than those of blacks. The mines prospered. Three hundred new companies were floated. Output of gold reached £27 million a year, a third of the world's production. But like so many of Milner's schemes, this one, too, loosened unexpected consequences. Both liberal and sensation-seeking newspapers in London began printing stories, hardly exaggerated, of inhuman working conditions in the mines, and of sodomy running rampant in the packed compounds. Slavery, in naked form, was being not only tolerated but officially encouraged by officers of His Majesty. Even though the slaves were only yellow, it was enough to topple a tired Tory Government already tarnished by its conduct of the war. The general election gave the Liberals a huge majority, which they promptly used to bring formal censure on Milner's policies.

The High Commissioner did no better with his cultural scheme. At Vereeniging, when the treaty ending the Boer War was being negotiated, Smuts and Botha had asked that their native language be considered as equal with English – it was, after all, spoken by more people in South Africa. The request was treated with the scorn it deserved. What need was there for schoolchildren studying the language of Milton and Shakespeare to be saddled with learning a barely pronounceable backwoods *patois*? As a concession from Milner, Article 5 of the Treaty read: 'The Dutch language will be taught in public schools ... where the parents of the children desire it, and will be allowed in courts of law when necessary.'

The result of repression was the springing up, where none had existed, of the beginnings of a new literature – history, fiction, even poetry. Soon enough Herzog would write – in Afrikaans, not Dutch – 'The nation has become aware of its national existence.'

On his final departure from South Africa in April 1905, Milner – now Lord Milner – left a private letter for his successor, Lord Selborne. In it he conceded that the war had not decided that South Africa would remain permanently in the Empire; it had only made that possible. He also warned Selborne that no Afrikaner politician could be trusted; every one of them was capable of 'duplicity and deceit'.

The warning came too late. It was now the turn of the Dutch to press for unification, and on their own terms. They had won everything else; the last remaining point of contention had to do with 'the native question'. The Cape Colony, following the traditional Imperial example, permitted natives to vote, provided they met certain requirements. That few had ever done so was immaterial; they had the right – and even, in theory, the right to hold office. The Boers, of course, could hardly conceive of such foolishness. In their mind, the entire native question had been settled once and for all by the Great Trek.

Smuts and Botha were inflexible, and the British press swung to support them. *The Times* even warned that 'Nothing could possibly be more unwise or more certain to prejudice [unification] than any criticism from this country which would suggest that South African statesmen were indifferent to their responsibility towards the coloured races.'

Only one dissenter was heard, and again it was W. T. Stead, whose *Review of Reviews* noted: 'If the South African white males wish to brand themselves with the stigma of imposing a colour bar, let them do their own dirty work on their own responsibility.'

But generous good feeling was in the air. With Smuts leading the fight for his side, the English capitulated by agreeing to leave the question to be decided later, when they would no longer have any say in the matter. The South Africa Bill was passed without a division.* On September 20th, 1909, King Edward VII, who had made his own position known by inviting Botha to dine privately with him, gave his Royal Assent, and on March 31st, 1910, the Union of South Africa became the Empire's newest Dominion.

In his speech opening the Union's first Parliament, the new Governor-General, Lord Gladstone – the great Prime Minister's fourth son, Herbert, but a nonentity in his own right – expressed the opinion that 'His Majesty well knows that you have passed through the fire of sorrow and trouble, and that misunderstanding and conflict have brought sorrow on the land. But all this is now peacefully buried in the past.'

It took only four years to prove him wrong. In August 1914, the guns began booming in Europe. Even before Britain had declared war, Australia and New Zealand put their armed forces at the disposal of the King. Canada followed suit. Botha, who had as expected become Prime Minister of the Union, telegraphed that his Government was prepared to undertake its own defence. London was grateful, but wanted to know whether it would also be possible for the Union to seize the high-powered radio transmitters which the Germans had built in their South-West Africa, and which were crucial in the battle for control of the South Atlantic.

Botha loyally agreed to do it, and prepared to move into the German colony in mid-September. But some of his former comrades-in-arms – de la Rey and de Wet, both of whom commanded high prestige and personal loyalty – could see no virtue in pulling British chestnuts out of the fire. To his embarrassment, Botha learned that this view was shared by Christian Beyers, another hero of the Boer War who was now serving as Commandant-General of the South African military forces.

The South African Rebellion, understandably, is played down in Imperial accounts of the Great War. Even the exact number of rebels –

* During the sketchy debate, Sir Charles Dilke raised a prophetic point: 'I do not wish to be an alarmist, but I do not think it can be said that we are strengthening the Imperial fabric, in an Empire where there are 360 millions of coloured people under our rule, by such conditions.'

well over 10,000 – is glossed over, and they are described as misled, be-
fuddled and seduced by German propagandists. There is little doubt that
the presence of German divisions on the Marne within weeks of the start of
fighting in France made an impression on Afrikaners. But for thousands of
young men who had been too young to fight, although not too young for
internment in the concentration camps, the opportunity to ride against the
English was irresistible. In what to Botha must have been a grim joke,
commandos began to form, gather strength as they moved across the
countryside, and demonstrate that they had not forgotten how to wage war.
In the end, he took the field himself and cut the heart out of the rebellion by
surrounding and capturing de Wet – something which nearly half a million
British troops had failed to do in three years of fighting.

After this exertion, the war against the Germans was, emotionally, an
anti-climax. South-West Africa was an enormous sea of sand defended by
some 6,000 poorly-armed Germans, almost all of them civilians. The
country's two harbours – Lüderitzbucht and Swakopmund, which the con-
querors found consisted largely of cinemas and beer gardens – were taken
bloodlessly by small naval detachments. Windhoek, whose radio station was
the second largest in the world, lay some 200 miles inland. With 67,000
troops committed to the campaign, Botha had more difficulty with heat and
lack of water than with the enemy – chivalrous to a fault, they poisoned
wells and lay minefields in his way, but always left a note behind reporting
what they had done. The war ended with the Germans' surrender on July
9th, 1915, just in time to permit Botha to return home and campaign for the
general election of 1915, the Union's first. In recognition for his services to
the Empire, his countrymen called him 'bloodhound', 'murderer' and
'Judas'; they defeated three of his cabinet ministers, and brought into
political prominence a former Reformed Dutch preacher named Dr Daniel
F. Malan, who was yet to have his say in South African affairs.

World War I so enmeshed and exhausted the Powers on the continent of
Europe that it left them scant resources to steal each other's African
possessions. Most of the fighting was done by colonial or native troops
under the leadership of white officers, and much of it had an unreal
quality.

In German East Africa, a stock-company Prussian colonel named Paul
von Lettow-Vorbeck had recently arrived at Dar-es-Salaam to take command of the minuscule military garrison – 216 Europeans and 2,540 native
troops. Upon declaration of hostilities, the colony's civilian governor, Dr
Heinrich Schnee, prepared to surrender, but von Lettow would have no
part of such a dishonourable course. He started his personal war by throwing back into the sea an invading force of two full Indian brigades, but-
tressed by a British line battalion and 2,000 bearers recruited in Zanzibar –

8,000 men in all. Before the battle, which the *Official History of the War* described as 'one of the most notable failures in British military history', General A. E. Aitken had voiced the opinion that 'The Indian Army will make short work of a lot of niggers.' It was, even for a British general, a rash prediction. After his first victory, von Lettow led his small force inland and, for four years, proceeded to play hide-and-seek with an Allied force that eventually totalled more than 150,000 troops commanded by a succession of some 100 British, South African and Belgian generals – including, for a frustrating year, Jan Christiaan Smuts. During all this time, von Lettow never lost a battle, never came close to being captured, but managed to inflict 20,000 casualties on his pursuers. (Including Captain Frederick Courtenay Selous, who although 65 years old and an African legend, had insisted on enlisting in the 25th Royal Fusiliers. He was killed during a fire fight on January 4th, 1917.) Von Lettow and his men subsisted – rather comfortably according to his own account – on what they took from British and Portuguese supply depots. They ranged over much of central Africa and ended the war deep within Northern Rhodesia, where von Lettow was considering plans to capture Salisbury when a British motorcyclist travelling under a white flag finally found him and delivered the news that an armistice had been signed the previous week at Compiègne. Sceptical about the outcome of the war – the occasional news reaching him from Europe had convinced him that the Allies were losing – von Lettow cabled the Kaiser for confirmation. When no reply came, he marched his troops into the central square of Abercorn – it could easily hold all of them – and surrendered. They had started the war equipped with 1871-issue German rifles; the arms they lay down included 38 machine guns, a field gun, and almost a quarter of a million rounds of ammunition.

In the Sudan, Wingate, who had remained in Khartoum as Governor-General and Sirdar of the Egyptian Army, took advantage of the Ottoman Empire's ill-advised alliance with Germany to precipitate the great Arab revolt. Its goal – to keep the holy cities of Mecca and Medina out of Turkish hands – turned out to be irrelevant to the outcome of the war. As side effects, however, it set General Allenby loose across Syria and Mesopotamia to create a muddle which is still far from resolution, and it produced one of the most stirring books in the English language.*

The revolt also emboldened a thug named Ali Dinar, who had proclaimed himself Sultan of Darfur, to take up the Mahdi's ancient cry of holy war. While he was still whipping up his reluctant host in the desert far west of the Nile, Wingate assembled a well-armed column of 2,000 men under a tough lieutenant-colonel named Kelly. The two forces met on May 22nd, 1916, outside El Fasher, Ali Dinar's capital, and for 40 minutes it was like old times again. The enemy lost 2,000 men to Kelly's 26, and the Empire

---

* *Seven Pillars of Wisdom* (Cape, London, 1935). Lawrence of Arabia – Captain T. E. Lawrence – was a young archaeologist attached to Wingate's Arab Bureau in Cairo.

was enlarged by another 150,000 square miles, and a little less than one million sullen, uncomprehending souls.

It was to grow still larger and more populous at the peace table, for the most important effect of World War I on Africa was the eradication, at Versailles, of the former German colonies. As newcomers to Africa the Germans had not done badly, and there was, after some genteel haggling, a little something for everybody. Britain awarded itself German East Africa, which it re-named Tanganyika, and agreed to divide the Kaiser's possessions on the west coast – Togoland and the Cameroons – with France. Belgium received Ruanda and Urundi to add to its Congo – it had long coveted the two provinces, and fought against von Lettow exactly hard enough to make sure its troops would be occupying them when peace came. South-West Africa, which nobody else claimed as strenuously, was turned over to the South Africans.

But this had been the War to End all Wars. In keeping with the new spirit of the times, the Powers wanted to make it clear that they were not just indulging in another cynical land-grab. Article 22 of the Covenant of the newly-created League of Nations therefore assured the world that:

> To those colonies and territories which as a consequence of the late war have ceased to be under the sovereignty of the States which formally governed them ... there should be applied the principle that well-being and development ... form a sacred trust of civilization. ...

And further, that

> The best method of giving practical effect to this principle is that the tutelage of such peoples should be intrusted to advanced nations who by reason of their resources, their experience or their geographical position can best undertake this responsibility, and are willing to accept it ... and that this tutelage should be exercised by them as Mandatories on behalf of the League.

One more word – Mandate – joined the lengthening glossary of Protec-torates, Suzerainties, Advisorships, Condominiums, Regencies. With peace, the military figures which had so long punctuated its history were gradually eased out of Africa – tutelage, with its promise of realizing deferred gains, was too important a business to entrust to generals. In their place appeared a new breed of professional colonial administrators. Their bible was a book, *The Dual Mandate in British Tropical Africa*, written by an Englishman named Frederick Dealtry Lugard – Lord Lugard. A man of self-discipline and energy, he had gone to Africa in 1888, early enough to take part in the campaigns against the Arab slave merchants, and remained to explore and then govern the territories which became Uganda and Nigeria. *The Dual*

Mandate, published in 1922 after its author's retirement, took its title from Lugard's thesis that colonizing nations had a double obligation: to raise the educational, economic – and eventually political – levels of native populations, while at the same time developing for the world's enrichment the natural wealth and resources of their countries. As he wrote: 'Europe is in Africa for the mutual benefit of her own industrial classes and of the native races in their progress to a higher plane. ... European brains, capital and energy have not been and never will be expended in developing the resources of Africa from motives of pure philanthropy.'

It was an unsentimental idea which nonetheless – in Lugard's mind – had elements of idealism and justice. It even sounded good in translation: France's Colonial Minister, Albert Sarraut, wrote in *The Development of French Colonies*: 'Henceforth relieved of the demands of conquest, French enterprise in its colonies may now be devoted to the full development of its patrimony. The sovereign interest of France is now consonant with the interests of each of its colonial possessions: to lay down the master plans which must guide and control the task of development.'

And his Belgian counterpart, Louis Franck, who had become Minister of the Colonies in 1918, echoed: 'What are we doing in the Congo? We are pursuing a double aim: the extension of civilization and the development of outlets for Belgium and Belgium's economic activity. These two aims are inseparable.'

Each country, according to its own experience and national preference, chose its own method of discharging its sacred trust to civilization. The British followed Lugard's example – imposed on him by the niggardliness of the Colonial Office – and elected the efficiency of indirect rule: a few whites administered enormous areas through their control of traditional native leaders. The French preferred direct rule. The Belgians, awed by the sheer size of their Congo, left education in the safe hands of the Church and stuck to their prudent shopkeeper's attitude of ruling by division. In 1934, there were more than 2,500 separate tribal chiefs in the Congo – and approximately 6,000 missionaries.

Although their techniques differed, the tutors all came to the same agreeable conclusion: that what was best for their own countries was also best for their colonies. The more copper, tin, cocoa, palm oil, cotton, coal, chromium, cobalt, sisal they could carry away, the happier everybody would be. The Congo's exports increased fourteen-fold; those of Northern Rhodesia twenty-fold.

It was hard work, emptying a continent, but fortunately Cecil Rhodes's foresight had provided the indispensable tool.* He had written in 1900:

---

* How impossible the exploitation of Africa's resources would have been without railways is demonstrated by one episode cited in Albert Sarraut's book. During World War I, the French needed to transport 4,200 tons of cereal in the Ivory Coast. It took 125,000 porters two and a half million working days to do it.

'The object is to cut Africa through the centre.' His railway had done just that. Rhodes had also said, 'The junctions to the east and west coasts, which will occur in the future, will be outlets for the traffic obtained along the route.' These junctions, pushing across desert, veld and jungle, spanning gorges and cataracts, edging down the coastal ranges, now reached the open sea at Beira, Benguela, Matadi, Dar-es-Salaam, Port Sudan. Africa's rivers had barred the European's way, so he built his own – tractable and willing.

There was still the main trunk line itself. War had halted construction, but in 1921 Robert Williams tried to revive interest in the project. Speaking before the African Society in London on April 21st, he reported that 'The Cape to Cairo Railway is working out as its founder planned that it would do,' and urged his fellow millionaires to 'devote some fair share of their money' to finish the work. To whet their appetites, he also alluded to some recent discoveries of gold made by one of his agents, a Major Cuthbert Christy, in the wilderness of the Nile-Congo Divide, in the southern Sudan.

Major Christy's report, along with more information – and mis-information – than any sensible man could care to have about Africa, appeared in 1923 in a massive, five-volume prospectus entitled *The Story of the Cape to Cairo Railway and River Route*. Weighing 38 pounds, lavishly illustrated, and dedicated to 'the ever-honoured memory of Cecil John Rhodes and to all those who gave their lives and life's work towards the completion of his great Imperial project,' the work spun out a strange history of Africa in which there were no villains, no wars that had been anything other than well-intentioned misunderstandings, no motives sullied by self-interest. The Congo, for instance, had been 'the achievement and the glory of King Leopold II'. The Mahdi had been a violent eccentric, and Lobengula an engaging but misguided old duffer.

One of the articles was a prediction of what the future might hold. The author wrote in part:

The future of Africa for good or ill is, and always will be in the hands of the white races. The Black Peril as such is a fallacy. ... I can see science as the Great Comocrat co-ordinating races and governments and administering a scheme of world reform. ... Egypt and the Sudan will show immense progress. Under the hand of wizard engineers, it will have blossomed into one gigantic garden plantation. ... The religion of Islam will have begun to merge into a world faith under the guiding hand of science. ... The Congo Basin will be outshining anything previously known in the Old World or the New. A huge combine of white races will direct its affairs. ... The Union lands of South Africa, with many mines working diamonds, coal and gold, all in a setting of beautiful farms and orchards, modern dairies, wide acres of wheat, vine and tobacco [will] indeed be a peaceful land flowing with milk and honey.

In fairness, it should be said that the author of this forecast was requested by the editors to look a full century into the future, so that he may still be proved right – although as of now the trend does not seem to be running in his favour.

The Story of the Cape to Cairo Railway and River Route has become a curiosity, a bibliophile's find. But the railway it described has not yet – Major Christy's gold strike notwithstanding – been completed. Its southern terminus at the moment is Wau, the capital of the Sudanese province of Bahr-el-Gazal. Northward from Cape Town, it is possible by rail and Congo River steamer to reach Kinsangani, formerly Stanleyville, in what is now the Zaire Republic. In between there still lie 500 miles of terrain, uncertain both topographically and politically.

It may yet be bridged, but if so it will be done under auspices entirely different from those of the original Dreamers. For what they – as well as the editors of *The Story of the Cape to Cairo* and a great many other people – failed to foresee was that a new, enormous wave was about to wash over the full length of Africa.

First to feel the force of this wave was the Union of South Africa. On May 26th, 1948, the country was to hold its first general election since the war. Prime Minister Jan Christiaan Smuts barely bothered to campaign. His United Party held 89 Parliamentary seats to the Afrikaner Nationalists' 49. He himself, at 78, was a revered world figure, a signatory of the Versailles Treaty and one of the chief architects of the new United Nations, the dean of the British Commonwealth, Winston Churchill's warm personal friend and close confidant, the most prestigious statesman his country – his continent – had produced in modern times. The Afrikaners, led by Dr Malan and running on the one-word slogan of *apartheid*, won a clear majority – their first in the country's history. As an added, cruel blow, Smuts was personally defeated for re-election in the Transvaal constituency of Standerton which he had represented for more than 25 years – defeated by an unknown newcomer to politics.

It was appropriate that Smuts should be the first to go: he was the continent's last living link with the nineteenth century. To a friend, he said after the disastrous election: 'My old comrades have turned against me.' The friend gently corrected him. His comrades could not have turned against him; they were all dead.

Smuts followed them on September 11th, 1950. For as long as anyone could remember, he had symbolized his country to the world, but his departure left no void. In October of the same year, an obscure Senator with academic credentials as a social psychologist was appointed to the critical cabinet position of Minister of Bantu Affairs: Dr H. F. Verwoerd.

The second shock struck the continent's other end. Even by Egyptian standards, Egypt had been going through hard, humiliating times. Cromer had at last retired in 1907, pointing with a bookkeeper's pride to what he considered the greatest accomplishment of his 24 years of absolute rule: he had reduced the country's debt – from £96,457,000 to £87,416,000. His successors continued to whittle away at it until 1914, when Britain imposed a Protectorate – a technical expedient made necessary, it was said, because Egypt and its Canal were politically still part of enemy Turkey. After the armistice, one pretext or another delayed the granting of independence until 1936 – and then under King Fuad, the son of Ismail the Magnificent. Fuad's portly figure, and later that of his son Farouk, became familiar to postage stamp collectors all over the world, but if there was any question of where real power lay it was dispelled on February 4th, 1942. With Field Marshal Rommel's columns rolling towards Alexandria, and nationalist demonstrators taking to the streets in Cairo, a squadron of British tanks and armoured cars crashed through the gates of the courtyard to surround the Abdine palace. Sir Miles Lampson, the British Ambassador, was calling on King Farouk to let him know that his country, which had been permitted to remain neutral, was about to go to war. In his hurry, the Ambassador had neglected to request an audience, so a court official offered to have him announced. Sir Miles brushed him aside, saying, 'I know my way.'

That war, too, ended, and the stately withdrawal resumed until, at last, a group of army and air force officers took Cairo and the country in a blood-less coup on July 23rd, 1952. For one lovely afternoon, history performed a reprise: the fat King, stuffed into the ceremonial white uniform of a full Admiral, rode out of the palace, shook hands with sorrowing old retainers and members of the diplomatic corps. Then he stepped aboard the royal yacht *Mahroussa* and sailed off for Naples, taking with him his immediate family and 200 trunks bulging with personal effects. There was one differ-ence, however. Last time, it had been British warships which had rendered the final honours. This time, it was Egyptian destroyers.

South Africa. Egypt. The Sudan was next. Since Omdurman, a tight group of British civil servants had played at running the country. On January 1st, 1956, they pulled out, leaving behind an admirable constitu-tion and a population so hopelessly divided by religion, colour and custom that it immediately plunged into civil war. North of the Equator the French, ever supple, devised a paper scheme which did away with the dis-credited term 'colonies', and substituted for it a concept of partnership with the Mother Country. In their inexhaustible treasure house, the Belgians clung on, hoping that the shield of ignorance and tribal rivalries they had so assiduously constructed would now serve its purpose.

In the wings, a new cast of characters waited. No fairy princesses, dashing generals, great engineers or financial titans this time – there was a mission house schoolteacher, a post office clerk, a witch doctor's grandson, a physician, a journalist, a public health functionary, a poet, a former seminary student, a trade union organizer. Cecil Rhodes would have had trouble with their very un-Anglo-Saxon names: Nyerere, Lumumba, Kenyatta, Banda, Aziwike, Houphouet-Boigny, Senghor, Nkrumah, Sekou Touré.

For better or worse, the time had come for the Africans to take back their continent.

NOTES ON SOURCES

PART ONE

The standard histories of South Africa are *South Africa, Rhodesia and the High Commission Territories* (*Cambridge History of the British Empire*, Volume 8, Cambridge University Press, 1963) and Eric Walker's *History of South Africa* (Longmans, Green, London, 3rd edn 1959). The Cambridge is, as always, a reliable reference equipped with exhaustive bibliographies. Walker is, in the words of a fellow-scholar, 'sound, well-balanced, but rather unreadable'. Not as thorough, but far more stimulating and perceptive is C. W. de Kiewiet's *A History of South Africa, Social and Economic* (Oxford University Press, London, 1941). The newest and best, however, is *The Oxford History of South Africa*, edited by Monica Wilson and Leonard Thompson (O.U.P., London, 1969).

Accounts of early visitors to the Cape – and a mixed bag they were – are collected in I. D. Colvin's *The Cape of Adventure* (T. C. & E. C. Jack, London, 1912). The *Journals* of Jan van Riebeeck are available in a handsome, annotated three-volume English translation published by the Society which bears his name. For the remainder of the Dutch period of occupation, one of the best works is Margaret W. Spilhaus's *South Africa in the Making 1652–1806* (Juta, Cape Town, 1966). It is not an inspiring account, but neither is its subject. Verve and charm came to the Cape in the person of Lady Anne Barnard, wife of the first British Colonial Secretary, whose *Letters, 1797–1802* (edited as *South Africa a Century Ago* [Smith, Elder, London, 1901]) ramble over politics, manners and morals, and are everything one would expect from an observant, intelligent and witty lady who could herself have stepped out of Jane Austen.

Britain's first unsuccessful attempt to colonize the Cape is described in J. E. Edwards's *The 1820 Settlers in South Africa* (Longmans, Green, London, 1924). There is also an account of the earlier Huguenot migration in C. G. Botha's *The French Refugees at the Cape* (*Cape Times*, Cape Town, 1919). The inevitable clash of nationalities and races, and its immediate consequences, are treated in two first-rate books: W. M. Macmillan's *Bantu, Boer and Briton, the Making of the South African Native Problem* (O.U.P., London, 1929), which is based in large part on the career of Dr Philip; and Eric Walker's *The Great Trek* (A. & C. Black, London, 1934), this time writing in fine, high style. A first-hand account of what the Boers faced when they turned their backs on the Cape will be found in *Louis Trigardt's Trek Across the Drakensberg*, edited by C. Fuller and issued in

Cape Town in 1932 as Number 13 in the Van Riebeeck Society publications. Jan Smuts's phrase became the title of a book, *A Century of Wrong* (*Review of Reviews*, London, 1900) for which he is responsible, but which is credited as being issued by F. W. Reitz. The process whereby southern Africa was divided into four separate states, and its aftermath, are neither especially interesting nor simply told. The best account is C. W. de Kiewiet's *The Imperial Factor in South Africa* (Russell and Russell, London, 1937). Another worthy attempt is J. A. Agar-Hamilson's *The Road to the North: South Africa 1852–1886* (Longmans, Green, London, 1937).

Finding diamonds was more fascinating both as an occupation and as a subject for chroniclers. Among the many accounts of Kimberley's early days, the most complete is J. T. McNish's *The Road to El Dorado* (Struik, Cape Town, 1968) and *Graves and Guineas* (Struik, Cape Town, 1969). Interesting for its portraits of winners and losers alike is Paul Emden's *Randlords* (Hodder & Stoughton, London, 1935) and George Beet's *The Grand Old Days of the Diamond Fields* (Maskew Miller, Cape Town, 1931). The original technical work on the fields is *The Diamond Mines of South Africa* (Macmillan, New York, 1902) by Gardner Williams, Rhodes's man. A colourful account of the early period's wheeling and dealing was compiled by his son, Alpheus F. Williams, in *Some Dreams Come Through* (Howard B. Timmins, Cape Town, 1949). Rhodes's chief rival rates a biography of his own: Richard Lewinsohn's *Barney Barnato* (Routledge, London, 1937). One only wishes, reading it, that Barney had taken the time to write his own. The descriptions in the text are taken from Anthony Trollope's *South Africa* (Chapman & Hall, London, 1878) and Bryce's *Impressions of South Africa* (Macmillan, London, 1900).

On Cecil John Rhodes, there is a lot to read. The *Bibliography* compiled by E. E. Berke to commemorate the centenary of his birth and published in *The Story of Cecil Rhodes* (Bulawayo, 1953) lists 1337 items. The latest 'definitive' biography is J. G. Lockhart and C. M. Woodhouse's *Rhodes* (Macmillan, New York, 1963). It is stylish, if a little awe-struck by its subject, but suffers most seriously – as suggested in the text – from what it chooses to omit. Rhodes's earlier biographers include associates and collaborators such as Sir Lewis L. Michell: the *Life of the Rt. Hon. Cecil John Rhodes* (Edward Arnold, London, 1910); Sir Thomas E. Fuller: *The Right Honourable Cecil John Rhodes* (Longmans, Green, London, 1910); Sir James G. McDonald: *Rhodes, A Life* (Philip Allan, London, 1927); and Rochfort Maguire, whose *Cecil Rhodes: a Biography and Appreciation* (Chapman & Hall, London, 1897) was published under the pseudonym of 'Imperialist'. Two of Rhodes's long list of male secretaries also contributed their reminiscences: Philip Jourdan in *Cecil Rhodes; His Private Life by his Private Secretary* (John Lane, London, 1910), and Gordon Le Sueur in *Cecil Rhodes, the Man and his Work* (John Murray, London, 1913). Each of these accounts adds touches of its own, but the collective portrait remains unmarred by shadow of any kind. The first attempts to come to grips with Rhodes as a force for harm as well as unalloyed Imperial good are Basil Williams's *Cecil Rhodes* (Constable, London, 1921), and William Plomer's *Cecil Rhodes* (Peter Davies, London, 1933). In a class by itself is Sarah Gertrude Millin's *Rhodes* (Chatto & Windus, London, 1933). Far more interested in the man than in the public figure, and in his motives rather than his achievements, Mrs Millin produced the most perceptive – and also the most critical – book yet written on the Colossus of Africa. One would have thought, given the nature of Rhodes's career, that some French, German or possibly even Belgian writer would have taken the trouble to do a methodical dissection, but if one exists it has escaped the author's attention. André Maurois's biography – *Cecil Rhodes* (Collins, London, 1953) – is an admiring gloss. Of other accounts, the only detail which sticks in the memory is that French writers habitually – and probably enviously – tend to refer to Rhodes as *Le Napoléon du Cap*.

Many of Rhodes's speeches, political and financial, have been collected in *Cecil Rhodes, his Political Life and Speeches, 1881–1900* (Bell, London, 1900) by Vindex, a pseudonym for John Verschoyle. Bechuanaland, the scene of Sir Charles Warren's expedition, is covered in great detail in John Mackenzie's *Austral Africa; Losing it or Ruling it* (Sampson Low, London, 1887). The Reverend Mackenzie clearly opts for the latter. The expedition itself receives the treatment it deserved in Sir Ralph Williams's *The British Lion in Bechuanaland* (Rivingtons, London, 1885). George Pauling, without whom the Cape-to-Cairo would not have got very far, speaks for himself in *Chronicles of a Contractor* (Constable, London, 1926).

PART TWO

The highlands of Central Africa which eventually, and in part temporarily, became Rhodesia have history that dates to antiquity. Within the scope of this book, however, the earliest accounts of the country and its inhabitants are largely the work of missionaries who, in this part of the continent, preceded the soldiers. *The Letters, Diaries and Journals* of two generations of Moffats – the patriarchal Robert and Mary, and the unhappy John and Emily – have been published as part of the Oppenheimer Series of early Rhodesiana which also includes Charles Rudd's diary of his momentous journey to Bulawayo. Completing the family chronicle, and casting considerable light on the business practices of Rhodes, Rudd and Company, is Robert Unwin Moffat's biography of his father, *John Smith Moffat, C.M.G., a Missionary* (John Murray, London, 1921). Among many early accounts, T. M. Thomas's *Eleven Years in Central Africa* (John Snow, London, 1872) is notable because the author witnessed and described Lobengula's coronation. Daily life at the court is depicted in J. Cooper

Chadwick's *Three Years with Lobengula* (Cassell, London, 1894), written by one of the resident white traders in Bulawayo; E. C. Tabler's *The Far Interior* (A. P. Balkema, Cape Town, 1955) collects the accounts of the earliest travellers to venture north of the Limpopo. The most famous of them, however, wrote his own: David Livingstone's *Missionary Travels and Researches in South Africa* (John Murray, London, 1851). It may well be the most impressive, haunting book ever written about the continent. In a totally different vein, but a classic of its kind, is Frederick Courtenay Selous's *Travel and Adventures in South Africa* (Rowland Ward, London, 1893). Most of the adventures end predictably with the skinning or decapitation of some large animal, but few people have enjoyed the preliminaries as much, or have written as enthusiastically about them.

The first attempt at a formal history of the region is E. P. Mathers's *Zambesia, England's El Dorado in Africa* (King, Sell & Railton, London, 1891), an engaging grab-bag of every legend, traveller's tall story and questionable account which the author, a cheerful jingoist journalist, could round up. His views on right and wrong are as simplistic as black and white, but such is his enthusiasm for the subject that there is hardly a dull page in the book. The same cannot be said for Hugh Marshall Hole's *The Making of Rhodesia* (Macmillan, London, 1926). Hole was a senior official of the British South Africa Company, and his account – intended as semi-official history – necessarily has to take some strange detours. An entirely different view is presented in *The Chartered Millions* (Swarthmore, London, 1920) by Sir John H. Harris, which, typically for the time, takes the Company to task more for its financial dealings in London than its administrative policies in Salisbury and Bulawayo. A spectacularly successful attempt to tell the story from the point of view of the victims is novelist-historian Philip Mason's *The Birth of a Dilemma: The Conquest and Settlement of Rhodesia* (O.U.P., London, 1958). In the same vein, but reaching farther back into the Mashona-Matabele past, is William Rayner's *The Tribe and its Successors* (Faber & Faber, London, 1962). L. H. Gann's *A History of Southern Rhodesia* (Chatto & Windus, London, 1965) brings the story up to date and provides a thorough bibliography, but is a reversal to the white man's point of view in tracing what is basically black man's history. This aberration is corrected in *The Zambezian Past* (Manchester University Press, 1966), a collection of symposium papers edited by Eric Stokes and Richard Brown. Standing alone is Stanlake Samkange's *Origins of Rhodesia* (Praeger, New York, 1968), which, the author states in his preface, was written in reaction to the version of his country's history as it was taught him in a native school. The style is sometimes uneven, and anger occasionally shows through the scholarly citations, but it seems fair to say that no one who has not read it can claim to know Rhodesian history.

Though it probably did not occur to Rhodes to include it, authorship was among the crafts and professions represented in the Pioneer Column of

1890. Two of the Pioneers wrote books, as dissimilar as their authors. *On the South African Frontier* (Sampson Low, London, 1899) by the American, William H. Brown, is the rambling account of a curious and observant amateur scientist – Brown had a commission from the Smithsonian Institution to collect samples of native flora and fauna which earned him the nickname 'Curio' Brown. Frank Johnson, as the text suggests, was something of a braggart or worse, and his autobiography *Great Days* (Bell, London, 1940) reflects it. The observations of Major A. G. Leonard are drawn from his *How We Made Rhodesia* (Kegan Paul, London, 1896).

On Rhodes's first visit to 'his' protectorate, there is a first-hand account in D. C. De Waal's *With Rhodes in Mashonaland* (Juta, Cape Town, 1896). The touring party stopped in Umtali, then little more than a handful of huts, and paid a call on the infirmary. This, along with other reminiscences, is described in Rose Blennerhassett and Lucy Sleeman's *Adventures in Mashonaland by Two Hospital Nurses* (Macmillan, London, 1893), which contains one of the pithiest assessments of Rhodes. Having met the great man, one of the authors noted: 'He is the darling of fortune, which does not often select her favourites from the Sunday school.' Lord Randolph Churchill's opinions, forcefully expressed, were published as *Men, Mines and Minerals in South Africa* (Sampson Low, London, 1892).

Lobengula is the subject of several full-length studies. Friederich Posselt's *Lobengula the Scatterer* (Rhodesian Printing and Publishing Co., Bulawayo, 1945) and Gustav S. Preller's *Lobengula, the Tragedy of a Matabele King* (Afrikaanse Press, Johannesburg, 1963) are both sympathetic to him more out of anti-British than pro-Matabele bias. Hugh Marshall Hole's *The Passing of the Black Kings* (Philip Allen, London, 1932) is surprisingly fair, considering its authorship. Stuart Cloete's *African Portraits: a Biography of Paul Kruger, Cecil Rhodes and Lobengula* (Collins, London, 1946) is an interesting idea which does not quite come off.

On the Matabele War, the contemporary account, W. A. Wills and L. T. Collingridge's *The Downfall of Lobengula* (*African Review*, London, 1894), is totally uncritical, not to say dishonest. All the pertinent facts are painstakingly collected in Stafford Glass's *The Matabele War* (Longmans, London, 1968), but the story is better told by Mason and Samkange. 'Doctor Jim', one of the main architects of the war, was a complicated man, better-rounded and in many ways more interesting than his celebrated friend. His portrait is admirably drawn in I. D. Colvin's two-volume *The Life of Jameson* (Edward Arnold, London, 1922).

PART THREE

Although the Jameson Raid is treated – at times with great reluctance and always with circumspection – in all the Rhodes biographies, it has also gathered a literature of its own. The immediate after-the-fact view of the

Uitlanders is probably best expressed by one of their leaders, Sir James Percy Fitzpatrick in *The Transvaal from Within* (Heinemann, London, 1899). Edmund Garrett provided a smooth but unconvincing explanation in *The Story of an African Crisis* (Constable, London, 1897), which originally appeared as a supplement to his *Cape Times*. Richard Harding Davis breezed through and composed *Dr. Jameson's Raiders versus the Johannesburg Reformers* (R. H. Russell, New York, 1897). John Hays Hammond's delayed *The Truth about the Jameson Raid* (Marshall Jones, Boston, 1918) fails to live up to its title. A major flaw in all these accounts was the unavailability of the private papers of Sir Graham Bower, deputy to Sir Hercules Robinson and everyone's choice as the scapegoat. The unsealing of these documents in 1950 enabled Jean van der Poel to produce what will probably be the definitive account, in *The Jameson Raid* (O.U.P., London, 1951), although the angry and well-informed W. T. Stead anticipated her in his own *The History of the Mystery* (*Review of Reviews*, London, 1897) which, in thinly-veiled fiction, caused considerable embarrassment in Whitehall by placing the blame exactly where it belonged – on the shoulders of Pushful Joe Chamberlain. The full text of the Lying in State in Westminster – the proceedings and minutes of the evidence – was issued by H.M.S.O. as *Parliament. Select Committee on British South Africa. Second Report, no. 311* (1897).

The occasionally odd doings of the poor, persecuted Johannesburgers before, during and after the Raid are given full treatment in Robert Crisp's *The Outlanders* (Peter Davies, London, 1964), which is entertaining enough to make one wish one had been there at the time. More scholarly is J. S. Marais's *The Fall of Kruger's Republic* (O.U.P., London, 1961), which carries the story to Chamberlain's successful provocation of the war, and is itself a fascinating study of a historian struggling with barely-contained indignation.

The gradual materialization of Rhodes's Prussian bogey is documented in the two works of Mary E. Townsend, *Origins of Modern German Colonization* (Columbia University Press, New York, 1921), and *The Rise and Fall of Germany's Colonial Empire* (Macmillan, New York, 1930), as well as in the more recent *L'Expansion Allemande Outre-Mer* (Presses Universitaires de France, Paris, 1957) of Henri Brunschwig. More thorough still is *Britain and Germany in Africa* (Yale University Press, 1968), a compilation of symposium papers edited by Prosser Gifford and Wm. Roger Louis. The effect, real or imagined, of Germany's African aspirations upon London, Cape Town and Pretoria is treated with lucidity and wit in an earlier work, Reginald Lovell's *The Struggle for South Africa 1875–1899* (Macmillan, New York, 1934).

There was little enough occasion for heroism during the Matabele and Mashona uprisings, but Herbert Plumer, who led the forces on the winning side, made the most of it in *An Irregular Corps in Matabeleland* (Kegan

Paul, London, 1897), and so, at second hand, did Frank W. Sykes in *With Plumer in Matabeleland* (Constable, London, 1897). Both are appropriate companion volumes to Baden-Powell's *The Matabele Campaign, 1896* (Methuen, London, 1897) which is cited and quoted in the text. Eyewitness accounts of Rhodes's peace-making in the Matopo hills are provided by Hans Sauer in his autobiography, *Ex Africa* (Bles, London, 1937), which also gives his side of the great smallpox debate with Jameson, and by Vere Stent in *A Personal Record of Some Incidents in the Life of Cecil Rhodes* (Maskew Miller, Cape Town, 1925).

Much nonsense was written about the Matabeles and Mashonas before and after the uprisings, including Frederick Courtenay Selous's amiable but simple-minded *Sunshine and Storm in Rhodesia* (Rowland Ward, London, 1896). It remained for a Soviet historian to set the record straight: A. B. Davidson in *Matabele i Mashona v Borbe protiv Angliskayi Kolonizatsii* (Moscow, 1958). More recently, his work has been amplified and superseded by T. O. Ranger's *Revolt in Southern Rhodesia 1896–7* (Northwestern University Press, Evanston, 1967) which must rank as a new mark of excellence against which all future books on the history of Africa – as contrasted to the history of white men's activities in Africa – should be measured.

Unlike the Khartoum campaign, the Boer War – the South African War, to give it its proper name – produced little in the way of first-rate reportage. Much of the same cast was on hand, but their books – G. W. Steevens's *From Capetown to Ladysmith* (Tauchnitz, Leipzig, 1900) and Winston Churchill's *Ian Hamilton's March* (Longmans, London, 1900) and *London to Ladysmith* (Longmans, London, 1900) – are disappointing. Part of the reason may lie in the nature of the war itself, which brought more credit to the vanquished than the victors, and generated violent protest within Britain itself. (For a compilation of anti-war writings, see H. J. Ogden's *The War against the Dutch Republics in South Africa* [National Reform Union, Manchester, 1901].) Sir Arthur Conan Doyle wrote a long account, *The Great Boer War* (McClure, Phillips, New York, 1902), which he expected would outlast the detective stories he had been dashing off. He was wrong. The fullest treatment of the conflict, L. S. Amery's *The Times History of the War in South Africa* (Sampson Low, Marston, London, 1900–1909) fills seven volumes and may be more than anyone cares to know about the subject. The narrative prepared for the German General Staff (authorized English translation by H. Du Cane and H. W. Walley, John Murray, London, 1904–6) has been mentioned in the text. There are in addition two excellent recent works: Edgar Holt's *The Boer War* (Putnam, London, 1958) and Rayne Kruger's *Goodbye Dolly Gray* (New English Library, London, 1967). The strange doings of General Sir Redvers Buller are given full-scale exposition in Julian Symons's *Buller's Campaign* (Cresset Press, London, 1963). In his preface the author notes that he had originally planned to write an account of the entire war, but chose instead to concentrate on Buller. It was a genial decision.

Other figures fared less well at the hands of biographers. J. L. Garvin's three-volume *Life of Joseph Chamberlain* (Macmillan, London, 1932–4) is a protracted and unconvincing *apologia*. Stephanus Johannes Paulus Kruger has yet to be properly assessed. His own *Memoirs* (T. Fisher Unwin, London, 1902) are turgid, and Marjorie Juta's *The Pace of the Ox* (Constable, London, 1937) is a noble and sympathetic attempt which fails to grasp the complexity of its subject.

H. F. Varian's *Some African Milestones* (G. Roland, Oxford, 1953) gives a graphic, authoritative account of the construction of the Victoria Falls Bridge. Another good account appears in Leo Weinthal's *The Story of the Cape to Cairo Railway and River Route* (Pioneer Publishing Co., London, 1923) which also contains the reminiscences of Sir Charles Metcalfe, Sir Robert Williams and Sir Harry Johnson as they pertain to Rhodes's project. A more comprehensive treatment of its effect on the entire continent will be found in Lois A. C. Raphael's *The Cape-to-Cairo Scheme: A Study in British Imperialism* (Columbia University Press, New York, 1936). Written as a superlative doctoral dissertation, Mrs Raphael's book is weighted towards the diplomatic aspect of her subject, but contains a wealth of documentation. More limited in time and space (it stops at the Boer War and the Zambesi), Anthony Nutting's *The Scramble for Africa* (Constable, London, 1970) is, as could be expected, both fluent and knowledgeable.

PART FOUR

Napoleon's invasion of Egypt kindled lively interest among Europeans in the long-forgotten country. Among the earliest products of this interest is Edward William Lane's *Account of the Manners and Customs of the Modern Egyptians* (London, 1831), a frequently reprinted classic which was originally intended as a companion volume to a study of Egyptian life in Pharaonic times. Undeservedly less well-known is *The Englishwoman in Egypt* (London, 1844–6) written by Lane's sister under the name of Sophia Poole. Another shrewd observer and seasoned travel writer was Prince H. L. H. von Pückler-Muskau, whose *Egypt under Mohammed Ali* (London, 1845) benefits from long private interviews with the subject. Somewhat later, another Englishman, Nassau William Senior, surveyed the chaos which Mohammed Ali's death had unleashed and described it without mincing words in *Conversations and Journals in Egypt and Malta* (Low, Marston, Searle & Rivington, London, 1882). Another perceptive and articulate observer was Lady Duff Gordon, whose *Letters from Egypt, 1862–1869* (re-edited, London, 1959) cover not only gossip and diplomatic doings, but life as it spun out in the smaller towns and villages along the Nile.

Most of the early visitors to Egypt, however, were French. Some stayed on to work for Mohammed Ali, like Antoine Clot who noted his experiences in *Aperçu Général sur l'Égypte* (Paris, 1840). Others, including Théophile Gautier, Flaubert and lesser lights, were satisfied to derive inspiration from what they saw – or thought they saw. The results of their investigation include serious works such as P. N. Hamont's *L'Égypte sous Mohammed Ali* (Paris, 1843) and Paul Mouriez's *Histoire de Méhémet Ali* (Paris, 1855–8), and bits of fluff such as Charles Didier's *Les Nuits du Caïre* (Paris, 1860) and the totally fictionalized and fascinating *Les Mystères de l'Égypte Dévoilés* (Paris, 1865) by one Madame Olympe Audouard, which endow the flesh-pots of Cairo with a wholly undeserved gloss. So numerous were passing-through French writers that Jean-Marie Carré compiled an intriguing critical anthology of their output in his two-volume *Voyageurs et Écrivains Français en Égypte* (Cairo, 1956).

With the accession of Ismail, European interest in Egypt shifted from belly-dancers and languid *houris* to hard cash and soft credit. Given the disparity between the two, virtually no contemporary writer had a good word for the Magnificent. Ungraciously, the sternness of the critics was almost in direct proportion to the degree to which they benefited from his munificence. Thus Edwin de Leon, who as United States Consul was one of the leaders of the diplomatic wolf-pack, produced *The Khedive's Egypt, or The Old House of Bondage under new Masters* (Harper & Brothers, New York, 1877), a colossal exercise in gall. Another American diplomat, Elliot E. Farman, chimed in with *Egypt and its Betrayal* (Grafton Press, New York, 1908). A visiting businessman, James C. McCoan, was a little more charit-able in *Egypt as it is* (Cassell, London, 1877), but resident journalists took readily to the London line – *The Times*'s C. F. Moberly Bell in *Khedives and Pashas as I have known them* (Low, Marston, Searle & Rivington, London, 1884), and the *Telegraph*'s Edward Dicey in *The Story of the Khedivate* (Scribner's, New York, 1902). It was only after Ismail's exile and death that the record began to undergo rectification. Theodore Rothstein's scholarly *Egypt's Ruin* (A. C. Fifield, London, 1910) does much to undo the portrait provided by Cromer. Pierre Crabites's *Ismail the Maligned Khedive* (Routledge, London, 1933) is a very readable and convincing attempt at a full-scale rehabilitation. The author, an American, was a long-time resident in Egypt who served as a judge on the Mixed Tribunals, and therefore had first-hand experience with some of the problems which undoubtedly bedevilled Ismail. Another and still more recent view of Ismail which cannot help but enlist the sympathy of the reader is contained in David Landes's *Bankers and Pashas* (Harvard University Press, Cambridge, Mass., 1958), which is both a technical and an entrancing study of Egyptian finances as seen through the operations – manipulations is the better word – of André Dervieu, one of the Khedive's principal Parisian bankers.

It was Ismail, of course, who inadvertently brought Cromer to Egypt, and with him the other British administrator-authors: Alfred Milner –

England in Egypt (Edward Arnold, London, 1892) – and Sir Auckland Colvin – *The Making of Modern Egypt* (Seeley, London, 1906). In the face of such massive self-assurance and stylistic polish, it required considerable courage for Afaf Lufti Al Sayid to undertake his *Egypt and Cromer* (John Murray, London, 1968) which, as may be imagined, reached independent and divergent conclusions. The attempt, however, was successful and is well worth consulting.

It is possible to read two entirely different accounts of the same events in the modern history of Egypt, depending upon whether the author happens to be writing in English or in French. During the 1930s King Fuad embarked upon a campaign – in scope, it was almost an orgy – of ancestor rehabilitation. Throwing open both his purse and the Palace Archives, he subsidized a large body of historians, nearly all of them French, to 'do' the dynasty of Mohammed Ali. The result is a large body of beautifully printed books, well written and exhaustively documented. Read alone, they would give a distinctly slanted version of what happened along the Nile during the nineteenth century, but they provide an essential balance to Cromer *et al.* Handsomest of the lot is the seven-volume, illustrated *Histoire de la nation Égyptienne* edited by Gabriel Hanotaux (Plon, Paris, 1931–40), who was a far better historian than politician. Volumes 6 and 7 cover the post-Napoleonic period and the conquest of the Sudan. On Ismail, there is also the four-volume *Histoire du Règne du Khedive Ismail* (Rome, 1933–6) by Georges Douin, which is heavy going, but contains the most complete accounts of the Khedive's trips to Europe and the ceremonies surrounding the opening of the Suez Canal. Another extremely well-documented work, part of an unfinished series because it is listed as Volume 3, is Angelo Sammarco's *Histoire de l'Égypte Moderne* (Cairo, 1937), which covers the period 1801–82.

In the same vein are two major works by the Egyptian historian Mohammed Sabry: *L'Égypte Sous Mohammed Ali* (P. Geuthner, Paris, 1930) and *Épisode de la Question d'Afrique: L'Empire Égyptien sous Ismail* (P. Geuthner, Paris, 1933). Both are well-reasoned and fully documented from Egyptian and foreign sources, and have served as the basis for most subsequent studies. Sabry also produced as a doctoral thesis *La Genèse de l'Esprit National Égyptien* (Paris, 1924), a study which has particular relevance in the light of recent developments in Egypt.

Mohammed Ali's career is traced in two works: Shafik Ghorbal's *The Beginnings of the Egyptian Question and the Rise of Mohammed Ali* (Routledge, London, 1928), and Henry H. Dodwell's *The Founder of Modern Egypt* (Cambridge University Press, 1931). Unclassifiable, but somewhere at the other end of the spectrum, is Lord Edward Cecil's *The Leisure of an Egyptian Official* (Hodder & Stoughton, London, 5th edn., 1935). The author was the son of Lord Salisbury, and the subject he chose is one to which he brings extensive personal experience.

On the Suez Canal, the last word, it would seem, has been said in D. A. Farnie's recent and monumental (860 pages) *East and West of Suez: The Suez Canal in History, 1854–56* (Clarendon Press, Oxford, 1969). The author traces the earliest attempts to pierce the Isthmus, the building of the overland route, the opening, and the all-important sale of the Khedive's shares to Disraeli. He also brings the story up to Egypt's repossession of the Canal and provides an exhaustive bibliography. Still of interest is de Lesseps's own *The History of the Suez Canal: A Personal Narrative* (Blackwood, Edinburgh, 1876), and another of Pierre Crabites's many books on Egypt, *The Spoliation of Suez* (Routledge, London, 1940). It is as frankly partial as its title suggests, but it manages to strike just the right combination of outrage and sympathy. Henry Morton Stanley, who seems to have been everywhere in Africa, covered the opening of the Canal, but his account in Volume II of *My Early Travels and Adventures in America and Asia* (Sampson Low, Marston & Co., London, 1895), is not up to his usual standard.

Arabi Pasha, who is dismissed as a misguided lunatic by most British writers, receives more meaningful analysis in the French works cited. The fullest treatment of his personality and movement – if it can be called that – is found in Wilfrid Scawen Blunt's *Secret History of the English Occupation in Egypt* (T. Fisher Unwin, London, 1907) which also contains Arabi's autobiography, composed while in jail awaiting trial.

On the Anglo-French conflict which marked the century, there are two first-rate works. Both are by French writers – the British apparently felt that since they ended up owning the country there was no need to write books explaining how it had happened. The first is Jean Darcy's *France et Angleterre: Cent Années de Rivalité Coloniale* (Perrin, Paris, 1904). The second, *L'Angleterre en Égypte* (Imprimerie du Centre, Paris, 1922) by Juliette Adam, contains among other material a compilation – far from complete because they lingered for another 14 years – of solemn British assurances that their occupation of Egypt was merely a temporary necessity.

PART FIVE

That the literature on the Sudan is so rich and varied is largely the result of a single man's decision to accept a job. Had General Charles Gordon gone to Kabul instead of Khartoum, and met his death under similar circumstances, we would all know a great deal more about Afghanistan than we do. On Gordon himself, Richard L. Hill's *Bibliography of the Anglo-Egyptian Sudan*, compiled in 1939 (O.U.P., London, 1962), lists more than 300 titles – from *Golden Gleanings from the Thoughts of General Gordon* to *An Estimate of General Gordon's Scientific Characteristics*. The best single work on the man – aside from his own *Journals*, of course – is probably still Bernard M. Allen's *Gordon and the Sudan* (Macmillan, London, 1931).

Travellers' books abound – the Sudan was both relatively accessible and eternally fascinating to Europeans in the nineteenth century. Among the best are: Frederic Cailliaud's *Voyage à Méroé* (à l'Imprimerie royale, Paris, 1823–7), J. L. Burckhardt's *Travels in Nubia* (John Murray, London, 1822), Schweinfurth's monumental *The Heart of Africa* (1868–73: new edition, Afro-Asia Books, Chicago, 1969), and W. J. Junker's *Travels in Africa* (Chapman & Hall, London, 1875–92). Less well known but equally interesting is *Egypt, the Soudan and Central Africa* (Blackwood, Edinburgh, 1861) by John Petherick, a sharp-eyed Welsh mining engineer who journeyed to Africa not for curiosity or the advancement of knowledge, but to turn a shilling or two. Of special interest because of the author himself is Romolo Gessi's *Seven Years in the Soudan* (Sampson Low, Marston, London, 1892), written by the most selfless of Gordon's small band of international lieutenants.

Much of what indignant Englishmen knew about the Mahdi and his movement was the single-handed work of Reginald Wingate, first by virtue of his own *Mahdiism and the Egyptian Sudan* (Sampson Low, Marston, London, 1892), and then because of the famous 'prisoner' books – Father Joseph Ohrwalder's *Ten Years' Captivity in the Mahdi's Camp* (Sampson Low, Marston, London, 1892), and Rudolf C. Slatin's *Fire and Sword in the Sudan* (Edward Arnold, London, 1897) – which he edited and translated. They made fascinating reading when they were first published, and they still do today – a fascination which is heightened rather than diminished by the knowledge that they were intended to be unabashed, inflammatory pro-war propaganda. (For contrast, see Charles Neufeld's *A Prisoner of the Khaleefa* [Putnam, New York, 1899]. Neufeld presumably fared no better than the others in captivity, but his book was published without Wingate's help.)

In general, the Mahdi does not come off well at the hands of the English writers, which is understandable under the circumstances. There is, however, a fascinating biography entitled *The Mahdi of Allah* by Richard A. Bermann (Putnam, New York, 1931), originally written in German. In the introduction which he contributed to the English edition, Winston Churchill, who knew something about the writing of history, noted: 'It is always interesting to know what kind of book the Devil would have written, but the theologians never gave him a chance. It is interesting for Britons to learn the Mahdi's point of view, and Richard Bermann has performed this in a remarkable book. ... '

As for Kitchener, despite his open contempt for the press, the Nile campaigns produced several abidingly readable books. Among them, in descending order of merit, are: Churchill's own *The River War* (Longmans, London, 1899); G. W. Steevens's *With Kitchener to Khartoum* (Blackwood, Edinburgh, 1898); Henry S. L. Alford and William Pennistoun Sword's *The Egyptian Soudan, its Loss and Recovery* (Macmillan, London, 1898);

A. Hilliard Atteridge's *Towards Khartoum* (A. D. Innes, London, 1897); Ernest N. Bennett's *The Downfall of the Dervishes* (Methuen, London, 1899); and Bennet Burleigh's *The Reconquest of the Soudan* (Chapman & Hall, London, 1898) and *Sirdar and Khalifa* (Chapman & Hall, London, 1898). On the purely military aspects of the campaign and especially the construction of the Desert Railway, the most complete account is E. W. C. Sandes's *The Royal Engineers in Egypt and the Sudan* (Institute of Royal Engineers, Chatham, 1937).

The best biography of Kitchener of Khartoum is Sir Philip Magnus's *Kitchener: Portrait of an Imperialist* (John Murray, London, 1958), which utilizes Salisbury's private papers. It supersedes both in style and fairness the older, official three-volume *Life of Lord Kitchener* (Macmillan, London, 1920) by Sir George Arthur. Wingate's biography, *Wingate of the Sudan* (John Murray, London, 1955), was written by his son Ronald, but disappointingly does not begin to do justice to its subject. An essential source on the subject of the Sudan, as well as every other parcel of the Empire on which the sun never set, is G. E. Buckle's edition of *The Letters of Queen Victoria* (John Murray, London, 1926). Italicizations, exclamation marks and all, they make fascinating reading at any time, and should be required on any extended ocean cruise.

In their effort to provide the Sudan with a model administration, the British did not neglect the compilation of history. Starting with Richard L. Hill's *Egypt in the Sudan, 1820–1881* (O.U.P., London, 1959) – he was a member of the Sudan Civil Service when he assembled his *Bibliography* (O.U.P., London, 1962) – we have a complete and uninterrupted account of the Sudan's troubles: *The Mahdist State in the Sudan, 1881–1898* by P. M. Holt (Clarendon Press, Oxford, 1958), and *The Mahdiya 1881–1899* by A. B. Theobald (Longmans, Green, London, 1951). Works on the period of the British Condominium tend to show the inevitable bias of authorship preceded by personal participation in the events described, as in J. S. R. Duncan's *The Sudan, a Record of Achievement* (Blackwood, Edinburgh, 1952). An excellent account, covering the entire period from Mohammed Ali's conquest in 1820 to 1956, is *The Independent Sudan* (R. Speller, New York, 1959), by Mekki Shibeika, the Sudan's foremost historian.

For the greater role which the Sudan played in Salisbury's calculations, and therefore in the diplomatic game which rippled out across most of Africa during the late years of the nineteenth century, there are three masterful accounts which, happily, agree on little more than dates and names: William L. Langer's *The Diplomacy of Imperialism 1890–1902* (Harvard University Bureau of International Research, Cambridge, Mass., 1935); G. N. Sanderson's *England, Europe and the Upper Nile 1882–1899* (Edinburgh University Press, 1965); and Ronald Robinson and John Gallagher's *Africa and the Victorians* (Macmillan, London, 1961). To any reader who enjoys fiction of international intrigue – the iron hand in the velvet glove, the double-cross and the double double-cross, the *agent provocateur* and the hugger-mugger behind chancellery doors – these three books are unhesitatingly recommended as supreme examples, fluidly written, of the genuine article.

PART SIX

The literature of the Marchand Mission and the incident at Fashoda – in French, Fachoda – falls into three categories: the accounts of the participants; the alibis and self-righteous moralizing of losers and winners; and the appreciations of modern scholars, cooled by time and enriched by long-withheld official papers.

In the first category, the best single work is undoubtedly the diary kept by Dr J. Emily and published as *Mission Marchand, Journal de Route* (Paris, 1913). For style, perceptiveness and power of expression, it ranks high in the output of physician-writers. Baratier's recollections are contained in three books, *Au Congo* (A. Fayard, Paris, 1914), *Vers le Nil* (Paris, 1923) and *Fachoda* (B. Grasset, Paris, 1942), the last of which contains a full account of his strange interview with Delcassé and the sorrowful meeting with Marchand in Cairo. Mangin, at all times a shrewd and unsentimental observer, wrote two books, *Regards sur la France d'Afrique* (Plon, Paris, 1924) and *Souvenirs d'Afrique* (Plon, Paris, 1936). His letters, in which frankness is heightened by immediacy, were published in the September 15th, 1931, issue of *Revue des Deux Mondes*. Marchand, as he had promised, never wrote either a book or an article on the Mission. His account of the meeting with Kitchener, however, appeared in *Le Figaro* on August 29th, 1904, and a somewhat more detailed version – originally given orally to friends in Thoissey – was published by *L'Illustration* on January 27th, 1934, on the occasion of his death.

For the other side, there is Wingate's account as it appears in his biography, and that of Major-General Sir Horace Lockwood Smith-Dorrien, who commanded the British force, in *Memories of Forty-Eight Years' Service* (E. P. Dutton, New York, 1925). Major H. W. Jackson gave a punctilious but generous account in *Fashoda, 1898* (Sudan *Notes and Records*, III, 1 [Cairo, 1920]). Kitchener's version, transmitted verbatim by Rodd to Salisbury, can be found as No. 193 in Volume I of *British Documents on the Origins of the War, 1898–1914* (H.M.S.O., London, 1927), by G. P. Gooch and Harold Temperley.

Except for the intentional inaccuracies in Kitchener's report, all of these accounts are in close agreement. Where writers differed was on the inspiration of Marchand's trip, and the consequences of his forced withdrawal. Two French cabinet ministers produced rather lame 'Who, me?' books, André Lebon's *La Politique de la France en Afrique 1896–1898* (Paris, 1901), and Gabriel Hanotaux's *Fachoda* (Paris, 1909). Among the many other volumes of lower-level finger-pointing, Fernand Vatin's *La Vérité sur Fachoda* (1923) stands out if only because it supports England's claim and demonstrates the fallacy of Marchand's premise. The British view, which Lt Winston Spencer Churchill was asked to clarify for his overseas cousins (in *The North American Review*, 1898), is fairly reflected by such articles as *Fashoda and Lord Salisbury's Vindication* (in *The Fortnightly Review*, December 1898), and *France, Russia and the Nile* (*Contemporary Review*, December 1898), which paints the entire episode as a pre-Bolshevik Russian plot, foiled by British pluck and determination. A scholar, Jules Cocheris, contributed a very shrewd reconstruction, *La Situation Internationale de l'Égypte et du Soudan* (Plon-Nourrit, Paris, 1903), which has since been largely borne out by the more recent work of M. B. Giffen in *Fashoda, the Incident and its Diplomatic Setting* (University of Chicago Press, 1930), and Pierre Renouvin's *Les Origines de l'Expédition de Fachoda* (*Revue Historique*, 1948) which remains the last words insofar as the French archives are concerned.

There are, as has been mentioned, more than a dozen biographies of Marchand. Most were intended by their authors or publishers as Examples to the Young, and deserve no other audience. The least unsatisfactory is Jacques Delebecque's *Vie du General Marchand* (Paris, 1937). There is also a very striking if entirely non-political portrait of the man in Charles Castellani's *Marchand l'Africain* (Paris, 1902). Castellani is the illustrator who had set out with the Mission, but turned back.

The latest and best life of Théophile Delcassé is Christopher Andrew's *Théophile Delcassé and the Making of the Entente Cordiale* (St Martin's Press, New York, 1968), a major work which places Fashoda in the context of the prior and later career of one of the least appreciated but most effective French statesmen of his time.

For the month-to-month progress of the Marchand Mission, and for a full contemporaneous account of goings-on in Africa, there are few sources better-informed or more lively than the monthly *Bulletin du Comité de l'Afrique Française*. Its editors not only knew their way around the continent, but played important back-stage roles in the shaping of colonial policy.

PART SEVEN

The story of South Africa's inauspicious birth as a nation is told brilliantly in Leonard Thompson's *The Unification of South Africa* (Clarendon Press, Oxford, 1960). Nothing, it seems, need ever be added to this definitive account, but for an exceptionally clear insight into history in the making – or unmaking – there is also *The Milner Papers: South Africa* (Cassell, London, 1931), edited by Cecil Headlam. They suggest that Milner was brilliant enough to realize he was failing even as he was making the decisions which rendered that failure inevitable. For the other key protagonists of this period, there is the excellent two-volume biography, *Smuts*, by Sir Keith Hancock (Cambridge University Press, 1962), and several lives of Louis Botha, one of the most readable of which is Earl Buxton's *General Botha* (John Murray, London, 1924). The descent into *apartheid* has been covered in many accounts, notably by Alan Paton, but none is more dispassionate and therefore impelling than *The Making of a Nation, 1910–1961* (Macmillan, Johannesburg, 1969) by D. W. Kruger, who is Professor of History at the University of South Africa.

World War I as it affected Africa is covered in Volume IV of Sir C. P. Lucas's *The Empire at War* (Milford, London, 1925). Like most official compilations of its kind, it is exhaustive in detail and defensibly accurate in fact, without at the same time really telling the story as it happened. Anyone reading about the East African campaign in Lucas, and then turning to Paul von Lettow-Vorbeck's *My Reminiscences of East Africa* (Hurst & Blackett, London, 1920) will perceive the distinction. For the background to the division of the spoils, G. L. Beer's *African Questions at the Paris Peace Conference* (Macmillan, New York, 1923) is useful. On the mandates themselves, the classic work still remains Quincy Wright's *Mandates Under the League of Nations* (Greenwood Press, New York, 1930).

No attempt has been made to follow the enormous literature of colonialism into its economic, political and sociological by-ways. Two of the most important works – perhaps the most important in terms of influence – are cited in the text: Lugard, and Sarraut. Useful because of their scholarship, scope and freedom from hypocrisy are Raymond Buell's *The Native Problem in Africa* (Macmillan, New York, 1928) and Lord Hailey's massive *An African Survey* (O.U.P., London), originally published in 1938 but revised in 1957. Just to reassure oneself that the assumption of colonialism as the naturally-ordered scheme of things was not unanimous, it may be refreshing to consult Leonard Woolf's *Empire and Commerce in Africa* (Allen & Unwin, London, 1920).

The writings of African freedom are beyond the scope of this book – as is the subject itself. Virtually all of the personages cited at the end of the section have written on the subject, or contributed collected speeches. There is one additional volume – Anwar Sadat's *Revolt on the Nile* (Allan Wingate, London, 1957) – which merits attention if only because its author is, at this writing, the chief of state of his native country, and because few books have ever packed more bitterness and hatred into so few pages.

Index

INDEX